Solon the Thinker

SOLON THE THINKER
Political Thought in Archaic Athens

John David Lewis

BLOOMSBURY
LONDON • NEW DELHI • NEW YORK • SYDNEY

Bloomsbury Academic
An imprint of Bloomsbury Publishing Plc

50 Bedford Square	1385 Broadway
London	New York
WC1B 3DP	NY 10018
UK	USA

www.bloomsbury.com

First published in 2006 by Gerald Duckworth & Co. Ltd.
First paperback edition 2008

© John David Lewis 2006

John David Lewis has asserted his right under the Copyright, Designs and Patents Act, 1988, to be identified as Author of this work.

All rights reserved. No part of this publication may be reproduced or transmitted in any form or by any means, electronic or mechanical, including photocopying, recording, or any information storage or retrieval system, without prior permission in writing from the publishers.

No responsibility for loss caused to any individual or organization acting on or refraining from action as a result of the material in this publication can be accepted by Bloomsbury or the author.

British Library Cataloguing-in-Publication Data
A catalogue record for this book is available from the British Library.

ISBN: PB: 978-0-7156-3728-9
ePUB: 978-1-4725-2114-9
ePDF: 978-1-4725-2113-2

Library of Congress Cataloging-in-Publication Data
A catalog record for this book is available from the Library of Congress.

Typeset by Ray Davies

Contents

Acknowledgments	vi
Preface	vii
Author's Note	viii
Abbreviations	viii
Introduction: Approaching Solon's fragments	1
1. 'I brought the people together': Solon's *polis* as *kosmos*	11
2. 'To know all things': psychic qualities and the *polis*	23
3. 'In time, retribution surely comes': necessity, *dikê* and the good order of the *polis*	42
4. 'A *kosmos* of words': archaic logic and the organization of poem 4	60
5. '*Moira* brings good and evil': *bios* and the failure of *Dikê*	74
6. 'We will not exchange our excellence': *Moira* and wealth	96
7. 'I set them free': tyranny, slavery and freedom	108
Appendix: glossary of terms used by Solon	131
Notes	135
Solon's fragments, translated by John Lewis	155
Bibliography	163
Index	174

Acknowledgments

Articles reflecting research used in this book include:

'Slavery and Lawlessness in Solonian Athens', in *Dike* 7 (2005): 19-40.
'The Intellectual Context of Solon's *Dike*', in *Polis* 18.1&2 (2001): 3-26.
' "*Dike*", "*Moira*", "*Bios*" and the Limits to Understanding in Solon, 13 (West)', in *Dike* 4 (2001): 113-35.

Earlier formulations presented at conferences:

'Slavery and Lawlessness in Solonian Athens', *Law and Public Order in Ancient Societies Panel, Colloquium on Ancient Law*, The American Philological Association Annual Meeting, New Orleans, 5 January 2002.
'Political Thought in Ancient Greece', *Second Renaissance Conference*, Palo Alto, California, 5-10 July 2002.
'The Horoi and the Bridge between the 4th and 6th Centuries', *Place and Genre in Greek Epigraphy Conference*, University of Cambridge, January 1999.

Preface

The research grew out of my PhD dissertation at the University of Cambridge. A dissertation, however, is one's final college paper, and few – certainly not mine – should become books. This book draws from the research, but is completely re-written. In the research I received patient help from Paul Cartledge, Paul Millett, Dorothy Thompson, Pat Easterling and many others, none of whom has seen the book. Thank you to Mary Beard for the chance to sit in the Museum of Classical Art and Archaeology in Cambridge, under the statue of the Sunium Kouros. Regular tea with A.J. Graham and Harold Mattingly, Jr, was like sitting between Zeus, who sees all, and Prometheus, who never hesitates to share the fire of his intellect.

I value the material and intellectual support that the Anthem Foundation for Objectivist Scholarship offered towards the pursuit of intellectual values and this book. I appreciate Ashland University's use of an Anthem Foundation grant to allow me course release so early in my academic career. I thank Fred Miller and Robert Mayhew for their kind words and comments, and Ed Harris for the chance to participate in the APA Panel. Thanks to Sean Templeton, who proofread it. I am especially indebted to C. Bradley Thompson for his encouragement, and for his example of one who understands his principles and stands by them. I edited the paperback edition while a visiting scholar at the Social Philosophy and Policy Center, Bowling Green State University.

Most of all, to my wife Casey, I owe more than I can write or say. I am so glad she had a chance to run off to Nice for a month, while I contemplated the sculptures in the Cambridge Classics Library.

Author's Note

Latinized forms of Greek names are used throughout the text, for ease of reading.

Attic forms of Greek terms are given, except where quoting from Solon or referring directly to his verses. For instance, I use Dusnomiê because that is Solon's form (and capitalized as such), but in discussing it I may compare it to anomia. Thus in some cases the Attic and Ionian forms may be mixed in a single sentence.

In the bibliography and citations, the cited date refers to the date of the edition used, not necessarily the original date of publication.

Abbreviations

Poems and fragments of Solon and other archaic poets are numbered as by M.L. West, *Studies in Greek Elegy and Iambus*. Ancient authors are generally abbreviated as in LSJ.

CAH = *Cambridge Ancient History*
DK = H. Diels and W. Kranz, *Die Fragmente der Vorsokratiker*
FGrH = F. Jacoby, *Die Fragmente der Griechischen Historiker*
HCT = A.W. Gomme, *A Historical Commentary on Thucydides*
IESS = D.L. Sills, *The International Encyclopedia of the Social Sciences*
IG = *Inscriptiones Graecae* (Berlin, 1873-)
KA = R. Kassel and C. Austin, *Poetae Comici Graeci*
LSJ = H.G. Liddell, R. Scott and S. Jones, *A Greek-English Lexicon*
KRS = G.S. Kirk, J.E. Raven and M. Schofield, *The Presocratic Philosophers*
MW = R. Merkelbach and M.L. West, *Fragmenta Hesiodea*
OED = *Oxford English Dictionary* (2nd edn, 1991)
PMG = D.L. Page, *Poetae Melici Graeci*
Smyth = H.W. Smyth, *Greek Grammar*

Introduction
Approaching Solon's fragments

A short time will show the townsmen whether I am crazy,
  with the truth coming out into the middle
                                                                Solon 10

The purpose of this book is to examine the poetic fragments of Solon as early Greek political thought. The focus is on Solon's preserved poetry, not on laws or institutional reforms attributed to him by later writers, and not on his place in a literary or historical tradition. What rises out of Solon's verses is an all-embracing way of looking at his world – a way of understanding Athens and the men in it, of grasping the certainty of justice and the arbitrariness of fate, and of judging rulers both bad and good – that is rooted in a new world-view that was sweeping the Aegean world. His preserved verses, even though fragmentary, often cast in epic form, and motivated by an opaque rhetorical purpose, nevertheless present an enlightened frame of reference, an energetic moral programme and a well-organized set of ideas. His words mark the birth of thought about the *polis* as a lawful, just community.

Solon, selected as chief official of Athens around 594 BC, is one of the most revered figures in Greek history.[1] The classical Greeks, the Romans and the American Founders crafted pedestals for him: Plato made him one of the Seven Wise Men; Aristotle thought him among the most serious lawgivers; Demosthenes used him to attack his opponents; Cicero saw him as a fount for Roman Law; Plutarch sensed a moral icon; James Madison admired the immortal legislator; and Woodrow Wilson said he gave to Athens 'a fixed and definite constitution'.[2] Yet Solon's reputation as a constitution-maker bears little resemblance to what is left of his poems. Numerous studies have focused on social reforms, political institutions, economic policies and laws, often in terms familiar to students of political science but anachronistic to early Greece. In reaction, many studies of his verses have reinforced his position in a Homeric–Hesiodic tradition, either basing his ideas on epic poetic forms, or showing him to be a less-than-great poet. But these vital examinations may obscure his own thoughts and distort his real importance. This book proposes an approach that looks to his verses neither to reconstruct Athenian history, nor to relate him to a poetic tradition, but rather to discern the remains of early sixth-century Athenian political ideas. To do so, we must take a deceptively simple approach, but one that is surprisingly controversial: we must look at everything Solon says about these ideas, in all of his fragments. Solon is not an extension of a genre – he is a person in his own right, with a distinct point of view, who should be read as such.

There has been an exciting revival of interest in Solon over the past five years, and a plethora of full-length studies dedicated to his poems.[3] Yet there remains an under-valuation of Solon's importance in the history of thought, and, given his early dates, an unwillingness to break from the idea that a progression of time corresponds necessarily to intellectual progress. Some scholars have recognized extraordinary innovations in Solon; Richmond Lattimore laments that 'the influence of Solon on tragedy seems to have been generally underestimated', since later poets 'tend to retire from the advanced position of Solon' with respect to the punishment of *hubris*. Victor Parker sees in Solon an understanding that is more definitive than classical-period writers. But the possibility that Solon's verses might take positions more advanced than those of the fifth century runs counter to expectations.[4]

All of our evidence supports one assumption about Solon in his own time: he was immersed into a swirling cauldron of political competition and clashing ethical values. Struggle and contest – whether expressed in private symposia, public shouting matches, tragic competitions or before magistrates and juries – is a feature of ancient Greek history at every point, and there is no reason to exempt early Athens from this agonistic way of doing business. Solon may have made his name by publicly challenging a law against advocating war with Megara, in his poem *Salamis* (only fragments 1, 2 and 3 remain); and a fragment that suggests a context for the delivery has the truth coming out 'in the middle', i.e. in public (fragment 10). Solon repeatedly refers to antagonists (fragments 4c; 5.5-6; 15; 33; 36.22-5). This was an energetic debate conducted on the normative level, over ideas such as *dikê* and the fundamental values of the *polis*. The recension of Homer, the creation of tragedy, the late sixth-century Athenian buildings, and indeed Solon's own references to his enemies, all suggest a cultural atmosphere that was much more lively than Solon alone.[5]

To reconstruct the intellectual foundations of this discourse, a historian would ideally examine the positions of the various speakers, finding agreement and conflict, and defining the ideas at work and how they affected the community. However, apart from scraps of poetry preserved in later historians and biographers, this material is lost to us. This presents a serious problem of evidence and interpretation. From archaic Athens only Solon's words survive, in a recension of personal and political observations, exhortations and aspirations, in a self-consciously identified Attic tongue designed to move his audience into support for his views.[6] The point demands emphasis: Solon's verses are all that is left of early sixth-century Athens from which we can determine any specific point of view

Introduction

without importing more material from other centuries than we have from Solon's own time.

How then can we approach these verses? It is obvious that the poems are too vague and fragmentary to allow a chronological reconstruction without relying heavily on later works. But the question remains as to where to start in understanding the ideas that are fundamental to understanding cultural and political history.

One approach – common to general histories – uses later historical narratives to set the intellectual and institutional contexts within which the verses are interpreted. Writers such as Herodotus, Aristotle or Plutarch are used to reconstruct a sequence of social crises ('debt slavery') and political upheavals ('a change in the *politeia*'), to lay out economic conditions ('interest rates'), to establish the institutional makeup of archaic Athens (a 'second council of four hundred'), or to establish the abstract ideas implicit in archaic thought ('*politeia*' or '*dêmokratia*'). This becomes the framework of interpretation for the poems. However, this runs the risk of turning the poems into malleable tools of support for secondary interpretations. Aristotle wrote some three hundred years after Solon's birth, and the gulf between the two men constitutes the intellectual revolution of the fifth century and the Platonic Academy. Likewise the legendary confrontation between Solon and Croesus – if used to understand Solon as a historical figure – should be evaluated in relation to the ideas found in Solon's verses, as a means to understanding how those ideas were understood, reformulated and transmitted by Herodotus. How wrong it would be to see Herodotus as presenting the 'real' Solon, and to make the poems fit that portrait.[7]

An objection may follow, that the extant verses were selected by later writers, who shaped the material when they decided to preserve certain verses and not others. A few readers might even conclude that there is no evidence for a 'Solon', beyond the character created by a literary tradition.[8] But it is more accurate to see Solon's poems as 'expressions of a specific purpose at a specific time, place and circumstance'.[9] In either case, our understanding of him does depend upon the choices of later writers, which may say as much about the principles of selection as they do about the original author. Yet such selection does not involve the level of creative intervention found in the wholesale manufacture of laws, institutions and economic reforms in Solon's name. Calhoun, for instance, found a principle of 'criminal law' in Solon, derived from later commentators.[10] Nor is Solon evidence for archaic 'economic' conditions – his concern is rather for the effects of material wealth on a man's disposition, his *polis* and his fate.[11] Economic conditions are better revealed through research into pre-monetary societies, pre-technological agricultural methods and classical archaeology.[12] It is a sobering thought to realize that what we have of Solon makes no reference to reforms of the Attic tribes, a second council, coinage, juries, or specific legal cases and laws, and that debts and wealth

3

requirements for offices are each mentioned solely by one ambiguous phrase. The poems are mercilessly silent on the status of women, foreign slaves and children – although young boys do get at least one lustful mention – and they say virtually nothing about the audiences, despite strong implications of *public* delivery of his poems. But to escape from the no-man's land between the vagueness of the poems and the unverifiability of later sources by mixing primary and secondary literary materials requires loyalty to primary materials.

With a very different aim in view, and often in reaction to such studies, scholars have worked to place Solon into a tradition of oral poetry. Such studies may rely upon a generic poetic form, a typology by which material from otherwise differentiated poets is selected, classified and compared. Elizabeth Irwin has produced an important study on precisely these grounds, establishing a 'genre' of 'martial exhortation elegy', exemplified by Callinus and Tyrtaeus, and then finding rich parallels between such works (as well as Homer and Hesiod) in Solon's poem 4, which is considered explicitly apart from any other works by Solon. Similarly, Eric Havelock has shown that Solon 4.5-8 exhibits important similarities to Hesiod *Works and Days* 202-85, particularly the actions of stupid and unjust men and the certainty of retribution by divine personifications.[13] These linguistic parallels are certainly real, and Solon clearly participates in a pan-Hellenic discourse using common poetic devices. But these devices must not be allowed to obscure the challenges he made to what came earlier – challenges that would grow, in the next century, into an intellectual revolution. Irwin stresses that 'The introduction to Solon 4 is indeed programmatic: martial themes throughout the poem play a continuous subordinate role analogous to their initial function as foil'. Further: 'Solon composes a poem in which the defining virtue in martial poetry – both epic and elegiac – is subordinated to his message, namely, the warning of the disasters awaiting those who disregard justice, and the suffering such behaviour lays on the entire community'. These martial themes, Irwin maintains, were 'performed' almost exclusively in aristocratic symposia, dominated by 'heroic role-playing' with 'political implications'.[14]

It is vital to maintain the proper subordination. Poems with generic similarities, e.g. those of Tyrtaeus and Solon, were from different *poleis*, were not intended for the same audience, do not always display the same understanding of 'excellence', and were written decades or centuries apart by men who probably never met. A common 'genre' or terminology does not imply that either they or their audiences understood their political concepts and values the same way, or that the latter drew on the former for more than the impact that an emotive poetic turn-of-phrase may offer.[15] Our literary evidence is punctuated in time and space. Solon punctuates the history of Attica in the early sixth century, and Hesiod, for example, punctuates Boeotia in the late eighth or so. To juxtapose Solon and Hesiod is to compare points of punctuation in an otherwise austere historical record. Such a comparison does not tell us to what extent (or even *whether*) the earlier man influenced the latter, and it need take no position on the historical development between the two men. The determination of 'influence' is a tricky business, and is dependent upon establishing some meaning for any given passage before its origins or effects can be determined. For instance, Irwin observes that Solon's fragment 11 is 'the explicit recognition of the deceptive use of political language'.[16] But this basic meaning – which is surely incontestable – leaves open the source of its poetic form, and the context of its delivery. Did Solon publicly chide the deceivers, condemn them in a symposium, or even praise them in private? We may disagree about whom he is referring to and his rhetorical purpose, but the basic meaning of his words is clear – and not dependent upon the audience.

But the elevation of genre and 'performance context' into primary considerations has led scholars to claim that each poem must stand alone from the poet's other works – and that using a poet's other works to understand that poem is simply wrong. By this approach, Solon's poem 4, the *Hymn to the City*, for instance, can be compared to Hesiod, but not to Solon 36.[17] But to use Hesiod to understand Solon's poem without the benefit of Solon's other verses would be akin to using phrases within Thomas Hobbes' *Leviathan* to understand Thomas Jefferson's *Declaration of Independence*, all the while eschewing Jefferson's *Notes on the State of Virginia* because of a difference in rhetorical purpose or audience. Hobbes will be useful here only if we have some understanding of the basic positions of the two men – which requires first reading each on his own terms.

By examining everything Solon and Hesiod say about, for instance, *dikê*, including their claims about the divine, human life and natural events, it becomes clear that the conceptual differences between Solon and Hesiod are profound, and transcend similarities in language. These include Solon's denial of divine power over the *polis*, the lack of any statement in his verses that a human deed results in a natural event, his focus on failings in *noos* as the reason men destroy the *polis*, and his joining of *dikê* to written laws enforced alike. It is in such differences that the mark of innovation may be discerned, and that the poetic tradition becomes a vehicle for profound transformation as well as evidence for homogeneity. But to understand the nature of the subordination, Solon must be taken on his own terms, by considering everything he says about *dikê*, in every verse. His words must be taken as a singular point of view at a particular time – not merely as an appendage to a poetic tradition.

Coming to grips with Solon's use of tyrannical language is a case in point. Terms such as *kratos* (power) may suggest that Solon was not far removed from tyrants, who used similar language to gain and legitimate their power. Perhaps Solon attained tyrannical power for himself, and only then created his famous laws, as a cover for single rule. But whether he acted tyrannically or not, and whatever his rhetorical purposes at any moment, his verses offer a powerful indictment of the tyrant's entire approach to life. This is their meaning, regardless of how he used them. Victor Parker has shown that, prior to Solon, little semantic distinction had been made between *tyrant* and *basileus* (chief) or *anax* (king). Further, Parker finds no negative evaluations of tyranny (as distinguished from kingship) before Solon, and that even fifth-century playwrights may not challenge the positive connotations.[18] Perhaps Solon used such language because no distinctions had yet been made between tyranny and other forms of single rule. But this does not mean that he accepts their equivalence without challenge. He condemns tyranny on multiple levels; we can infer a rhetorical purpose – or deny a difference between tyranny and kingship – only by first recognizing the meaning of tyranny as Solon gives it to us.

Solon's importance in the history of political ideas is precisely in such challenges. Embedded in his exhortations are the first extant descriptions of a tyrant in terms of psychic corruption, the first equations of slavery and tyranny in political terms, and the first descriptions of how and why a crowd grants power to tyrants. He also offers an alternative – the protection of all Attic-speaking men from slavery under written laws – that constitutes the first statement of political freedom in western thought. Firm differentiations between just rule and hubristic aggrandizement – and of existing as a slave from being free politically – are thematic in Solon's verses. To test such claims about the verses, while bearing in mind his archaic forms of thought, requires us to consider everything extant from Solon's words about what it means to fall into the slavery of tyranny – to discover how he uses important terms in different passages, to find his place in the shifting values of his age, and to ask whether he is consistent across the verses. To begin an investigation by lifting a 'tyrannical' passage out of a poem and building a series of linguistic parallels to earlier poets, without establishing what *Solon* claims is essential about the idea, is to elevate linguistic similarities over the content of the ideas. This may empower the ideas of the past to obscure the new message of the present.

But should we expect consistency from a poet like Solon? Mark Griffith, citing multiple inconsistencies from poets other than Solon, draws the conclusion that a 'proto-philosopher' and a 'religious sage' such as Xenophanes or Parmenides may need coherence across his thought, but this is not so for a 'wisdom poet' such as Solon. As a matter of policy such poets rely upon deceit to win a contest; their vision is necessarily limited to the contest that is immediately before them.[19] But Griffith's conclusion depends upon the premise that Solon is a member of this category (a 'wisdom poet') who thereby possesses the quality of deceit. Griffith offers this without citing any examples from Solon's own works. A reader who considers Solon to be one of the 'proto-philosophers' may draw precisely the opposite conclusion. The conclusion is only as good as the categories,

Introduction

and it is difficult to place Solon or even a poet-philosopher like Xenophanes, into one category or the other. In his day, a wisdom poet *was* a philosopher, and a lawgiver *was* a poet. A wise man can, after all, be consistent in his overall world-view (if not in every particular detail), all the while engaging in a contest of words, and pursuing a political purpose.

An *a priori* assumption of inconsistency, if used as an interpretative strategy, can condition its own result. Solon's direct disavowal of tyranny can be used to turn him into Shakespeare's Julius Caesar, ostensibly refusing the crown in order to gain power. Anything in the poems can support this conclusion; a call for freedom or a demand to obey the laws can be read as ironic or rhetorical ploys to establish tyranny, and ambiguity becomes a Procrustean bed of selective redefinition. But it is improper to conflate, at the outset, archaic political verse with fiction, or a speaker's exhortations with lying, in order to create a self-fulfilling prophecy. Since *any speaker and any position* can be so deconstructed, including those who adopt this method of analysis, the approach is not reliable.

There is an even more important point here. The premise behind using a range of the poetic fragments to understand any particular verse is not that the poet is always consistent. The point is that we always understand any particular item – whether in reading, conversing or writing – in context with other knowledge. I am an American of the late twentieth and early twenty-first century, who learned Greek late in life, and who understands politics in post-Lockean terms of limited government, liberty and individual rights. Solon comes from a very different time. The best evidence I have for his intellectual context is what remains from him – his views of divine figures, his statements about the men of Athens and their motivations, his grasp of *noos*, *dikê*, *moira*, *doulosunê* and *eleutheros*. Hermann Fränkel observed a certain archaic method, 'to circle around its subject', a point that I interpret as understanding an idea in a widening context of related ideas.[20] Solon suggests precisely this method, as he returns to similar topics from different directions before unknown audiences. What we discover in one place may support or challenge what we find elsewhere, and we may find ourselves uncertain of a particular point – as I am not at all certain what Solon means by the *horoi* ('boundary stones') that he tore up in poem 36 – but we should not ignore what he has said elsewhere.

In contrast to literary and historical approaches, philosophical studies have often been directed towards particular concepts, focusing on Solon's place in an unfolding tradition of heroic, martial, aristocratic and democratic values, or on the development of duty, responsibility and moral consciousness.[21] Such a narrow focus on Solon's ideas is understandable; he leaves not even an outline of a 'natural philosophy', a 'cosmology', or an 'ethics' or 'politics'. Nor does he rise to political philosophy or theory by speaking of the *polis* and its constitutions as types. Consequently, philosophical studies have seldom connected Solon with the Ionian philosophic revolution on any fundamental level, at best seeing him as part of a wide cultural phenomenon and de-emphasizing his position between Homer and the Presocratic philosophers.[22] There are many exceptions, of course: the studies of Gregory Vlastos, for instance, are powerful and important.[23] But beyond localized comparisons, philosophers have generally not paid attention to Solon, and most histories of philosophy do not deal with his poems.[24] Solon has had his own poetry little examined as a source for the political ideas that illuminated the intellectual life and history of archaic Athens. To cite one example of neglect, von Fritz, in his study of *nous* and *noein*, jumps from Hesiod to Xenophanes, noting that Xenophanes is the 'first Greek thinker ... who uses the word in fragments of indubitable authenticity'. Yet *noos* and derivatives appear eleven times in Solon's extant verses, and Solon directly connects failures in *noos* to civil strife.[25]

Solon deserves such an examination. A.A. Long, attempting to define a 'scope' for early Greek philosophy, proposes an 'account of all things' that is (1) explanatory and systematic, (2) coherent and argumentative, (3) transformative, (4) educationally provocative and (5) critical and unconventional.[26] Solon's lack of concern for 'all things' in the extant verses is indisputable, as is his lack of explicit theories. But can we say with assurance that Thales was 'systematic' and that Solon was not? Can we be certain that Thales was more 'educationally provocative' than Solon? Is it not possible that Anaximander's cosmology is a wider application of ideas developed by thinkers about the *polis*? If Anaximenes has a 'system' of cyclical rain / sea / mist / clouds / rain, has he not closed a circle that began with verses such as those of Solon, that 'snow and hail comes from clouds, and thunder comes from lightning'? Does Solon not show concern for an 'ethics' – if not formally systematized, at least pregnant with implications for a system of some kind? The lack of systematic thought in Solon about the *polis* as a type, for instance, does not mean that he is not thinking about his *polis*, and that what he has left us is not 'political thought' in the form that he understood it.[27] Thus I can accept Adkins' admonishment that in Solon's poem 4 'there is no political theory', and yet consider the nature of 'political thought' at the time. The key is to distinguish thought about the *polis* of Athens – which is surprisingly well developed in Solon – from thought about the *polis* as a type. Only after the former could the latter develop.

This book will not attempt a historical reconstruction of Solon's actions in Athens, including his laws, institutional 'reforms', or even the specific audiences before whom he spoke. Nor will it attempt an exhaustive review of scholarship on Solon, a systematic commentary, or a chronological ordering of the poems. No systematic epistemology or epistemic position will be developed for Solon. The question here is how Solon understands the *polis*, his world and the men in it, in exhortations that do not present theories but nevertheless do reveal a rational point of view. The primary importance of Solon's verses is as sources for intellectual history: the ideas that shaped his world and that of his descendants.

The first four chapters are structured around ideas that are unveiled in poem 4, *The Hymn to the City*, but are also found in Solon's other verses. In broad outline, the first three chapters read the poem in order. Chapter 1 reads lines 4.1-4 alongside the first two lines of fragment 11, in which divine will is disavowed as responsible for the *polis*. This leads to a hypothesis, that Solon sees Athens as a self-supporting *kosmos* – a human realm set apart from the gods – that functions without threat of external destruction. Chapter 2, centred on lines 4.5-10 but also considering fragment 6, delves into the internal energy of the *polis*, unpacks the psychic qualities that Solon sees at the heart of the *polis*, and connects them to *koros* as both satiety and excess. Chapter 3 then turns from this internal perspective to a wider view of Solon's *polis*, his ideas of necessity, *Dikê*, *Eunomiê* and the 'Good Order' that are distributed throughout a just *polis*. Chapter 4 addresses Solon's claim to have created a '*kosmos* of words', by examining the internal organization of poem 4 and the archaic logic at its heart. Chapters 5 and 6 deal with a fundamental problem in Solon, his fatalism – the deep divide in his thought between the certainty of *Dikê* in the *polis* and the uncertainty of *Moira* in each person's pursuit of wealth – that sets poem 13 at odds with his more political verses. Chapter 7 turns to the intellectual and physical aspects of tyranny, slavery and freedom, using poem 36 but also shorter fragments such as 9 and 11 to unveil Solon's lawful solution to the disorder of his day.

The limited size of Solon's extant corpus imposes serious difficulties on the organization of this book, which emphasizes different ideas in the same verses at different points. Solon's two perspectives on the *polis* is a case in point; he may see it both in terms of its abstract form of arrangement, and in terms of the psychic conditions of the men in it. Myriad applications of this dual perspective follow; for instance, Solon's concepts of *hêsuchia* (broadly, 'calmness'), *Dikê* and *Eunomiê* must be considered in relation to the disposition of each man, as well as to the condition of the *polis* as a whole. It is not the case that Solon understood a concept such as 'perspective', or that he was aware of the implications of his own approach. But this idea does allow us to draw inferences about his thoughts about the hectic world of Athens, either standing on the acropolis and looking down at the city, or walking among its inhabitants.

Solon's claims to understand the implications of events beyond what is immediately before his eyes led him to a strong prediction of his own place in the Court of Time. His foresight was essentially correct; whether accidentally or by merit, he has gone down as the most important of the earliest Athenians. To read him is akin to looking at a plaster copy of a sculpture, housed in a museum effaced and broken, ripped from its context, remoulded with the tools of a later age, but nevertheless projecting an underlying order that refuses to be suppressed. To understand

Solon we must not take him anachronistically, either by attributing later philosophical concepts to him, or by undervaluing his position as 'not quite philosophical' and therefore trapped in epic prehistory. To do either would be to drop the context of his achievements, which stand in relation to the *Politics* of Aristotle as the Sunium Kouros stands in relation to the sculptures of Praxiteles: as proud in their own right, state of the art for their own time, and precursors of later glories.

1

'I brought the people together'
Solon's *polis* as *kosmos*

> I brought the people together for these reasons,
> How did I stop before I accomplished them?
> Solon 36.1-2

We will never know the exact nature of the crisis that swept over Attica in the last decades of the seventh century BC, but that it was a crisis is beyond doubt. Solon's verses, the suggestions of archaeology, and the evaluations of every commentator to follow, all agree that deeply rooted social problems threatened to engulf Athens in civil strife. Whether fuelled by claims to aristocratic honours, the desperation of subsistence farmers or the pressures of regional factions, tensions between the Athenians rose to threaten their way of life If our information is at all accurate, they tried a series of remedies: Draco was appointed to write laws, probably to translate customs of revenge into stone; this could not solve the problems that had been fuelled by those same customs. A strong-man such as Cylon, possibly a supporter of a rival city, tried to attain power; he was killed by another gang, who brought a grievous pollution onto the *polis*. To cleanse Athens of the crime and bring the city back to good order, a Cretan religious figure, Epimenides, may have been summoned to purify the city. We cannot verify the accuracy of all this – Draco in particular may be mythical – but it is evident that the crisis was not alleviated.[1]

The Athenians then did something truly remarkable: they took control of the situation, and, to the extent of their ability, ceased to settle for rule by an unchallenged aristocracy, chance, divine will or tyrants. Still mindful that their gods were powerful, and that a past crime was a pollution that would lead to further conflict, they chose one of their own – Solon, a man of the middle in some sense – to bring a solution to their problems. If his own words are any guide, neither tyranny nor shamanism was his claim to fame; the *polis* was understandable and actionable, a self-supporting cosmetic unity that worked in an understandable way, and it was the responsibility of human beings to preserve or to destroy it.

Such ideas were part and parcel of new forms of thought that were sweeping the Aegean world. In Solon's day, Greek thinkers had begun to search for a singular principle underlying life on earth. This does not mean that they had a cosmology, a systematic view of the earth and the heavens. But their 'world-view' had a meaning more fundamental than cosmology:

Solon the Thinker

a basic understanding of how the world operates, and of their place in it.[2] Such a world-view establishes, among other things, whether man is to be a plaything of omnipotent deities, a pawn in a capricious world without consistency, an autonomous being able to control his own fate, or an unstable and ill-defined mixture of these ideas. Such a world-view may be well thought out and explicit, or it may be implicit, unexamined and unconceptualized, expressed as an emotional 'gut feeling' or as an absolute that defies challenge and explanation; it may be riddled with contradictions, but it is implied in any generalization about the nature and purpose of human life in the world.

For a peasant the world may not extend beyond the closest village, and the cycles of life may be no wider than agricultural seasons, religious festivals and wars. But the world-view of an archaic Greek thinker was expanding, encompassing wider ideas about the nature of life and offering answers to its basic questions. This is most sharply highlighted in his views of his city, and in the powers he grants to his gods. The first is the centre of life on earth, the stage for human activities and the arena in which life unfolds. The gods look down on the human contest from a high seat, and they may or may not be concerned to involve themselves in the affairs of men.

The new understanding was growing out of earlier developments, in which the creative acts of individuals added up to a cultural revolution. Over a century earlier, Hesiod had placed the gods at the centre of human affairs. His *Works and Days* describes the whims of immortal persons as the source of the human need to work and struggle, with human beings under the personal thumb of Zeus and his informant Justice. Profound consequences follow for Hesiod's views of justice and human action, consequences that shape his verses and the lessons they offer. Zeus' autocratic power over human affairs is doubly manifested. He has the ability both to command particular events and to determine the general tenor of life on earth:

ὅν τε διὰ βροτοὶ ἄνδρες ὁμῶς ἄφατοί τε φατοί τε
ῥητοί τ' ἄρρητοί τε Διὸς μεγάλοιο ἕκητι.
Hesiod *Works and Days* 3-4

ἀλλὰ Ζεὺς ἔκρυψε, χολωσάμενος φρεσὶν ᾗσιν,
ὅττί μιν ἐξαπάτησε Προμηθεὺς ἀγκυλομήτης.
τούνεκ' ἄρ' ἀνθρώποισιν ἐμήσατο κήδεα λυγρά·
Hesiod *Works and Days* 47-9

Ἰαπετιονίδη, πάντων πέρι μήδεα εἰδώς,
χαίρεις πῦρ κλέψας καὶ ἐμὰς φρένας ἠπεροπεύσας,
σοί τ' αὐτῷ μέγα πῆμα καὶ ἀνδράσιν ἐσσομένοισιν'.
Hesiod *Works and Days* 54-6

1. 'I brought the people together'

Through him mortal men are famous or not,
spoken of or not, as great Zeus wills.

But Zeus hid it [*bion anthrôpoisin*, the means of life to men], being angry in his *phrên*,
because Prometheus, crooked of counsel, deceived him;
for this, he designed sorrow and mischief against men.

'Son of Iapetus, greater than all in wiles,
you cheer because you have stolen fire and outwitted me in my *phrên*,
to you and to men that shall be a great misery'.

Hesiod's language strengthens the capriciousness of the scene: Zeus acts by his own will (*hekêti*) to contrive great pains for men, motivated by anger at the deceptions of a minor deity, and responding with anger against innocents. The result is a transformation of the *bios* of men; the need for work and struggle to stay alive is due to the whims of Zeus, and the men of iron look back with longing towards a less trying age. Present here is the essential element of a magical view of the world: despite a relationship with the divine that lacks a lightning blast of commandment, the presence of a capricious divine authority over human life leaves open the possibility of such intervention, and makes a non-arbitrary explanation of human events impossible. Indeed the 'why' of anything is explained by 'the assumption of quasi-human intentionality, his more or less inscrutable will'.[3]

Zeus was angry in his *phrên* and was motivated by revenge. Kurt von Fritz has demonstrated an element of will to act in the psychic quality *phrên* and its compounds in Homer, Hesiod and Xenophanes, a will that is linked to the deeper understanding that is *noos* but is not divorced from sensory data.[4] Contrary to *thumos*, *phrên* is never used of blind passion or emotion, and contrary to *noos*, it combines intellectual, emotional and volitional elements with the potential or actual start of an action. As Xenophanes said of Zeus, 'without toil (*apaneuthe ponoio*) he shakes all things by active will (*phrêni*) proceeding from insight (*noou*)'.[5] *Phrên* is the will to act, in combination with *noos*, the characteristic insight of Zeus that allows him to grasp that which is not available to immediate sight. The term 'divine will' here is intended to convey the intellectual, emotional and volitional aspects of an immortal figure, with a capacity to act as desired, considered from a human perspective as a capricious presence presiding over human affairs. This bringing of cares to mankind by Zeus forces men to rely upon the mythic figure as an explanation for the past and as an expectation for the future, a reliance that is ultimately all-encompassing. As Hesiod put it, 'Zeus sees all ... therefore I hope (or expect) for the future ...' (Hesiod *Works and Days* 267-73). On the whole Hesiod's linking of natural events to human actions, especially his conflation of weather and just action, go hand in hand with his reliance on a vertical divine power.

13

Solon the Thinker

How could it be otherwise? By controlling the weather, Zeus controls the means of life for a peasant farmer. Hesiod is motivated by his world-view to think this way.[6]

Solon's early sixth-century world-view is also intimately connected to divine figures, but, compared to Hesiod, their power has been restrained. Solon was a religious man; he lived in a world of religious sanctuaries and poetic maxims, in which wisdom was musical, the world was in constant growth and metamorphosis, the gods spoke to people, and inexplicable forces might arise. There was a later tradition that Epimenides had been summoned by Solon to cleanse Athens; Solon has too many associations with Delphi and Egyptian priests to be ignored.[7] In his world ideas are closely associated with mythic figures, and he moves easily between Earth *qua* goddess, the Black Earth beneath his feet and the myths that unite them.[8] He often expressed himself in mythological terms; the Odyssean and Hesiodic reverberations in Solon's poem 4, the *Hymn to the City*, are undeniable. But these similarities must not be allowed to obscure the evidence for the movement by Solon away from the world-view of epic poets and into the world of the philosophers. With respect to the *polis*, the contrast between Solon and Hesiod is fundamental: divine intentionality and responsibility are precisely the elements that Solon denies:

> ἡμετέρη δὲ πόλις κατὰ μὲν Διὸς οὔποτ' ὀλεῖται
> αἶσαν καὶ μακάρων θεῶν φρένας ἀθανάτων·
> τοίη γὰρ μεγάθυμος ἐπίσκοπος ὀβριμοπάτρη
> Παλλὰς Ἀθηναίη χεῖρας ὕπερθεν ἔχει·
>
> Solon 4.1-4

> Our city will never be destroyed by a dispensation
> from Zeus or the plans of the blessed immortal gods,
> for truly a great-hearted daughter of a mighty father
> Pallas Athena holds her hands over it.

The separation of the city from the gods is also assumed in fragment 11, given the problem of tyranny as it arises from the actions of the citizens (see Chapter 7 for the entire fragment). Solon holds the men of Athens responsible for their problems, and he refuses to allow them to blame the gods for their own choices; is not the will, purpose or intentions of the gods that will bring ruin to the *polis*.[9] The same idea is expressed in a different couplet, preserved in a fragment of six lines that has been divorced from its wider context:

> εἰ δὲ πεπόνθατε λυγρὰ δι' ὑμετέρην κακότητα,
> μὴ θεοῖσιν τούτων μοῖραν ἐπαμφέρετε·
>
> Solon 11.1-2

> If by your own actions you have suffered these most grievous calamities
> do not place the blame for your lot (*moira*) on the gods.

1. 'I brought the people together'

There are many linguistic parallels to epic verse here: the *aisa* 'portion' or 'destiny' of the immortals is found for example at *Iliad* 17.321, *huper Dios aisan*, the achievement of men beyond that provided by the gods, but denied to the Greeks by Apollo. *Iliad* 16.780 allows men to achieve *huper aisan*, 'beyond expectation' given that the Gods have not intervened.[10] But there remains an important distinction in Homer between situations in which the gods are involved, and those in which they are not. Homer speaks famously of men who wrongly blame the gods for their own shortcomings. But in Homer any failure by the gods to protect a favourite is always preceded by deliberate withdrawal, never a defeat by human force.[11] In Solon's verses Athena continues to protect Solon's *polis* even as Athens faces ruin, her pledge of protection empty before hubristic men, who manipulate the passions of the crowd for the sake of power. This may seem to place Athena in the unenviable position of being an incapable protector, but her role is not to protect men from themselves. Emily Anhalt, citing Athena as among the best of the witnesses and guardians in Homer, wonders whether Solon has redefined the city into a 'tacit agreement'. Athena as *episkopos* in Solon might be the protector of that bond.[12] But Athena would not guard any particular agreement, nor could she prevent the social breakdown to follow were such agreements broken. The whole point to the problems in the *polis* is that men have failed to guard their agreements for themselves.

The presence of pre-existing linguistic and mythic forms in Solon's words is not an unambiguous indication of irrational mental processes or non-political thought. To assume as much threatens to elevate the modern connotations of the symbol over what it represents to Solon. Oswyn Murray has hypothesized that the presence of such forms has influenced modern investigators, leading to the manufacture of pre-political conditions which the classical Greeks had to rise above. Murray disagrees: 'archaic rationality' rather serves up new concepts under the old mythic signs, and the sign is not a direct guide to the content. Murray cites the Athenian Kleisthenic reforms, which created new relationships in a way that does not admit to institutionalized 'tribal' baggage held over from a rigid, religious past. Terms such as *phulai* (and the translation 'tribes') have led historians to associate erroneously the archaic institution with the modern referent and its primitive connotations.[13] The remedy is to consider what the symbol refers to rather than the modern referent to the translation. Similarly, Solon's use of Athena is not necessarily the reiteration of a primitive deity but may be the expression, in mythical language and form, of a world-view that is highly naturalistic, even if expressed in traditional language, akin to new (conceptual) wine served up in old (linguistic) bottles.[14]

Athena's energy is directed upwards, hardening the separation between men and gods, and defining a place for each. Athena affirms the independence of Athens from divine 'intentions', or 'plans' as well as *aisa*

Solon the Thinker

('dispensations'); men must not blame the gods for their lot (*moira*).[15] Athens is to be free of the capricious changes that Zeus brought to Hesiod's fifth race of men.[16] Homer lacks such a barrier: the gods turn against Troy, Athena brings active assistance to Achilles with the agreement of Zeus, and Apollo deserts Hector when the scales of death turn against him in *Iliad* 22. Similarly *Dikê* in Hesiod sits next to Zeus and tells him of human misdeeds, to which Zeus responds personally.[17] Solon, however, exhibits a different world-view, and consequently a very different idea of justice. His city is not under divine control. It belongs exclusively to us.

In literary evidence, Athena as *episkopos* of a *polis* is unique to Solon.[18] She may be Solon's special point of focus for the stability of the *polis* and its distinct place in the world, and the expression, in archaic language and form, of a world-view that confirms human responsibility for the *polis* while holding external forces at arms length. Athena's removal of divine dispensation is consistent with the general decline in the power of Zeus across Solon's fragments, which is suggested not only by the number of citations but by the reduced scope of their authority. Of the six mentions of Zeus in the fragments, 4.1-4 explicitly denies the ability of the gods either to protect or to destroy the *polis*. The two hexameter lines constituting fragment 31, possibly a preface to his laws, appear ritualistic and formulaic, asking Zeus for *kudos* 'renown' and *agathê tuchê* 'good luck' for his statutes, but making no claims for their divine origin.[19] This fragment may be spurious. First, it is the only extant hexameter line in Solon. Second, Plutarch says that 'some say' that he put his laws into epic form – neither he nor Plato or Aristotle claimed to have solid evidence. Third, his laws were so important that it is difficult to believe that later Athenians would not have preserved – or reconstructed – them, had they existed in this form. The fragment may represent a set of oral customs associated with Solon, an unwritten *ethos* spoken in epic metre, with no theological implications for Zeus. Only in poem 13 is Zeus shown as doing anything connected directly to human affairs, and such analogies are in the context of the pursuit of material sustenance (*bios*) by particular men without mention of the *polis*.[20] The upshot is that Zeus does not run Solon's *polis*, whatever his role in our individual lives.

The result is that the source of motion and change for the *polis* is now internal and not external, and the responsibility for it rests on the Athenians themselves. This establishes the terms by which Solon can understand the *polis* as a self-supporting *kosmos* with its own internal energy and self-sufficient principles of conflict and harmony.[21] This then demands that he offer an explanation for how it works.

Solon's verses suggest an implicit but growing understanding that the *polis* – like natural phenomena – must be grasped in terms of horizontal interactions between neuter, internal factors rather than vertical despotisms directed by wilful, external forces. Solon – like the Presocratic philosophers – may have increased the use of neuter adjectives as abstract

1. 'I brought the people together'

nouns. Charles Kahn has noted the development of neuters in the Presocratic philosophers, e.g. *to apeiron, to chreôn, ta enantia, to periechon*, as a 'linguistic stamp' replacing mythical personalities with regular powers: 'The strife of elemental forces is henceforth no unpredictable quarrel between capricious agents, but an orderly scheme'.[22] This is consistent with Solon's general approach, which stresses factors *inside* the *polis* – such as psychic qualities, *hubris* and wealth – and their consequences to explain its condition. Perhaps Thales was also looking for a source of motion and change inside phenomena such as magnets and amber, rather than an external power.[23] His *panta plêrê theiôn* (all things are full of gods), contemporary with Solon if authentic, may have been the only form of expression available to him, in an age before distinctions such as animate and inanimate, or material and motive, had been made. As Thales' statement puts a non-wilful power into objects, and allows them the power of self-generated action, so Solon's denial of divine will places the motive power of the *polis* into the citizens, and forces a reliance on an embedded rather than authoritarian conception of necessity to explain its movements. To speculate further about Solon's relationship to Thales will not be fruitful, although it is worth stressing that Thales was contemporary with Solon, and was no doubt aware of his ideas.

What is certain in Solon's extant verses is that, in contrast to Homer and Hesiod, Solon never has Athena intercede actively into human affairs, and never speaks of a natural event to follow from a human action. Solon's view of the *polis* rather belongs to the world of his young contemporary Xenophanes, whose explanations for natural events constitute denials that the gods create such wonders *ex nihilo*.[24] Xenophanes' criticisms of anthropomorphic theology reverse Hesiod's creation myths and acknowledge that human beings created the gods. Although he does not go that far, Solon does say that Zeus will not alter the order in the *polis*, a prerequisite to Solon's creation and establishment of his own order in Athens. Each man to some degree replaces divine whims with rational explanations, Xenophanes in the world at large and Solon in the *polis*, and each man places human actions at the forefront of his conclusions. Each understands that human knowledge is limited, a view possibly necessitated by the lack of a substitute for the poetic forms that each man was coming to challenge, but also founded upon a real inability to know the future.[25] With men unable to reach the gods and the gods no longer coming down to men, shortcomings in human ability to grasp the unseen will hold the gravest consequences for Solon, as for Greek thought in general.

The differences between Solon's *Hymn to the City* and Hesiod's *Works and Days* cannot be explained as Solon simply replacing Zeus with *Dikê*, or replacing *Dikê* the cosmic person with *dikê* the cosmic power. The difference between my interpretation and that of Elizabeth Irwin turns on what we each see as most important. Irwin observes that the arbitrariness of Hesiod's Zeus has been removed, yet preserves a Hesiodic interpretation of Solon 4 by claiming that Solon bypassed the problem by 'simply leaving Zeus out'. Because of its Hesiodic use of language, she concludes, Solon 4 'nevertheless does advance with a line of thought that is quintessentially Hesiodic'. The problem, as she explains it, is that 'to be Hesiodic without Zeus verges on the oxymoronic. Solon's "thoroughly Hesiodic" poem chooses a depiction of *dikê* which both is, and is not, obviously and thoroughly Hesiodic, depending on what are considered to be the essential elements of Hesiod'.[26] In my view, to elevate Solon's poetic form of expression over his explicit message is an improper subordination. The most important thing about Solon is precisely his replacement of the arbitrary wilful interventions of Zeus – and *Dikê* personified – with an explanation based upon the internal operation of the *polis*. Solon's use of Hesiodic language indicates the form of expression that he and his audience had available, but is not the essence of its content. Epic formulations can neither explain Solon's two disavowals of divine efficacy over the *polis*, nor account for the patterns of necessary consequences, expressed in neuter terms, which run throughout his verses. Solon's poem is not, in the deepest sense, Hesiodic.

A fundamental difference has been indicated here between Solon and Hesiod. Hesiod's *Works and Days* and *Theogony* are both predicated on Zeus' power. His absence in Solon's verses about the *polis* is more than a poetic agenda or simple reworking of the ancient vision. Zeus' absence is a consequence of a shifting world-view, an implicit understanding of causal necessity that redefines profoundly and publicly the lawgiver's understanding of the *polis*, and that makes true *political* thought possible. Indeed it is the connections between justice and Zeus in poem 13 that are the anomalies in his verses, and to which we shall later return.

Solon's elevated perspective on the *polis* – best understood by standing on the acropolis and looking down at the area where the archaic village had lay spread before him – would have allowed him to see Athens as a self-supporting, independent community, taking shape before his eyes, moving under its own energy and understandable in its own terms. Solon's view of Athens may have strong connections to early Greek conceptions of *kosmos*, in which particular things are seen as integrated into a larger phenomenon, which has an internal principle of order, not an external power imposed on it. This is a working hypothesis about Solon's view of the *polis* as *kosmos*.

The first use of a *kosmos* form in Homer refers to the two sons of Atreus as *kosmêtore laôn* ('marshals of the people'); the first *kosmos* in Homer is a body of soldiers arranged in lines, and the first organizing principle is a military leader's command to come to order.[27] The Greeks are a disorderly heap until they form ranks; only then do they exhibit the coherence necessary to act in unison; only then are they integrated into a military *unit* with a single organization and purpose. It is the lines into which the soldiers are arranged that demonstrate the presence of a *kosmos* and allow

1. 'I brought the people together'

an observer to understand the unit. The greatest danger to the troops is to break the order and revert back to a mob. If a soldier speaks above his station, as did Thersites in *Iliad* 2, 'the worst of the Achaeans' who is *ou kata kosmon,* 'out of order', he destroys the unit and becomes a threat to everyone.[28] A growing awareness of the importance of speech to good order is suggested by the increasing use of *kosmos* with respect to speech in the *Odyssey*. '*Ou kata kosmon*' is of course not 'falsely', but rather 'inharmoniously'; whether true or not, the speech is inappropriate because it brings forth the unpleasant emotions that lead to strife.

Other examples of *kosmoi* in Homer imply the ability to see an orderly arrangement in specific things in the world; *kosmoi* include vegetable beds and clothing.[29] From the underlying idea of a *kosmos* as something 'neat and physically trim', Charles Kahn shows *kosmos* as preparing a meal, cleaning a house or setting an arrow to a bow as 'neat arrangement'. Kahn sees a 'transfer' to the 'wider decorative sense' of 'finery, rich adornment', and 'the good order of the assembled host ... ordered by a leader'.[30] The political implications of an ordered arrangement are found in men 'arranged in three groups ... dwelling apart by tribes'; it is the arrangement by tribes that establishes the identity of the political unit.[31] But as with all such examples, it may be misleading to assume that the Greeks had different meanings for the different uses, and to select meanings from a list. It may be more consistent with the outlook of the Greeks themselves to find a core meaning that is fundamental to all the applications. This is especially true in the case of *kosmos*, given that its 'ordering', 'adornment', 'marshalling' and 'beauty' senses are all used in Homer. At *Iliad* 4.145 the bridle is a *kosmos* to the horse and a *kudos* to the rider. The bridle is a *kosmos* because it brings order to the horse; it makes the horse fit for use and the rider worthy of praise; the result is a thing of beauty.

An integrated understanding of the earth and sky may have first occurred systematically in Hesiod's *Theogony*: 'the confusing variety of phenomena are reduced to a few principles, so they can be grasped by the mind'.[32] A similar integrative function and cognitive purpose are found in Hesiod's *Works and Days*, where the injunction to Perses 'let it be dear to you to order (*kosmein*) your work (*erga*) properly (*metria*)' urges him to arrange the multitude of operations required to run a farm into a manageable order.[33] The poem seeks to unify and clarify the farming calendar, and thus to provide points of reference for the farmer's activities within a graspable arrangement of seasons. In the archaic poets such a systematic integration may be sought for reasons of beauty or utility, and it may have an application to the organization of a *polis*.[34] But the idea that is fundamental to these examples is that an integrative order is used to bring complex phenomena into the reach of man's intellect and actions. To create an order among particular things (*kosmein*), or to order something well (*kata kosmon*, or *eu kata kosmon*) is to create such an arrangement.

The *kosmos* is an 'organized whole', with 'distinct parts that comprise the union'.[35] It is the nature of the parts and the principle of their arrangement that makes the multiplicity a *kosmos*. The size and scope of a *kosmos* is contextual to whatever is under view. In terms of scale, G.S. Kirk describes an ambiguity in the Presocratic use of *kosmos* 'which could signify either the world as a whole or more localized arrangements within it'.[36] But this is not an ambiguity; it is rather the application of the same idea on various scales of integration, on multiple levels. As a brooch (an arrangement of gems) on the lapel of a well-dressed woman is a *kosmos*, so is the woman's total outfit (including the brooch), the *polis* in which the woman lives, and the universe of which the *polis* is a part. This integrating way of mind is fundamental to how the Greeks understood their world. Hussey, discussing the *kosmos* that is the universe, observes that its intelligibility 'as a whole' is vital; 'the assumption that the cosmos is *piece-meal* intelligible is surely implicit in all cosmologies'.[37] Once properly ordered the *polis* itself becomes a *polis-kosmos*; freed from external forces both divine and foreign, its justice is found in the arrangement of its internal factors, and their dispositions towards one another, understood as a whole.

This may be how Solon understands his beloved Athens. Explicit confirmation of this hypothesis cannot be found in his extant verses – but it is fundamental to his entire approach to the *polis*. He speaks of *kosmos* terms three times: his verses as a *kosmos* of words (1.1), the failure of hubristic men to order (*kosmein*) present festivities properly (4.10), and wealth improperly gained as *ou kata kosmon* (13.11). In each case there is an arrangement – of words or activities – that demonstrates an internal order and beauty of form. Solon's sense of the *polis* is as an integrated phenomenon, governed by its own power, understandable by its internal relationships. Solon expresses this in *hêmeterê de polis* – 'Our *polis*!', the first linking of *hêmeteros* with the *polis* – as an impetus to preserve its order by 'bringing the people together' under a common system of justice.[38]

Solon had a wealth of tools at hand to bolster this sense of integration and identity: the war over Salamis, a feeling towards the fatherland as god-founded, a sense of *dikê* as the means to preserve the *polis*, and claims to Homeric heroism received through a rich palette of mythic stories. His festival calendar may be an attempt to synchronize the order of the agricultural seasons with the festivals and the public life of the *polis*.[39] The seven-year seasons of life in fragment 27 bring an orderly arrangement to the stages of human life.[40] Fragment 6 connects the psychic qualities to the condition of the *polis*. *Eunomiê* in poem 4 integrates the various aspects of a just *polis* into a single point of focus, anchored to a proper state of mind in each one of us. The statutes of poem 36 become the focus of civic integration, for a *polis* in which individual judgments are harmonized around a common, enforced, sense of justice. Elizabeth Irwin, guided by the genre of 'martial exhortation elegy' and the assumption of 'heroic role-playing' through performance in aristocratic symposia, sees Solon's

1. 'I brought the people together'

claim in 4.10, that the leaders did not properly '*kosmein*' the festivities, in military terms: Solon undercut the leaders' pretences to martial prowess. Perhaps, although there are other applicable meanings of *kosmos*, and other contexts of delivery apart from the symposium. For Solon, of course, the most important point is that martial prowess is not a value inside the *polis*.[41]

Such a view would demand that Solon look for reasons for tumult within the *polis*, to show the relationships between each one of us and the *polis* as a whole, and to ask why we all too often act to disrupt its harmony. A science of politics, connected to theories of the soul, would be a natural outgrowth of such views Much in what follows in this book is intended to ask whether, and to what extent, the self-governing nature of the *polis*, and its proper form of organization, are found in the verses, and how far such an order extends in human life. How does each one of us relate to the *polis*? Where is its energy? (Chapter 2) What is its organizing principle? What constitutes good order, and does it apply to all areas of life? (Chapter 3) Are Solon's own poems a *kosmos* of words, with an internal arrangement of their own? (Chapter 4) What are the limits to Solon's capacity to understand how such an organizing principle applies to human life beyond the *polis*? (Chapters 5 and 6) How does Solon actually change the order in Athens? (Chapter 7).

It is valuable to consider two visual perspectives on the *polis*. Standing on the acropolis, akin to an architect who sees a plan view of his building, or a city planner or cosmologist who takes an external perspective on his subject, Solon could have seen the *polis* as a whole. Its streets and buildings would have betrayed an underlying order, as if from the elevated vantage-point of a god. His mind could have searched for its hidden patterns, understanding those buildings and the men in them according to an immanent order not unlike that in the sky above or the sea in the distance. He could have considered the need to 'bring the people together', not in a physical sense, but in terms of a common standard of justice and written laws. From his higher perspective he could have recognized what was needed to establish such an order in his audience, or what was setting them into conflict. Looking down he might have seen conflicts in the *polis* as akin to wounds on a body.[42]

Then, stepping back into the *polis*, from an internal, street-level vantage point, as a mediator in a dispute, an official surrounded by rival claimants, or reclining at a symposium, Solon would have seen not the whole, but the particular people in it. He could have come to understand the *polis* in terms of what drove his fellows, for good or bad – akin to an architect who sees the elevation view of the building and works on its joints. Looking for an internal source of motion and change in the *polis,* he could have drawn connections between the psychic factors in each person and the condition of the *polis* in which they lived, and expressed them in terms of the poetry he knew. He saw not just a disparate bunch of people, acting with neither rhyme nor reason, but rather a singularity – a living-together, or *sunoikism* – that could be understood and sculpted into a proper shape. To do this he would have to reach each person, and persuade him to bring order and restraint to his own dispositions and actions.

2

'To know all things'
Psychic qualities and the *polis*

> Now one ought to know all things [well]
> Solon 9.6

It is impossible to know the nature of the audience, and the actual state of Athens, when Solon spoke the words preserved as poem 4, his *Hymn to the City*. Did he speak before an aristocratic clique, at a time of great challenges to their prerogatives, or rather in a public area, full of tumult from a gathering mob? Did he harangue his audience and challenge their views, or leverage their support for his own ends by feigning agreement? Was he reflecting calmly upon earlier events that had been resolved, or calling passionately for an end to a crisis now? Was he an archon laying down a *diktat* and acting with the power proper to that office, or rather guiding his fellows under an informal authority, perhaps decades after holding formal office? This information is forever lost to us. But what we do know is that Solon was immersed in the gritty affairs of the *polis*, as a mediator of some kind within the tumultuous interactions of his fellows. Rather than standing apart, as an impartial observer of distant phenomena, he was an actor of first rank within the very affairs he was trying to guide.

This difference in perspective – between the *polis* as a cosmetic whole, as if seen from without, and the direct experience of its internal energy – is not explicit in his verses, and doubtless not conceptualized by him. If he did see the *polis* in these two ways, it is the holistic, cosmopoetic view that would constitute the greater intellectual leap – as Anaximander's cosmology was a greater feat of intellectual integration than isolated observations of the sky. But as a lawgiver and teacher, Solon solidly connected the condition of the *polis* to the thoughts and actions of individual men, through their psychic qualities. The men are the individual stars that make up the political *kosmos*. The key link between the individual and the *polis* is the attitudes and dispositions of the men, those aspects of the *psuchê* that govern their relations with one another. Progressing further into poem 4, and following his denial that the gods will destroy Athens, Solon places the blame for the destruction of the city squarely on the shoulders of its people:

Solon the Thinker

αὐτοὶ δὲ φθείρειν μεγάλην πόλιν ἀφραδίῃσιν
ἀστοὶ βούλονται χρήμασι πειθόμενοι

Solon 4.5-6

The townsmen (*astoi*) themselves by their foolishness are willing
to destroy the great city, persuaded by material goods

Solon's use of a form of *boulomai* ('I am willing'; 'I choose'; 'I wish') with the infinitive form *phtheirein* ('to destroy'; 'to corrupt'), directed at the *polis*, is unattested in archaic Greek sources apart from Solon. *Phtheirein* here means 'to destroy' rather than 'to corrupt', given the slavery, civil strife and war (*doulosunê*, *stasis* and *polemos*) to which the corruption of the leaders necessarily leads. Solon emphasizes the point by slowing the metre in the first colon of the elegiac line 4.6:

– – – – – –∪∪–∪∪–

This is not an uncommon construction, but it occurs elsewhere in poem 4 only in lines 24 and 35. The impact of this line on his audience would have been powerful. It is an unmitigated statement that the townsmen have wilfully chosen to destroy the *polis*.

In Solon's time the meanings of *ethelô* and *boulomai* had not yet fused; they denoted different aspects of volition and choice, and implied a different basis for any resulting action.[1] The translation of *ouk ethelô* as being 'unable' to act differently can be distinguished from the active choice implied by *boulomai*. If I acquiesce in the decision of another then I *ethelô* by force or by habit, whereas if I make my own considered decision I *boulomai*.[2] An example in Solon of *ethelô*, applied to material objects, is found in the doors to a man's home, which the public evil breaks through even though they are *ouk ethelousin* ('not willing', or 'non-compliant'), i.e. locked – and if they are breached, it is not by their agreement.

In poem 13 Solon claims similarly that material goods may follow unwillingly because wealth, seen almost anthropomorphically, has been forced in a way contrary to its natural dispositions. Masaracchia illustrates this 'unwillingness' with a comparison between Sol. 13.11-13 and *Iliad* 13.570, equating Solon's 'by *hubris*' (*huph' hubrios*) with 'by force' (*biê*):[3]

ὃν [πλοῦτος] δ' ἄνδρες τιμῶσιν ὑφ' ὕβριος, οὐ κατὰ κόσμον
ἔρχεται, ἀλλ' ἀδίκοις ἔργμασι πειθόμενος
οὐκ ἐθέλων ἕπεται

Solon 13.11-13

ὁ δ' ἑσπόμενος περὶ δουρὶ
ἤσπαιρ' ὡς ὅτε βοῦς, τόν τ' οὔρεσι βουκόλοι ἄνδρες
ἰλλάσιν οὐκ ἐθέλοντα βίῃ δήσαντες ἄγουσιν.

Iliad 13.570-2

2. 'To know all things'

[wealth] which men honour (*timôsin*) by *hubris* comes not with proper order,
   but persuaded by unjust deeds
does not follow willingly[4]

   and he, writhing over the spear
struggles, as an ox does when the herdsmen in the hills
have bound him strongly in twisted ropes, and drag him unwillingly.

These passages suggest acquiescence to the will of another by necessity rather than agreement, because no other possibility exists. But *ethelô* can also indicate a willingness to do a thing because one is used to doing things in that way, or has been foolishly persuaded against a wise choice, each of which is in contrast to proper deliberation and decision *Boulomai* refers to a higher faculty capable of controlling a person's actions, the faculty that can override one's customary actions if one so decides. Homer provides examples in which *boulomai* can override *ethelô*, for example, at *Odyssey* 17.228, as at 18.364, in which Odysseus, disguised as a beggar, is derided, 'since he learned (*emmathen*) evil deeds, he will not care (*ouk ethelêsin*) to busy himself with work, but is minded (*bouletai*) rather to go stalking about the land'.[5]

Once Solon tells the Athenians that their leaders are minded (*boulontai*) to act as they do, those who continue with their *hubris* can no longer claim that they have not been warned. Their *implicit* desire to gain loot perforce is transformed into an *explicit* choice to continue on the path of destruction, which Solon roundly condemns. As Adkins put it, *boulontai* 'characterizes the citizens' actions as not merely likely but voluntarily accepted'; 'the *polis* is a relatively new institution: powerful inhabitants might be willing to allow it to perish' if their own, or friends' *oikoi* were safe. In these terms, Solon's own disposition is very different from that of his fellows. How his vision affects his own passionate desire to act on behalf of Athens is revealed in his own poignant and personal statement:

γινώσκω, καί μοι φρενὸς ἔνδοθεν ἄλγεα κεῖται,
   πρεσβυτάτην ἐσορῶν γαῖαν [Ἰ]αονίης
κλινομένην

Solon 4a

I come to know, and many pains lie in my heart
   as I look on my most ancient land of Ionia
declining

Looking upon the degradation of his homeland he comes to understand (*gignôskô*) the implications of what he sees, an inchoate process that he elsewhere mused as coming to poets from the god Apollo (as in *egnô*, poem 13 line 54).[6] Solon's *noêsis* – his grasp of the deeper implication of the situation – is conditioned by his evaluation of Attica as *presbutatê*; the

Solon the Thinker

basic meaning 'most aged' is also 'most venerable'.[7] From this sight and understanding come pains (*algea*) that lie in his *phrên*, which lead him to a passionate desire to act on behalf of Athens.[8] He is in a sense persuaded to do so, by his evaluation of the scene before his eyes. Solon's responses again imply a connection between *phrên* and the onset of an action, albeit it his own and not that of the immortals. By looking on he comes to know; the pains lie in his heart because he has become aware of the implications of what he sees. There is conjecture involved in *klinomenên*. The basic idea must be related to 'declining', 'tottering', or 'burning'. Although things are going downhill, Athens is still at a point where she can still be saved. He – not Zeus – wants to do something to end the decline. Other verses suggest that the range of his motivations is even wider, given what it meant to be an Athenian. For example, a series of myths connected Athenian identity to the war with Megara for the control of Salamis; Solon's poem *Salamis* explicitly connected his own Athenian identity to the war, and a failure to fight the war to personal shame. Solon's fragments 1, 2 and 3 may represent a single passage, connected to civic pride.[9]

Many of his fellows might agree with him on the war, and he stimulates their support by recalling the martial *ethos* they share, but inside the *polis* the same *ethos* does not apply. They do not yet grasp that assertions of martial prowess must not be directed at their fellows. Far from excellence, this has become injustice. They see the same things that Solon does, but through either defective dispositions, lack of poetic wisdom or conscious choice their *hubris* leads them to act for short-term loot. If Solon had his way, they would channel their desires for wealth or power into a deep attachment to justice in the *polis*, similar to Thucydides' account of Pericles' admonishment to the Athenians to love Athens rather than entreat with the Spartans. In either case, the emotions of the audience should properly rise against those bringing trouble to that *polis*. But the earlier Athenians were not in this frame of mind. Given the different *ethos* each follows, they were struggling with one another for some mixture of advantage, honour, reputation, loot, status or slaves, and taking the *polis* into strife. The key problem in poem 4 is the leaders of the people – those standing forth and claiming a pre-eminent position before 'the people' of Athens, whoever they are – whose *noos* is corrupt because they fail to grasp the new excellence of the *polis*. This redefinition of the civic *ethos* is the key to Solon's condemnations.

Poem 4 continues:

δήμου θ' ἡγεμόνων ἄδικος νόος, οἷσιν ἑτοῖμον
ὕβριος ἐκ μεγάλης ἄλγεα πολλὰ παθεῖν·
οὐ γὰρ ἐπίστανται κατέχειν κόρον οὐδὲ παρούσας
εὐφροσύνας κοσμεῖν δαιτὸς ἐν ἡσυχίῃ

Solon 4.7-10

2. 'To know all things'

and the *noos* of the people's leaders is unjust; they are about
  to suffer many pains from great *hubris*.
For they do not understand how to restrain their *koros*
  nor to order (*kosmein*) the present festivities of the banquet in calmness
                                                    (*en hêsuchiêi*)[10]

It is evident that Solon sees a necessary sequence of *koros* ('satiety') leading to *hubris* when the *noos* ('disposition', 'outlook' or 'understanding') is imperfect. *Hubris* is, in essence, arrogance in action, including larceny and assault, directed against the proper prerogatives of another person, the gods or the *polis*. It is not merely an attitude or disposition.[11] Noussia comments to Solon 13.11, that *hubris* is ' "violenza" et la componente antisociale', and contrasted with *kosmos*.[12] *Koros* is associated with larceny and ill-gotten wealth at 4.8, 13.11 and 16, and with *isomoiria* 'equal shares' at 6.3. It is contrasted with *Eunomiê* at 4.34. *Hubris* does not end with each person and his immediate opponent; poem 4 extends the *hubris* of men whose *noos* is not appropriate from the banquet into *polemos, stasis* and *doulosunê* ('war, civil strife and slavery'), reaching everyone, whether directly involved or not. The condition of the *polis* is vitally, and immediately, dependent upon the *noos* of the leaders of the people, and *hubris* is an action that destroys it. The identity of the *dêmos* here is not clear – whether the entire population, the townsmen or some upper or non-farming class – but that does not change the necessary sequence that Solon sees.

In fragment 6, musing to an unknown audience about the *dêmos* and their leaders, Solon also connects a flawed *noos* to *hubris* through *koros*:

δῆμος δ' ὧδ' ἂν ἄριστα σὺν ἡγεμόνεσσιν ἕποιτο,
  μήτε λίην ἀνεθεὶς μήτε βιαζόμενος·
τίκτει γὰρ κόρος ὕβριν, ὅταν πολὺς ὄλβος ἕπηται
  ἀνθρώποις ὁπόσοις μὴ νόος ἄρτιος ᾖ.
                                                    Solon 6

In this way the people would follow their leaders best,
  neither allowed to overreach nor oppressed too much.
For *koros* breeds hubris, whenever great wealth follows
  men whose *noos* is flawed.

Lines 3-4 in fragment 6 make the same essential claims as found in poem 4, albeit in a different order. Poem 4 line 7 begins with the flawed *noos* of the leaders of the people, extends the consequences through *koros* and *hubris*, which the remainder of the poem takes into civil strife, war and slavery. Fragment 6.3-4 is a generalized form of the claim in poem 4, that *hubris* in the *polis* is the inevitable result of *koros*, the excess that follows men of unjust *noos*. Conversely, the entire sequence in poem 4, from *hubris* to *stasis*, is an application of the general condition in 6.3-4 to the political ordering of Athens, in terms of the propensity of the people or their leaders to act immoderately. To understand *stasis* one must grasp *hubris*, and to understand *hubris* one must grasp *koros*, which is explained by a flawed *noos* in the presence of wealth (*ploutos*) or power (*kratos*) that it cannot handle. In such formulations Solon in effect isolates the specific psychic factors that determine the condition of the *polis*, and considers them in terms of their necessary relationships, all the while condemning the men involved.[13]

Whose *noos* is flawed in fragment 6 is ambiguous; the likelihood of sarcasm or irony is real. On the one hand it may be that of the leaders – not the *dêmos* – given the blame that Solon assigns in poem 4 towards the leaders of the people. If a leader's *noos* is bad, yet he has access to material resources or factional loyalties, then the *koros* that accompanies his position will lead him to *hubris*, by forming a gang, mobilizing his family or appealing to a crowd. On the other hand, the real source of the problems may be in the mob, which must be restrained properly, i.e. neither too much nor too little. That they cannot control themselves is probably a given for Solon. Taking fragment 6 in this light, it may be the immoderation of the people – either grasping beyond their appropriate level, or failing to keep budding tyrants in check – that is to blame. The best overall interpretation of the lines may be that Solon directed his warnings towards everyone – rich and poor, powerful and not – and that *hubris* must be avoided in every case. Irwin notes that lines 3-4 of fragment 6, *anthrôpois hoposois*, are 'more universalizing' than a similar phrase in Theognis 153-4: *kakôi ... anthrôpôi kai hotôi ...* 'a base man and one [whose mind is not fit]'.[14] Any conclusion that all blame falls on 'the rich' – or 'the poor' – would fail to capture the universal nature of Solon's moral admonishments, and would exempt some men in the *polis* from responsibility for its condition.

In two fragments of six and eight lines, preserved as poems 9 and 11 (reproduced and discussed in Chapter 7), Solon also placed the blame for the destruction of Athens on the flawed *noos* of its citizens. In fragment 9, the connection between *noos* and the condition of the *polis* is immediate: the slavery of tyranny comes from *aidriê* 'ignorance', and the remedy is to 'know' (*noein*) all things, which may mean to intend that all things be well.[15] In fragment 11, the *noos* which is empty (*chaunos*) in the people leads them to a similar result, given their willingness to accept a speaker's words while ignoring the things he does. Such verses illustrate the naturalism in Solon's thinking – his ability to relate the city to phenomena in the sky in fragment 9 – as well his grasp that *noos* is the key factor in the *polis*, akin to the wind that destroys the calm. There is much more to say about these fragments; at this point it is important only to note that in the last four passages, Solon directed blame at the men for their failures in *noos* and the injustice that accompanies ignorance, while he, of course, does not suffer from their noetic failures.

We should certainly not assume that these poems were heard in se-

2. 'To know all things'

quence, or even by the same crowd; but they do suggest that Solon was able to present similar ideas in different ways, at different times and before different audiences. Solon describes a causal sequence that stretches from an internal psychic state to the entire *polis*. Solon has no concept of 'cause'; but he knows that big things follow from small beginnings, see 13.14-15, and poem 4 clearly shows civil strife as following upon *hubris*. In fragments 9 and 11 the process is causal because each step is preceded by antecedent factors that make the consequences necessary; once begun it continues inevitably to its end. The innovations here are not the effects of *hubris* and *atê*, but rather Solon's reliance on a necessity that underlies *koros*, *ploutos*, *atê*, *hubris* and *stasis*. Scholars have noted Solon's innovative associations between these factors.[16] In essence, he replaced the gods – such as Homer's Athena, who motivated Achilles to leave his sword in his sheath, at the start of his conflict with Agamemnon – with neuter psychic qualities. These qualities have no personalities themselves; they are rather part of the human personality (if it is permissible to use a word so far beyond Solon's own conceptions). Rather than an anthropomorphized figure whispering in the ear of a man or a god – as Athena spoke to Achilles, and as *Dikê* whispers to Zeus in Hesiod's *Works and Days* – the whisper each man hears is his *noos*, the restraint of 'conscience' necessary to a proper disposition towards a situation. The mature expression of this idea would be Socrates' *daimon*, which never tells him what to do, but only restrains him.

Koros is a vital concept for Solon, a symptom of the failure to restrain one's *noos*, and Solon's use of it illustrates how a term can be re-defined normatively. Prior to Solon, *koros* ('satiety'), contrasted with any state of need, was not a bad thing. *Penia* ('poverty'), not *koros*, could drive a man into violence. Satiety applies to many things – e.g. *ploutos* (wealth) versus *polemos* (war) – but in any case *koros* means that one has enough; it ends any competition or conflict associated with pursuing its object.[17] In *Iliad* 13.64-5 Menelaus, standing over the body of Pisander, speaks of the Trojans as never satiated by war; if they were, they would hand over the woman and end the bloodshed. Menelaus is unaware of the grim irony of his stripping the armour off his dead foe, and of his responsibility for the problems of the Greeks, given his failure to restrain his own desire for more. His own position, at the top of the Greek social and military hierarchy, leads him to expect greater rewards and honours, relative to his social position. This is the root, at best only implied in Homer, of *koros* as 'excess': it is too much loot in relation to one's heroic *arête*, based on birth, good counsel, success in battle, and loot. But *koros* itself remains satiety, not excess.

In Hesiod's *Works and Days*, *koros* is also good. Good *eris* is the beneficial strife between productive persons, which Hesiod's relative Perses should embrace by renouncing fraud, and which contrasts with the detrimental strife between unjust men. The need to fill a barn full of hay is the practical reason for diligent work, and becoming satisfied in this endeavour brings one to the point at which it is permissible to raise disputes in town.[18] The poetic contrast with *koros* is poverty; in the poet's words, 'there is no advantage in destroying Poverty (*oulomenês Peniês*), only in Satiety (*Koros*)'.[19] But *koros* is not itself a motivation for *hubris* in Homer or Hesiod; what drives a man to violent action remains a lack, and the desire to overcome it, not the fulfilment of one's needs. *Koros* 'satisfaction' can give a man good cheer, and increase his strength to fight, but it is not a motivation to start or prolong a fight.[20]

Solon's verses are the first instances in extant Greek literature in which *koros* is cited as unambiguously bad; perhaps 'Solon was participating in – or even originating – the discourse on greed that Aristotle engaged with so deeply'.[21] Solon's concept of *koros* is all the more pointed since the personal corruption of *koros* leads to *hubris* and the destruction of the *polis*. On the face of it, this is a contradiction in terms; satiety is a condition in which desire has been fulfilled, not one that creates further desire. But Solon describes it as a corruption in *noos*, a blind, wanton desire for more beyond one's proper measure. The key development here is an explicit shift in the meaning of *koros* from 'satiety' to 'excess', and from the satisfaction of actual needs to the desire for unjust gain. *Koros* becomes excessive greed, an irrational desire that recognizes no limits to the ways in which wealth or power can be obtained, and that strives for acquisition from *hubris*, looting and slavery. Material success leads to the demand for more, at the expense of others, with dire consequences for the *polis*. Solon makes explicit the psychic factors that necessitate this shift.

For Solon, this desire for more at any price is not a function of material wealth itself, any more than receiving a pay-cheque today might lead one to commit robbery tonight. It is rather a person's attitude or disposition towards wealth and power that motivates a man towards violence, slavery and larceny. If *noos* is not *artios* ('proper', or 'appropriate') then the effects of material goods will be negative; 'satiety' becomes 'excess'. The level of wealth appropriate to a man of noble birth might destroy a base man who becomes newly rich, whose *noos* is unable to cope with it. Perhaps this is an early form of what would become Aristotle's ethical 'mean relative to us', an idea that connects virtue to what is appropriate to each individual, all the while preserving the general categories by which it is grasped.

Taking a counter-example from later history, given his ascetic premises, an archetypical medieval saint will reject material success in favour of poverty, seeing himself as good through self-abnegation. Material wealth has a very different effect on him than on a Greek, who values it and wants to live well. Solon realized that a person's actions are dependent upon his disposition, and that a man with the greatest wealth can do the most damage if his disposition is inappropriate. Leaving aside the question of whether Solon thinks anyone has *noos* that is capable of avoiding the corruption brought by material goods, 'success' becomes 'excess' if, and

2. 'To know all things'

only to the extent that, the *noos* is flawed. Solon, of course, is surrounded by men in this condition – as any experience at any gathering of Athenian citizens could verify. Their debased psychic conditions are destroying his world.

But what is *noos* in Solon?[22] *Noos* is a psychic quality with two main aspects. The first is the *locus* of a man's 'disposition' to think and to act, including his ambitiousness and willingness to strive; it is his general frame of mind. The second is the intellectual grasp or 'understanding' of a situation that transcends immediate sight. *Noêsis* is the complex process by which one may 'read' or 'recognize' (*anagignôskô*) the 'deeper significance' (*sêma*) in a situation; it is the capacity that Solon knew was at best difficult for us.[23] Solon does not distinguish *noos* as a deeper understanding from a proper disposition; they are mutually affective and self-supporting aspects of a single idea. A man is disposed to act according to his understanding, and if he changes his disposition he can change his understanding. Nor, of course, does Solon distinguish the moral from the intellectual; an intellectual failing is a moral failing because it leads to *hubris*.[24]

The nature of *noos* as a proper disposition is elaborated in Solon's use of *noos* and *noein* words to indicate some kind of psychic failing that is the ultimate reason for *hubris*. An excess in *noos* would of course not mean knowing too much, but rather being improperly disposed to understand how one should control one's pursuit of power, prestige or wealth in the *polis*. Poem 27, which orders the seasons of a man's life from early years to a *telos*, links a mature *noos* to the lack of a desire to act improperly. Apart from this poem, every passage in Solon's verses citing *noos* as a human attribute uses an emotionally potent modifier to indicate an improper mental state and its consequences, linking *noos* by association with injustice, immoderation, imperfection, etc. A normal, *dikaios* state of *noos*, connected to *hêsuchia* and moderation in the *polis*, is left entirely to implication, for example by an indirect analogy to a calm sea, in fragment 12. Solon's linking of a faulty *noos* to *hubris* is his way of condemning the martial values that he sees as destructive when practised inside the *polis*.

Noos is the key to grasping civil strife. *Koros*, *hubris* and *stasis* are mutually supporting and amplifying, in a man whose *noos* is flawed, through specific actions and the corresponding psychic dispositions. Without some regulation, the cycle of *ploutos*, *koros*, *atê* and *hubris* will spiral out of control, leading to *stasis*. To control these effects each person must control his own thoughts and actions with respect to his relations with other men. This establishes a politically causal role for *noos* that is both stronger and more anthropocentric than that of Hesiod, given the earlier man's reliance upon the divine to bring retribution, and given his failure to connect the misdeeds of Perses to the political condition of Ascra.

In addition to being a psychic disposition, *noos* is the faculty of understanding the implications of a situation that are not immediately

31

observable by one's eyes. Semonides 1 remains the classic statement of man as without *noos*, living like grazing cattle and 'subject to each day':

ὦ παῖ, τέλος μὲν Ζεὺς ἔχει βαρύκτυπος
πάντων ὅς᾽ ἐστὶ καὶ τίθης᾽ ὅκῃ θέλει,
νοῦς δ᾽ οὐκ ἐπ᾽ ἀνθρώποισιν, ἀλλ᾽ ἐπήμεροι
ἃ δὴ βοτὰ ζόουσιν, οὐδὲν εἰδότες
ὅκως ἕκαστον ἐκτελευτήσει θεός.

Semonides 1.1-5

O child, Deep-thundering Zeus holds the end
of all things, as it is and which he establishes as he wishes.
There is no understanding (*nous*) in men, but they live
upon the day, like cattle, knowing nothing
of how the god will bring each thing to an end.

For Semonides we are stuck with our immediate sense perceptions, unable to grasp the abstract meaning of what we are seeing, and incapable of projecting the consequences beyond the present moment. The issue is neither the changing day nor the brevity of life.[25] The issue is rather epistemological: our perceptual consciousness (our senses) cannot give us conceptual knowledge, including an understanding of what will be. Thus, we are stuck with the present moment, like cattle. Knowledge of the unseen is reserved for Zeus, who has control over it and alone knows what it will be. The contrast here between the observable (the grass of the cattle) and the ultimate end may be read as an early form of the later distinction made between the senses and reason, in which the latter is thought to be concerned with ideas apart from sensory referents. But the Greeks at this early stage had not separated thought from their senses; all they knew was that many things are beyond sight and beyond *noos*. Being concerned for what is real, they directed themselves towards understanding the consequences of what they saw. All we have beyond immediate vision, they grasped, is our hopes, which are imperfect and misleading. Semonides expressed a common, and fundamental, theme that resonates across Greek culture: the inherent limits to human understanding, especially of the future.

Greeks of all sorts – as found in contexts from Homer to Plato – were concerned with knowing that which is beyond immediate sight or memory. In *Odyssey* 13.312-4, Odysseus says to Athena that it is hard for a man of good understanding (*mal'epistamenôi*) to recognize (*gnômai*) you since you take on every shape; although I know well (*eu oida*) your past kindnesses. In the *Iliad* Achilles does not draw his sword, because Athena tells him he will get more later; the ephemeral Agamemnon cannot grasp this idea and demands loot now. Hesiod asks Perses to turn away from present gossip and lawsuits, in order to arrange his life across a span of seasons. In Aeschylus, Cassandra speaks of a future that no one else understands, and

2. 'To know all things'

thus cannot avoid. To Sophocles, Oedipus cannot recognize his mother and father, and his search for knowledge dooms him to a bad end. Herodotus has Croesus dismiss Solon as a fool, because Solon elevates an unseen end over present wealth, a decision that Croesus would later rue. In the Melian Dialogue of Thucydides the Athenians demand that the Melians focus on the present moment – the force that stands before their city now – and reject all concern for the past or the future. In Plato's cave the incapacity to see what abstract thinkers understand leads the mob to reject the philosophers as incoherent babblers. In Stoic thought, the job of the sage is to reveal that which is hidden to non-philosophers.

The Herodotus passage represents the reception of Solon as a figure of moral wisdom in the mid-fifth century.[26] After Croesus demands to know why *he* is not the most blessed of men, Solon lectures him precisely in terms of long-range understanding versus short-range focus on the present moment. Over much time, says Solon, there are many things to see (*idein*) that one would wish (*ethelei*) not to be so, and many things to experience (or suffer, *pathein*). After all, no day is similar (*ouden homoion*) to the next in what it brings. 'You appear (*phaineai*) to be blessed', said Solon, 'but I will not answer you until I know (or perceive, *puthômai*) that your life has ended well *(prin teleutêsanta kalôs ton aiôna)*'. Great wealth is not more blessed than that possessed upon a day *(tou ep' hêmerên echontos)* unless luck allows him to continue prosperously into the end. To move past the state of an *ephêmeros* and understand the true blessedness of a man, 'One ought to look (*skopeein*) to the end of all things (*pantos chrêmatos tên teleutên)*'. The entire passage is framed in terms of knowing and seeing, and the deepest problem in human life is our inability to see that which has not yet come to be.

In Solon's verses, the inability to see the long-range consequences of one's actions – to live like Semonides' cattle with concern only for the present day – is the greatest threat to the *polis*. In a tetrameter fragment of seven lines, excerpted here, Solon himself mimics a critic who would have acted precisely this way, had he been given power in the *polis*:

'ἤθελον γάρ κεν κρατήσας, πλοῦτον ἄφθονον λαβὼν
καὶ τυραννεύσας Ἀθηνέων μοῦνον ἡμέρην μίαν,
ἀσκὸς ὕστερον δεδάρθαι κἀπιτετρίφθαι γένος'.
                                                            Solon 33.5-7

'Had I come upon power, taking lavish wealth
and subjecting the Athenians to tyranny for one day alone (*mounon hêmerên mian*),
I'd be willing to be flayed into a wineskin later (*husteron*), my family obliterated'.

Solon's caricature of a critic, anticipating Croesus, calls Solon *ouk ... bathuphrôn* 'shallow minded', and *oude bouleêis* 'not of good counsel', for

Solon the Thinker

failing to cash in on his position. Solon may have here inaugurated two new terms: *bouleeis* appears only in Solon, and *bathuphrôn* appears elsewhere only in Pindar.[27] Solon vivifies the critic's fate in order to make him culpable; such a man would follow his corrupted *phrên* and *thumos* to conscious destruction. Solon's rejoinder to his critic, in fragment 32, says that he would suffer no shame for having foregone tyranny – implying that his fellows would expect him to grasp at the power and renown – for in challenging their present evaluations he would seem (*dokeô*) to be going to be victorious (*nikêsein*) in the future:

εἰ δὲ γῆς <φησιν> ἐφεισάμην
πατρίδος, τυραννίδος δὲ καὶ βίης ἀμειλίχου
οὐ καθηψάμην μιάνας καὶ καταισχύνας κλέος,
οὐδὲν αἰδέομαι· πλέον γὰρ ὧδε νικήσειν δοκέω
πάντας ἀνθρώπους.

Solon 32

If I spared my fatherland
and did not grasp tyranny and implacable violence,
staining and disgracing my reputation,
I am not ashamed. For in this way I think that I shall
be superior to all men.

The critic lives for one day only (*mounon hêmerên mian*) while Solon denies shame now and looks ahead for greater rewards in the future. Solon's verses are filled with this idea: the *dêmos* fails to see what a wily orator does because it is locked onto his immediate words and not the consequences of his actions; a man who strives with honest diligence fails to see ahead and falls into ruin; it is difficult to know the end of all things; the mind of the immortals is hidden; men with flawed understanding ruin the city, but *Dikê* knows what is and was; we mortals both base and noble are deceived; a man with evil in his heart will become visible in the end, even if he hides now; in the Court of Time I will be exonerated. On its face such passages do not support claims that Solon was a 'wisdom poet' who cared for nothing beyond immediate sight.[28] Even if he created these verses to win the contest, he did so with an understanding of a wider issue.

Elizabeth Irwin discusses fragment 32, with a special view to its ambiguity and its use of language associated with tyranny.[29] In conclusion, she states that Solon 'exploits the language of tyranny while seeming explicitly to reject it'. 'Solon seems to have achieved what a tyrant achieves anyway, νίκη, only πλέον ("more") – the rewards of seizing tyranny without having its particular κλέος.' But this analysis fails to consider the long-range nature of what Solon is saying, both as a foil to the critic of fragment 33, the different sense of victory in his words versus those of his critic, and his use of the future infinitive *nikêsein*. He has no good reputation now and no victory, but will have it in the future, only after the terms of a good

2. 'To know all things'

reputation have been redefined. It is by rejecting tyranny that he made his claim to future exoneration 'in the Court of Time' in poem 36. Of course, over history, Solon's prediction has come true. His reputation today is due not to his wielding of power, but to his sense of justice, his claimed reforms, and his written laws. This reflects a normative redefinition, such that what was once valued is not valued today. This long-range interpretation of Solon's ideas requires us to see more than what seems, and to hold his words in context with his other ideas.

As a *sophos*, Solon's ability to see the deeper implications of a situation, and thus to avoid long-term harm and attain long-term victory, is his primary claim to virtue over both the potential tyrant and his witting supporters. Solon demonstrates his wisdom by claiming to peer inside the would-be tyrant's *noos*, the deeper, unseen cause of tyranny. His own purported interchange with a critic recreates the hidden, yet essential difference, between the lawgiver and the tyrant: the tyrant's concern is for the power or loot of the moment, while the lawgiver's focus is long range, which is reflected in the later tradition that he swore his fellows to live by the laws for years into the future. Plutarch's sarcastic witticism that 'tyranny is a lovely stronghold' is consistent with Solon's view that tyranny is established for superficial goals by short-range minds.[30] But Plutarch's 'there is no coming down' would, in Solon's terms, also relate to the noetic effects of tyranny on the tyrant – of which Croesus' *hubris* would be a prime example.

It is not only the tyrant who looks favourably upon power; the crowd is also easily deceived. In the *polis* there is a relationship between seeing with one's eyes, *noos* and the context of a political assembly, in which the functioning of a person's *noos* is adversely affected by the crowd and the speaker. Shirley Darcus Sullivan observes, in passage 11.6, that 'all together the *noos* in you is empty' prevents the Athenians from seeing 'the truth of the present situation' and 'the significance of their deeds'. 'Lack of activity in the *noos* may affect how the eyes see or fail to see', with the result that a poorly functioning *noos* perceives and accepts what the leaders say while evading what they do.[31] The group undercuts the process of *noêsis*, by what Fränkel called mass psychology, 'the surprising contrast between the intelligence of the individual and the stupidity of the collected multitude'.[32] Fragment 34 demonstrates that these misevaluations can work in the other direction; those blinded by expectation of loot may be deceived about Solon's own *noos*:

οἱ δ' ἐφ' ἁρπαγῆσιν ἦλθον· ἐλπίδ' εἶχον ἀφνεήν,
κἀδόκ[ε]ον ἕκαστος αὐτῶν ὄλβον εὑρήσειν πολύν,
καί με κωτίλλοντα λείως τραχὺν ἐκφανεῖν νόον.
χαῦνα μὲν τότ' ἐφράσαντο, νῦν δέ μοι χολούμενοι
λοξὸν ὀφθαλμοῖς ὁρῶσι πάντες ὥστε δήϊον.
οὐ χρεών· ἃ μὲν γὰρ εἶπα, σὺν θεοῖσιν ἤνυσα,
ἄλλα δ' οὐ μάτην ἔερδον, οὐδέ μοι τυραννίδος

ἁνδάνει βίη τι[..]. ε[ι]ν, οὐδὲ πιεί[ρ]ης χθονὸς
πατρίδος κακοῖσιν ἐσθλοὺς ἰσομοιρίην ἔχειν.

Solon 34

They came as upon plunder, and held hope of riches,
and each one of them expected to find much wealth,
and that I, babbling smoothly, would show a rough *noos*.
But they spoke foolishly then, and now, angry at me,
they all look askance as upon an enemy.
But it is not necessary. For whatever I said, I have done with the gods,
I did not take pointless measures, nor did it please me
(to compel?) with the force of tyranny nor to subject
my rich fatherland to an equality of shares between good and evil men.

The distorted vision in line 5 ('they looked cross-eyed at me') describes the faulty evaluation of Solon's own *noos* by those in search of unearned wealth or honours from the city's leader. For each one of them, the persuasions of others, combined with his own desire for loot, result in a failure to understand the true nature of the speaker, whether bad (e.g. the budding tyrants) or good (Solon himself). Their rising anger and desire for loot bolster their reaction against him; like the assembled fools in fragment 11, each fails to see what the man before him does.[33] Persuaded by the crowd (like Hector), they want their loot now (like Agamemnon), and fail to stay their rage (like Achilles). The result is *ou chreôn*, an accusative absolute that may mean 'not usefully', or perhaps 'not justly' or 'improperly', but that certainly did not have to be.[34] Of course, this is also self-representation on Solon's part, who is as concerned with persuading *his* audience as *he* wishes. Even if this became a contest of moral counter-accusations, the terms that Solon argues with demonstrate a moral attitude that is unfriendly towards tyrannical power.

The issue of persuasion is vital to their noetic failures and the resultant *koros* and *hubris*. Solon, true to form, brings the issue and its consequences down to the level of those immediately involved, by explicitly connecting the improper *noos* to exceeding one's proper measure in fragment 4c. He frames the response in terms of an unwillingness to be persuaded:

ὑμεῖς δ᾽ ἡσυχάσαντες ἐνὶ φρεσὶ καρτερὸν ἦτορ,
  οἵ πολλῶν ἀγαθῶν ἐς κόρον [ἠ]λάσατε,
ἐν μετρίοισι τίθεσθε μέγαν νόον· οὔτε γὰρ ἡμεῖς
  πεισόμεθ᾽, οὔθ᾽ ὑμῖν ἄρτια τα[ῦ]τ᾽ ἔσεται.

Solon 4c

You, calm yourselves in your hearts,
  who drag yourselves into a *koros* of material goods,
moderate your *mega noos*; for we will not
  be persuaded, nor will things turn out right for you

2. 'To know all things'

The context of the fragment is not at all clear; was he purporting to stand up for poor farmers being stripped of their resources by a hereditary or wealthy aristocracy, or rather mocking the powerless threats of the *dêmos* in an elite symposium? Whatever the case, Solon again ties *koros* to *noos*, while offering a clue as to how the Athenians can be affected, or resist being affected, by their fellows: through persuasion. In line 6 of poem 4, he has already made the claim that the leaders are *chrêmasi peithomenoi*, 'persuaded by wealth'. As he continues in poem 4, he repeats the formula, that the leaders of the people are deficient in *noos* because of certain improper persuasions, this time making the issue not just one of material wealth, but of their own deeds or actions. This elegiac line is preceded and followed by a lacuna, making it impossible to know the precise context, even within the poem itself:

. . . .
    πλουτέουσιν δ' ἀδίκοις ἔργμασι πειθόμενοι
. . . .

                                                    Solon 4.11

. . . .
    They grow rich, persuaded by unjust deeds.
. . . .

In Solon the dative that accompanies the *peithomenos* form – the idea, thing or action that has persuaded him – is, in modern terms, an example of a premise that conditions his thinking. A 'persuasion' is an intellectual counterpart to the action of 'obeying'; a person who is 'persuaded' obeys because he is convinced that he should do so, either after deliberation or through habituation. The primary use of *peithô* forms in Homer, Hesiod and the Homeric Hymns is to exhort obedience, or a hearkening, by men towards gods or towards other men as Athena claims that Achilles will stay his anger, 'if you are persuaded by me'.[35] Buxton stresses the actional aspects of *peithô* by noting that *peithomai*, translated as 'obey, trust or believe', includes the notion of the 'acquiescence in the will of another'.[36] A translator must select whether he wishes to stress the element of intellect or action, of persuasion or obedience.

Solon expands the use of the *peithomenos* descriptor; he provides the first extant example of a person's being *peithomenos* by something other than gods, men or words, using the present participle to indicate that one has been persuaded by external factors such as material goods. These persuasions have effects that are deeper than what is manifest in particular situations; they affect how a person is generally disposed towards the *polis*, its laws and how he acts in it – a point that Democritus would make explicit.[37] Deceptions in the mind were a concern in far earlier times, and it would be dangerous to ignore the formulaic nature of Homeric poetry in ascribing too much importance to this. But Solon's lines are significant.

Solon the Thinker

For one thing, he is implanting the language of persuasion into discourse in Attica. Further, he is making explicit the idea that wealth in combination with an inappropriate mental state increases the motivation to obtain loot by unjust means. Success at injustice heightens the drive towards greater injustice, so that a person becomes persuaded by his own unjust practice; if so, this may be an early conception of 'vice' or 'virtue' as related to habituation. The number of uses of *peithomenos* forms followed by datives in Theognis suggests an increased awareness in the sixth century of a person as persuaded by such factors.[38]

Solon's placement of the participle at the end of the line heightens the impact on his audience; in 4.6 and 4.11 we hear that '[to destroy the great *polis*] some citizens are willing, by money persuaded' and that 'they grow rich, by unjust deeds persuaded'. In 13.12 we hear that the wealth 'which men honour by *hubris*, comes not according to order, but by unjust deeds persuaded'. The combination of the dative and *peithomenos* in the second colon of the elegiac line may have later become formulaic, appearing in thirteen epigrams in the *Palatine Anthology*.[39] In each case the reference to themselves as improperly persuaded would be the last thing to hit the audience, prompting the listener to examine his own psychic state as well as that of the unjust man. The connection Solon makes between improper persuasions and the thoughts, practices and possessions of his audience was a powerful indictment of those who, in the past, may have looked to blame the gods or corrupt leaders for their own immoderate actions in the *polis*.

In Solon's world, the internal regulation of the *polis* would not have been exclusively, and perhaps not even primarily, through judgments by magistrates or officials, but would have included persuasive pressure by friends, relatives and acquaintances to act in accordance with accepted norms, in context with powerful myths and ritualized conduct. Such non-institutional factors were central to Solon's use of persuasion as it relates to Good Order, especially in the symposium, the sacrificial banquet and other ritualized assemblies throughout the *polis*, all of which depended upon moderation by the participants, but which could also be highly competitive both internally and in relation to other groups. Noussia draws out Solon's possible engagement with *mageirikê technê* 'cookery', and 'second tables' practices, in fragments 38-41.[40] Seen in this light, to assume that the banquet or symposium were purely metaphors for the city is improper; such gatherings may have been a real source of power in the archaic *polis,* and the conflict in poem 4 literal. To Solon an appropriate measure is found in proper understanding; the hubristic do not *understand* how to restrain their excess (4.9). This compares to his application of an *epistamai* form to a poet in poem 13 line 52, literally 'the one understanding the metre of lovely poetry' (*himertês sophiês metron epistamenos*), the poet as 'expert' in the 'metre of delightful skill', imparted by Apollo.[41] Solon elevates the nature of that which hubristic men fail to

2. 'To know all things'

understand to the level of poetic inspiration by using the same verb reserved for the wisdom of a poet.[42] By implication, the expert poet is able to do what the unjust person in the city cannot: to understand the measure of wisdom, and to persuade others of it.

To interpret civil strife primarily in terms of *actions* would fail to recognize Solon's focus on the *noetic* foundations of this problem. Ultimately Solon's moral *kosmos* is a knowing *kosmos*, and a good man is one who is disposed to know well, and to act in moderation and not from *hubris*. Anhalt emphasizes how 'Solon seems to share the traditional archaic view which considers as intellectual deficiencies what we might term "moral" failings'. Sullivan sees *noos* in Solon 4.7 and 6.4 as the 'seat of someone's inclination to admirable or immoral behaviour'. *Noos* then is a faculty of virtue.[43] If such interpretations are right, then Solon's use of persuasion in the archaic *polis* challenges, and perhaps socially isolates, those who act in a way contrary to its harmony. This elevates the ethical standard of moderation into central importance, redefining the categories of factions in terms of the friends and enemies of Athens, and clearing a space for what Solon sees as a proper disposition towards Athens.[44] Solon may have been central to the transmission of moderation as an ideal to later Athenian culture, which also remained competitive in public contexts.[45] Greenhalgh's view, however, that Solon's denial of tyranny was 'an altruistic decision' should be challenged.[46] Solon's embrace of moderation in the pursuit of power was rather self-interested: the *stasis* in poem 4, rampaging into each man's house, is a direct warning to each person that the ramifications of injustice will be personal and swift. Solon's rejection of improper pursuits would be altruistic only in the terms of the critic in fragment 33, who would feel shame for not grasping at power and loot now.

In fragment 32, a self-referential response to a critic, Solon rejects his critic's values by adopting this new standard of moderation, and denying the shame normally associated with the refusal to 'haul in the net' and take the power that one can. Douglas Cairns, comparing Solon to the moral values of the *Iliad*, evaluates the importance of fragment 32 as Solon's reliance on 'his own interpretation of his actions'. The internalization of a standard, Cairns claims, allows him to ignore present taunts and to rely upon 'his own conception of the honourable, directly controverting the belief that failure to achieve competitive success is dishonourable with a claim that such success, improperly gained, is itself dishonourable'.[47] If this is true, Solon was again anticipating Democritus and the formal repudiation of the shame morality, his ability to 'ignore present mockery' based upon his own rational appraisal of what is right, considered from a long-range perspective.[48]

In my interpretation, Solon has shifted – implicitly of course – not from an 'external' to an 'internal' standard of evaluation, but rather from a 'dependent' to an 'independent' standard. This interpretation differentiates Hector (and Solon's critic in fragment 33) more fundamentally from

Solon. 'Independent' acknowledges the higher value placed on one's own conclusions than on the pressures of the crowd; it is a focus on the facts and not on other people. Philosopher Leonard Peikoff's definition of 'independence as primary orientation to reality and not to other men' is virtually a restatement of Solon 11.7-8.[49] Such a focus is strongly implied in the exhortation to focus on the deeds and not the words of the shifty speaker. 'Internalized', however, does not specify whether the standard is independent; it is possible to internalize a dependent standard. Hector's standard is internalized in that he thinks it is his own decision to attain value popular in Homeric society – the approval of others. Such approval is, after all, a value to him. That Hector's *thumos* bids him may indicate that 'his own feelings are no less important than public opinion',[50] but those feelings remain connected to that public opinion and are unable to guide him apart from that opinion. Hector – and Solon's critic – have 'internalized' their dependence upon that opinion so deeply that they never question that dependence. Solon is rather independent; he refuses to feel shame while breaking from the values that motivate those around him. His own position in an agonistic context of impassioned argumentation must be inferred from the explicit positions he takes in his poems, which are tools of persuasion on behalf of his values. Despite the rhetorical purposes, or perhaps because of them, there is little reason to doubt that Solon identifies himself strongly with the values he espouses, and that he does so in a context in which established values were being challenged.[51]

Democritus has been given credit for the first injunctions to look introspectively at the state of one's *psuchê*. Kirk, Raven and Schofield observe, with respect to two fragments from his work 'On Cheerfulness', that 'what is certain, and highly important, is that Democritus here is directing our moral attention inwards, as Socrates did, to the state of our souls'.[52] Kirk, Raven and Schofield continue: this care for the soul is 'not a quest for universal truths' but rather concern for that which 'may seem great and enviable to you', and an injunction to take those less fortunate as one's 'point of reference'. This turns to a political motive, the prevention of wrong-doing and concern for the state. The state of the *polis* in fragment 248 is connected to such inner states: 'law can only be a benefit, if people are willing to obey it', and they will be willing to do so only if they desire to live well and if the are properly *peithomenoi*.[53]

The introspection credited to Democritus should be considered in comparison to Solon's exhortations. Solon did not search for abstract forms in the *psuchê* divorced from particular situations, but he did observe relationships between the condition of the *noos*, the state of affairs in the *polis*, and physical actions. Solon may have taken important steps towards understanding the citizen as an individual with a definite relationship to the *polis*, and he saw the need for cognizance of psychic factors in understanding our place in the *polis*. As Balot puts it, 'The civic definition of the individual begins, I think, with Solon's formulation of individual identity

2. 'To know all things'

within the civic context'.[54] Solon shares with Kirk, Raven and Schofield's evaluation of Democritus neither an abstract 'state of the soul' as the object of his consideration, nor those 'less fortunate' as his point of reference. He remains a consequentialist in that the consequences of improper action remain the standard for determining what is just; the focus on the end is fundamentally unbroken.[55] But he moves past the epic view in seeing the need to examine one's own mental condition, and the condition of others, in context with those wider consequences. Solon's similarity to Democritus is not moral but cognitive. The Delphic inscription 'know yourself' (*gnôthi sauton*), attributed to Solon and to others, makes explicit the groundwork needed for the later abstract considerations of the ethical philosophers, and for examination of the role of rhetoric in shaping the understanding of an audience.[56] By founding the *polis* on psychic qualities, Solon made it necessary for later thinkers to develop theories about human virtues and vices and to connect them to the order that is proper to a just Greek *polis*.[57]

3

'In time, retribution surely comes'
Necessity, *dikê* and the good order of the *polis*

> *Dikê* surely comes later.
> Solon 3.8

The dangers of private revenge would have been palpably real to the people of Solon's time, and abstract analyses must not be allowed to obscure the immediate threats that faced Solon's fellows in the *polis*. In condemning unjust men – his political enemies, of whom he surely had more than a few, and who might have turned his own words back onto him in public acrimony – Solon was making certain members of the community visible, exposing them as threats to Athens, and fulfilling his own claim that they will become visible in the end. We don't know who these malfeasants were, but doubtless his audience was not in the dark; his stinger may have been as pointedly effective as Aristophanes' jabs against Cleon, and perhaps equally accurate. Perhaps Solon intends to bring the sack of Troy to mind, as Irwin suggests;[1] but if so, those warriors with their desires for honour and loot have become foreign enemies of the city. But Solon's claims to wisdom do not stop with his own particular enemies; his is the *noos* of a god – although it would be *hubris* to say this outright – that penetrates to the necessity underlying the rhythm of movements in Athens. These two levels in Solon's ideas – his concern for particular men and their *hubris*, and his sense of inevitability within the *polis* as a whole – lead to vital questions about how Solon sees each one of us in relation to the *polis*, and the nature of the necessity and justice by which he grasps its overall organization.

As poem 4 continues, Solon shifts between levels, seeing the 'entire *polis*' ('*pasei polei*') but always in relation 'to each one' of us (*hekastôi*). The first ten lines of the poem have shown the *polis* to be an independent arena of human life, which is vulnerable to men who fail to restrain their *hubris*. They do not order well (*kosmein*) the present festivities, which may not be a metaphor but rather a literal description of a confrontation at a ceremonial meal. Solon then expands on this idea, moving from the unjust assaults of individuals to an elevated, even divine sense of *dikê* that brings retribution to the entire *polis*, then turning back to the effects upon each one of us:

3. 'In time, retribution surely comes'

πλουτέουσιν δ' ἀδίκοις ἔργμασι πειθόμενοι
....
   οὔθ' ἱερῶν κτεάνων οὔτέ τι δημοσίων
φειδόμενοι κλέπτουσιν ἀφαρπαγῇ ἄλλοθεν ἄλλος,
   οὐδὲ φυλάσσονται σεμνὰ Δίκης θέμεθλα,
ἣ σιγῶσα σύνοιδε τὰ γιγνόμενα πρό τ' ἐόντα,
   τῷ δὲ χρόνῳ πάντως ἦλθ' ἀποτεισομένη,
τοῦτ' ἤδη πάσῃ πόλει ἔρχεται ἕλκος ἄφυκτον,
   ἐς δὲ κακὴν ταχέως ἤλυθε δουλοσύνην,
ἣ στάσιν ἔμφυλον πόλεμόν θ' εὕδοντ' ἐπεγείρει,
   ὃς πολλῶν ἐρατὴν ὤλεσεν ἡλικίην·
ἐκ γὰρ δυσμενέων ταχέως πολυήρατον ἄστυ
   τρύχεται ἐν συνόδοις τοῖς ἀδικέουσι φίλους.
ταῦτα μὲν ἐν δήμῳ στρέφεται κακά· τῶν δὲ πενιχρῶν
   ἱκνέονται πολλοὶ γαῖαν ἐς ἀλλοδαπὴν
πραθέντες δεσμοῖσί τ' ἀεικελίοισι δεθέντες
....
οὕτω δημόσιον κακὸν ἔρχεται οἴκαδ' ἑκάστῳ,
   αὔλειοι δ' ἔτ' ἔχειν οὐκ ἐθέλουσι θύραι,
ὑψηλὸν δ' ὑπὲρ ἕρκος ὑπέρθορεν, εὗρε δὲ πάντως,
   εἰ καί τις φεύγων ἐν μυχῷ ᾖ θαλάμου.

Solon 4.11-29

They grow rich, persuaded by unjust deeds.
....
   Sparing the wealth of neither public nor sacred treasuries
with rapaciousness they rob from one another,
   and fail to guard the sacred foundations of Justice,
who silently knows what is and what was,
   and, in time, surely comes to exact retribution later,
and now this inescapable wound (*helkos*) comes to the
                           entire *polis* (*pasei polei*),
   which falls swiftly into an evil slavery;
it awakens civil strife and sleeping tribal war,
   and destroys the beautiful youth of many;
and from its troubles the much-loved city is swiftly
   worn out, friendships destroyed in unjust factions.
These evils turn on the people; and of the poor
   many are going into foreign lands,
sold and bound in shameful fetters
....
Thus the public evil comes to the house of each man,
   it jumps high over the court-yard fence, breaks down
the locked doors, and finds any man for certain (*pantôs*),
   even if he flees into the farthest corner of his bedroom.

It is striking how individualized the connections are between the *polis* and each one of us. It would be an understatement to say that for Solon this is not an abstract exercise; his criticisms of his fellows are direct and personal. Archaic Athens was not a large city in modern terms; it was a village, and it is not likely that the audience failed to recognize those whom Solon was blaming. Solon's radical affirmation that each one of us is the target of the civil strife ties his exhortations into a *polis*-wide wound – war, civil strife and slavery, which mean youth killed, unjust friendship groups, and many poor in chains – and then completes the circle back to those in fancy estates who, despite memories of escaping civil strife by retreating behind private walls, will be found 'for certain'. This 'feedback' of political consequences onto each person is unprecedented. Of course the rage of Achilles brought mass death to the Greeks, and Hesiod knew that one man can affect the entire community, 'for often a city all together (*xumpasa polis*) suffers for one bad man', who devises 'foolish things' (*atasthala*, *Op*. 240-1). But, prior to Solon, the connection between the city altogether to 'each one of us' had not been made explicit. This forms the essential background to Solon's grasp of *dikê*. It is only after this idea was made clear that more complete theories connecting politics to ethics could be worked out in a later century.

The raging civil strife comes 'to the home of each one', *oikad' hekastôi* (4.26). *Hekastos* is one of Solon's favourite words; he uses it six times, always to stress that 'each one of us' is responsible and pays the price for a wider crime. In explaining why he was mobbed with people hoping to gain from his position, he distinguished their particular motivations: 'and each one of them (*hekastos autôn*) expected to find much wealth' (34.2). To describe more pointedly why the people fall in to tyranny, he reduces the decisions of a crowd to each person in it: 'each one of you' (*humeôn eis hekastos*) walks in the steps of a crafty fox, but 'all together (*sumpasin humin*) your *noos* is empty' (11.5-6). To remedy the decline of the *polis*, he wrote laws alike to the *kakos* and the *agathos*, brought *eis hekaston*, 'to each man's case' (36.18-19). The anger of Zeus, he tells us in his poem 13, the *Hymn to Memory*, follows 'not upon each particular thing' or 'each particular occasion' (*oud' eph' hekastôi*), which might lead a mortal to anger, but rather against 'whoever has an evil heart' (*hostis alitron thumon echei*) (13.25-8). Zeus is focused on deeper, hidden conditions.[2]

To demonstrate our flawed understanding of ourselves, Solon continues: 'We mortals, both *agathos* and *kakos*, think we understand, and 'each one himself has an expectation' (*autos doxan hekastos echei*) that things are going well' (13.33-4). To make this even more pointed, 'Whoever is oppressed by miserable disease deems he will be healthy, this he thinks. Another man (*allos*) being cowardly (*deilos*) thinks himself brave (*agathos*); and the ugly man thinks he is handsome' (13.37-9). To lift such passages out of the context of surrounding verses is in no way sufficient to grasp the totality of what Solon is saying. Yet even in isolation these passages suggest that Solon thinks of his wider claims in relation to individual or even particular men.

Solon does of course speak of the *dêmos* as if it were a singular thing, often without enough context to know whether he is talking about 'the

3. 'In time, retribution surely comes'

poor' as distinct from 'the rich', 'the new rich' verses 'the noble born', or all of 'the people', and without revealing whether he sees it as a crowd of individuals or a unified whole of some kind. Fragment 37 is an example, a difficult nine-line trimester passage in which the *dêmos* is contrasted sarcastically with *hoi ameinones*, 'the better sort' – whoever they are, perhaps his immediate audience – whom Solon claims as friends.[3] In other cases Solon does vivify the scene as if a contest between two parties, which suggests a factional view of the *polis*. He stands, for example, like a strong shield between the *dêmos* and the men with power and ability (*dunamis*) in fragment 5.5-6:

> ἔστην δ' ἀμφιβαλὼν κρατερὸν σάκος ἀμφοτέροισι,
> νικᾶν δ' οὐκ εἴασ' οὐδετέρους ἀδίκως.
>
> Solon 5.5-6

> I stood with a powerful shield around both sides,
>   not permitting either to claim an unjust victory.

Solon clearly recognizes a contentious situation between two parties, and his own position as a mediator between them. But should this be read as a metaphor for the *polis* as a whole, divided into factions, or rather as a concretization of one of the conflicts tearing it apart? With many variations, factional and class interpretations of the *polis* as a whole have often followed the Aristotelian *Constitution of the Athenians*, Plutarch and their successors, who claim that Solon placed the blame for the problems in Athens on 'the rich', opposed to 'the poor'.[4] Some interpreters have defined the *agathoi / kakoi* as a hereditary elite struggling to maintain or to re-establish their dominance, against certain well-to-do farmers who had risen in the previous century.[5] Others accept that there are no firm classes in ancient Greece, but even if 'classes' are anachronistic or inapplicable, this does not mean that 'class struggle' is not a useful 'heuristic and analytical category'.[6]

But, considering everything that Solon says about Athens and those in it, it is not at all clear that this is Solon's view. Solon's metaphor of the shield may not represent the city as whole, divided into feuding parts; it may rather be his way of showing how the strife between 'each one of us' plays out, in real altercations between men that he, as a mediator, might have personally stood between, and that might spread if not contained. Poem 4 reduces the 'wound' to 'each one of us'; fragments 11 and 34 stresses the improper motivations of 'each one' in a crowd; Solon's reforms in poem 36 include legal judgments 'for each man's case'. We should take Solon at his word: he saw both the *agathoi* and *kakoi* not as organized classes, but rather as akin to a pack of hounds, each one of them expecting loot, forming gangs for the moment only, against whom he makes a defence 'in all directions' (*pantothen*). More deeply, Solon's exhortations depend more upon the psychic factors that motivate each man to act as he does than upon the legal, institutional or class structures that men might create in acting as they do. When any one of them abandons justice, then justice abandons the *polis* – and strife follows by necessity, since that what forsaking justice *is*.

If so, then Solon's *polis* would be a *kosmos* not of competing forces or factions, but of competing men, and a person of any status could be *agathos* or *kakos*. A just *polis* is as one in which just dispositions are *distributed* among the people, not *collectivized*, and the result is a *polis* that exhibits the same just disposition (it is *dikaios*). A lawgiver's desire to change the condition of the *polis* would focus on those dispositions and their necessary consequences. This is exactly what Solon does. His *Dikê* is not a balance between forces, but rather a promise of later retribution, a sense of necessity that might be used to compel each man to restrain his *hubris*. To understand the *polis* in these terms, later thinkers would need a theory of individual ethics, in which virtues of character could be understood in a social context. Such a view would suggest a move towards *dikê* as a moral virtue, in the Aristotelian tradition. Thus Aristotle ends his *Nicomachean Ethics* with the injunction that to complete the philosophy of human affairs, one must now read the *Politics*. One needs to see the moral virtue of justice in terms of the character before seeing it in the *polis*. The preservation of the harmony in the *polis* is accomplished through the moderation in each one of us.[7]

To moderate the impetus towards *hubris* in his fellows, Solon must get them to make the connection between their immediate, visible interests and the necessary consequences for the *polis*, by demonstrating the relevance of the latter for each one of them. Solon's terminology of 'seeing' – the public evil *finds* him in every way, making *visible* all those who flee; *Eunomiê* makes all things *appear* (*pant' apophainei*) well-ordered – suggests Solon's need to draw out the inevitable, but unseen, consequences into a vivid poetic image that stands with the clarity and force of a real event. This comprehensive sense of necessity, understood in a community of real people, is the glue that binds the *polis* into a *kosmos*. It is to this that we now turn.

The nature and scope of necessity in Solon's thought are especially opaque, given his metaphorical formulations and hidden purposes, as well as the bareness of the historical record. Solon's explanations for thunder (fragment 9) and storms (12), read in context with his political exhortations, provide the raw material for an archaic understanding of causal necessity, which may share a common heritage with the explanations of the Presocratic philosophers. This first step is to note that every commotion necessarily begins with something that sets it off. Fragments 9 and 12 are typically distinguished – as in West's edition – but Plutarch rather places the first two lines of fragment 9 before fragment 12. Continuing Plutarch's juxtaposition by reconstructing both fragments into a single

3. 'In time, retribution surely comes'

passage strengthens the naturalistic context of Solon's understanding of the *polis*:

ἐκ νεφέλης πέλεται χιόνος μένος ἠδὲ χαλάζης,
βροντὴ δ' ἐκ λαμπρῆς γίγνεται ἀστεροπῆς·

Solon 9.1-2

ἐξ ἀνέμων δὲ θάλασσα ταράσσεται· ἢν δέ τις αὐτὴν
μὴ κινῇ, πάντων ἐστὶ δικαιοτάτη.

Solon 12

ἀνδρῶν δ' ἐκ μεγάλων πόλις ὄλλυται, ἐς δὲ τυράννου
δῆμος ἀϊδρίῃ δουλοσύνην ἔπεσεν.
λίην δ' ἐξάραντ' <οὐ> ῥᾴδιόν ἐστι κατασχεῖν
ὕστερον, ἀλλ' ἤδη χρὴ <καλὰ> πάντα νοεῖν.[8]

Solon 9.3-6

The force of snow and hail comes from a cloud,
   and thunder from a flash of lightning.
The sea is stirred up by the wind. And if something
   does not move it, it is justest (most calm) of all things.
But the ruin of the city comes from unjust men
   and the people fall into the slavery of a tyrant by ignorance.
Having raised these men up it is <not> easy
   to restrain them later. Now it is right to know all things <well>.

Poseidon and Zeus must be on leave here, because the causes of such upheavals are found in factors that are each as natural as the event they cause. Gregory Vlastos was correct to stress the naturalism in Solon's thinking.[9] To understand thunder or a storm, one must look into the sky or the sea to find what made it necessary – as one must look *into* the *polis*, also a deceptively simple thought, to find what made civic strife necessary. Solon's widest and most direct statements of immanent necessity in human life include the idea that *Dikê* brings retribution *pantôs*, 'in every way' (4.16), a thought repeated succinctly in poem 13 line 8, albeit without personification in our texts. At this point, it is important to note only that the idea would stick in each person's thoughts as a reminder of the inevitability of *dikê* and why one should act properly: πάντως ὕστερον ἦλθε δίκη ('*dikê* surely comes later', Solon 13.8).

Solon's grasp of what it means for something to occur *pantôs* stands in contrast to the ideas of those before him. Neither the word nor the idea is essential to epic; the anthropomorphic deities at the centre of human affairs serve as explanations for how things happen in Homer, and Hesiod tells us that Zeus has changed the very nature of life on earth on whim. *Pantôs* is used thrice in Homer, with an *ou* denoting an inability to avoid an outcome. In *Iliad* 8.450 Zeus is irresistible *pantôs*, and all the gods together cannot turn him. In *Odyssey* 19.91 the old handmaiden will not remain hidden *pantôs*, and in 20.180 Odysseus cannot avoid a fight 'in any way'. In the Homeric Hymns, *pantôs* is repeated at the *Hymn to Apollo* lines 19 and 207, where the god is worthy of a song 'in every way', and at line 11 of a fragment of *Dionysos*, on the need for festival sacrifices every three years. The term adds an emphasis but not any new idea of inevitability. The gods retain the powers to do largely as they will, within the limits of fate, even as the boundary between the gods and fate is subject to negotiation and compromise.[10] At this stage, the idea of a comprehensive necessity to which even the gods must subscribe is problematic at best.

Solon describes things as occuring *pantôs* seven times, all of them in poems 4 and 13: 4.16 and 28; and 13.8, 28, 31, 42 and 55.[11] Despite serious problems of interpretation concerning their views of *dikê*, poems 4 and 13 agree about the meaning of *pantôs*. In each case the poet widens the comprehensiveness of the scene and extends its temporal length, while adding a vivid sense of inevitability to human affairs. In poem 4 Solon expands the locative range (into a bedroom), the social range (the 'entire *polis*', *pasei polei*: youth, poor, friends, slaves, wrong-doers), and the temporal range (*tôi de chronôi*, 'in time') of the consequences into multiple aspects of life, with a force that brings the hidden implications of a scene into immediate awareness for the audience. This expansion is also suggested by the other *pan-* words in the fragments, which may denote a god's capacity to know all things, the inevitability of justice, or a person's own claims to know his own condition (about which he is often deceived). When Solon tells his listeners that something occurs *pantôs* the picture becomes sharper – the intensity rises – and the consequences appear more drastic, personal and inevitable, even if they cannot see them now.

In this way *pantôs* adds certainty to one's understanding; certain consequences come always and in every way, surely, without a doubt, even with respect to things that are not obvious to us now. The emphatic, comprehensive and long-range aspects of *pantôs* lend the term an epistemological dimension that is among its most important implications. For these reasons I translate *pantôs* as 'certainly' or 'surely'. It is the comprehensiveness of this thought that brings Solon closest to the universalized world of the Presocratic philosophers.[12]

Solon the Sophos is again taking on the most difficult and persistent problem the Greeks faced, that of grasping that which cannot be seen. Solon describes as *pantôs* precisely those things that are not visible now, but are necessary in the end. To say that something occurs *pantôs* would be superfluous if it could be seen. If one could literally see, for instance, that a man's *hubris* – caused by *koros* that accompanies a flawed *noos* – always leads to civil strife and tyranny, then this would not require argument, for the end would be in front of one's eyes. But the end is not so easily seen. The poet makes the hidden implications explicit in a vivid scene, e.g. the 'justice' or 'injustice' found in an orator's assertions, in a slave's chains, or in a fist-fight. A brawl becomes a matter of justice with

3. 'In time, retribution surely comes'

far-reaching implications. A speaker's actions may lead to tyranny and slavery, despite short-range gain to his supporters. A confrontation at a meal rises to the level of a cosmic altercation, and the effect on the *polis* is like the wind on the sea or a wound on the body.

Seen in this light, the *polis* becomes more than the immediate situation; it swells to encompass aspects that are out of sight or may not even have happened yet. This is a literal expansion of the range of the human mind beyond the present moment, an awareness of an underlying order that governs all things, and where its hidden connections lead. It provides the framework for moderation that Achilles did not have at the start of the *Iliad,* when Athena had to tell him not to draw his sword. It demands that we order our own affairs in ways consistent with the broad sense of order that is embodied in *Dikê* and that bores deeply into the foundations of Solon's world. Solon's Festival Calendar – like his laws – may have been just such an order, established within the regularity of the seasons, ordered by *Dikê*, intended to unify the rituals in the *polis*.

Solon's turn to *Dikê* in poem 4 makes a strong claim for her: she knows what is and what was; silently discarded, deadly retribution follows inevitably, onto the entire *polis* and each person in it. Unlike Hesiod's *Works and Days, Dikê* is not dragged from the city kicking and screaming, after which she brings reports to Zeus on high. In Solon she rather waits silently, and retribution comes inevitably *inside* the *polis,* without reference to Zeus. *Dikê* is in some way natural, operates apart from human wishes otherwise, and cannot be escaped. But *Dikê* is also limited. She does not know 'past and future wrongs';[13] this knowledge is reserved for the inspired poet and the lawgiver, who calls on Memory for guidance. Irwin draws the parallel in language between Solon's formulation and Hesiod's *Theogony* 38, where *Dikê* sees 'things happening now and that which is before', but then omits the rest of Hesiod's formulation: 'the things that will be'. This is a key difference between Hesiod and Solon: Solon's *Dikê* does not know what will be. The ability to see beyond memory and immediate perceptions is the central problem. It is Hesiod who skirts the problem, by simply calling on *Dikê*. The parallels in language between the two poets remain subordinated to the differences in their ideas.[14]

Dikê in Solon is, in one sense, inevitable and self-regulative, but in another sense, not; people must actively work to preserve her, or else the *polis* will not be *dikaios*. But how is Solon's idea of *dikê* both natural and inevitable for the entire *polis*, and yet subject to human choices? Does *dikê* in Solon refer merely to the mediation of real disputes between particular men, despite abstract terminology and metaphors? Or, does it subsume an abstract principle of ordering that has universal or even metaphysical import? Is *dikê* what people create in the *polis*, or is it a fact of nature that we must be cognizant of, if the *polis* is to remain at peace? If it is in nature, meaning apart from human creation, then is it a force imposed on the *polis* from the outside, or a principle of order that is observable in the actions of just-minded persons?[15]

Modern interpretations of Solon's *dikê* have fallen into a continuum. One pole of this continuum was defined by Eric Havelock, who sees justice as pragmatically determined for each dispute. In Havelock's view any attempt to establish a *principle* of justice applicable to more than one case overestimates the nature of archaic conceptualizations. Considering poem 36 as encapsulating Solon's views of *dikê*, in which Solon claims to have written 'statutes alike (*homoiôs*) to the base man and to the noble, fitting straight justice onto each man's case' (36.18-19), Havelock writes: 'The symbols of justice here are procedural ... Justice, however, is something he adjusts to each case, making a "straight fit" '. Havelock's position is immediately suspect on linguistic grounds, given his translation of the adverb *homoiôs* as '[and laws] *according with* [the noble and the lowly]' (emphasis added), which obfuscates the comparative meaning of the adverb, 'similarly', or 'alike'. *Homoiôs, homoioô* and related forms all have comparative meanings closer to 'likeness' than equality. The question of the adverb *homoiôs* in Solon turns on the force of this likeness; 'equal' may be too strong, and carry anachronistic egalitarian connotations. Rather than accepting that written laws do offer a means of dealing alike with various particular cases, Havelock grants *dikê* to each of those men according to their place in archaic society, thus begging the question as to why Solon said *homoiôs*, what he meant by it, or why his laws needed to be written anyway. We must also wonder if poem 36 exhausts the range of meanings that Solon understands for *dikê*; should we not consider *everything* he says about *dikê*, in all the extant verses?

The other pole of this continuum is Havelock's characterization of Jaeger, Vlastos and Solmsen. Havelock sees German idealism as motivating these writers to reify *dikê* into a cosmic principle or force. He sees in these writers '(1) an accepted political principle informing the existence of the early city-state, and (2) a comprehensive cosmic principle of metaphysical proportions'. But this deserves criticism, for Vlastos' view of *dikê* as the 'observable consequences of human acts' and 'self-regulated' does not claim that justice is 'metaphysical'; he rather claims it is 'immanent' from human actions – or perhaps manifested in those actions. In these terms Solon may be drawing general conclusions about how he sees his fellows acting, which is an entirely different matter from postulating a cosmic force governing human actions. Further, Vlastos stresses the practical implications of Solonian justice, in particular the distinct break made with the doctrine of blood pollution, which implies procedures that correspond to the principle. Accordingly, these two poles of scholarly interpretation are based upon Havelock's interpretation of these writers and not the writers themselves, since Havelock's interpretation does not accurately represent their views. The important distinction is between

3. 'In time, retribution surely comes'

justice as particular and procedural, versus justice as a systematic principle governing the *polis*.

A similar interpretative issue has been raised for Aristotle's concept of *stasis* by Kostas Kalimtzis.[16] The prevailing view of *stasis*, Kalimtzis observes, is of factional strife: 'civil war', 'sedition', 'faction', 'revolution', or the like. *Stasis*, in this view, is 'quintessentially a condition of violent, internal conflict', and it can be understood in terms of conflict theory. Adapting this view to Solon, passages such as the 'inescapable wound' in 4.17 become metaphorical treatments of real instances of violence. Breaking with this interpretation, Kalimtzis claims that the central concept governing Aristotle's *stasis* is *nosos* 'disease', and that the literal meaning of *stasis* was a wound or a symptom of disease over the body politic. What is needed to understand *stasis* is a theory of disease. Dichotomizing the 'disease' view of *stasis* in Aristotle against the 'strife' view implies a distinction similar to the 'principle of justice' versus 'procedures of justice' dichotomy. Does Solon understand *stasis*, for example, as a single, *collectivized* 'wound' imposed upon the whole *polis*? Or does he see it as a manifestation of the failures of individual men, *distributed* throughout the *polis*? Or, might we understand his *dikê* to be both an abstract principle by which he understands his *polis*, and an order that is observable in the actions of its members? I will formulate the question as it relates to *dikê* in this way: what aspects of *dikê* as real dispute mediation (if any) are in the poems, and what aspects of *dikê* as an abstract, governing principle (if any) can be found?

Two aspects of *dikê* – as the resolution of particular disputes, and as an overarching principle governing the *polis* – may be suggested in Hesiod.[17] Michael Gagarin has seen in the *Works and Days* 'a separation between proper behavior and lawful behavior', reflected in the different meanings of the adjective *dikaios* 'behaving properly' and the noun *dikê* 'settlement', 'litigation, legal system, law', which is always limited to human judgments. A person could be 'traditionally wrong' – opposed to the wide standards of society, which are perhaps legitimated by Zeus – while receiving a favourable judgment in a corrupted court; consequently, Hesiod's justice is 'two-tiered'.[18] Although Hesiod knows that men must take the steps to achieve straight justice, the standard, the operative agent and the motivation to act justly are ultimately centred on divine persons. This higher reach of traditional, divine *dikê* is ultimately beyond evaluation since it is the source of evaluations; *dikê* as retribution is 'a punishment the justice of which is never questioned'.[19] But men can act in a manner contrary to these standards, as Hesiod claims they have. If the *dikê* of dispute resolution is undercut by the 'bribe-eating judges' the result will be the perverted *dikê* of *Works and Days* 192, the justice 'by main force' that corresponds to the revenge actions that develop into Solon's *stasis*. In West's words, 'The law of the stronger will replace fairness and decency'.[20] A monist interpretation of Hesiod as exclusively 'legal' and particular fails to account for the influence of the divine and of traditions on Hesiod's real disputes. Conversely, a purely divine interpretation would fail to acknowledge the central place of just decisions by magistrates or officials in the archaic village.

Gagarin also holds that every use of *dikê* in Solon is a concrete legal procedure not significantly distinguished from that of Hesiod.[21] This interpretation has the merit of considering the level of abstraction that Solon has attained, and it does not attribute anachronistic concepts to him. However, monist interpretations of *dikê* in Solon are also problematic, as parallel passages in poems 4, 13 and 36 strongly imply. In 4.16, retribution comes to the entire *polis* by necessity, following upon unjust actions of the leaders, including the unjust decisions of magistrates; this subordination of particular decisions to the wider standard of *dikê* is embodied as *Eunomiê*, who brings retribution for injustice and 'straightens crooked judgments', *euthunei de dikas skolias*, in line 36. Poem 13 line 8 also presents a programmatic statement of *dikê*'s inevitability, and the sole case in Solon's verses of justice as analogous to the will of Zeus: 'justice surely comes later'. *Dikê* here is a generalized consequence of unjust actions; it follows whenever wealth is gained unjustly (*adikôs*), which also implies fraudulent judgments. In this poem Solon, we shall see, tests his broad conception of *dikê* against the experiences of each one of us.

In poem 36, Solon also claims *dikê* is inevitable 'in the Court of Time', perhaps recalling the retribution to come *tôi de chronôi* 'in time' in poem 4. *Dikê* here invites metaphorical interpretation:

συμμαρτυροίη ταῦτ' ἂν ἐν δίκῃ Χρόνου
μήτηρ μεγίστη δαιμόνων Ὀλυμπίων
ἄριστα, Γῆ μέλαινα

Solon 36.3-5

In the Court of Time (*en dikê Chronou*) these things will be witnessed
by the testimony of the great mother of the Olympian
gods, Black Earth

It is possible, I maintain, that Solon had actually been put on trial in Athens, and was perhaps even convicted, and that he was here appealing to a point of exoneration beyond the present moment, when *dikê* would triumph over the unjust judgments of the Athenians. As the poem continues, Solon would elevate his own case into one of importance to the entire *polis* – a matter of slavery for all – in a way similar to the later orators, who would one day elevate their own petty cases into claims of importance for the laws and freedom of Athens. This can never be more than speculation. Whether there was a real trial, or rather a turn of opinion against Solon, *dikê* here also has stands above particular human judgments, and the consequences of ignoring her are inescapable.

As Solon continues in poem 36 he also connects this broad view of *dikê*

3. 'In time, retribution surely comes'

to slavery, which could occur both apart from or according to a legal judgment, or by forcible necessity without regard for an appeal to a judge. For Solon himself as for nameless others, one can arrive at a decision under *dikê* that is not consistent with *dikê* in the *polis*. Again, human *dikê* is judgeable within a wider framework of *dikê*:

> πολλοὺς δ' Ἀθήνας πατρίδ' ἐς θεόκτιτον
> ἀνήγαγον πράθεντας, ἄλλον ἐκδίκως,
> ἄλλον δικαίως, τοὺς δ' ἀναγκαίης ὑπὸ
> χρειοῦς φυγόντας
>
> Solon 36.8-11

> Many men I brought up to their divinely founded
> fatherland, men sold, one illegally,
> another legally, and others by forcible necessity
> fleeing their debts

Whether lines 9 and 10 mean 'according to and against a legal judgment', or rather 'improperly and properly' according to traditional norms, Solon uses a deeper standard to judge slavery as wrong. In either case, *dikê* is not only a procedural term in Solon; it again rises above particular judgments to stand for a wider sense of order and propriety. This may be called 'natural *dikê*', which promises retribution for all unjustice, even if cloaked in the decision of a magistrate. In all of the passages cited here, there is no basis for limiting *dikê* to particular legal judgments. Solon is explicit: unjust judgments lead inevitably to *polis*-wide retribution, or to long-range exoneration, because human justice has become unjust. *Dikê* has natural (inevitable) and man-made (volitional) senses.

However, Solon's *dikê* is not always an inevitable result of human actions or an abstract principle of order that occurs independently of man's actions. In many cases it is humanly created, subject to human volition, found in the decisions of magistrates and officials ('legal' judgments), and applied to each man's case. These particular judgments will be just, as he says in poem 36, only if the proper laws have been written and enforced:

> ἐλευθέρους ἔθηκα. ταῦτα μὲν κράτει
> ὁμοῦ βίην τε καὶ δίκην ξυναρμόσας
> ἔρεξα, καὶ διῆλθον ὡς ὑπεσχόμην·
> θεσμοὺς δ' ὁμοίως τῷ κακῷ τε κἀγαθῷ
> εὐθεῖαν εἰς ἕκαστον ἁρμόσας δίκην
> ἔγραψα.
>
> Solon 36.15-20

> I set men free. By my own power (*kratei*),
> fitting together force (*biên*) with justice (*dikên*),
> these things I did, and I came through as I promised.

53

> And statutes alike to the base man and to the noble
> fitting straight justice onto each man's case,
> these I wrote.

As was the case for the corrections that *Eunomiê* makes to the *dikas skolias* in 4.36, and the chasing of a debtor in 13.29-31, *dikê* here must refer to the humanly created justice that is brought to each man's case through a magistrate or other official.[22] Linforth saw *'eutheian dikên'* 'impartial justice' as a singular abstract substitution for *'eutheias dikas'* in poem 4, where Solon uses *harmosas* to show the adaptability of his 'flexible instrument'. Linforth is surely wrong to see the basic issue as a change from 'unconstitutional oligarchy to constitutional democracy', and to frame the adaptability in those terms. But the point remains: both passages refer to concrete, human judgments. It is not a natural regulatory procedure; it is something that people must regulate for themselves. The *dikê* of human judgments remains subject to evaluation in terms of 'natural *dikê*', but the consequences that fall on the entire *polis* are the result of neither divine intervention nor a metaphysical force; they are inherent in the contention between the parties. Justice, even on the *polis* level, is not 'self-regulatory', since the result of injustice is not balance and quiescence, but strife and slavery.

To this point Solon's *dikê* also has two 'levels', or perhaps 'applications': *dikê* as an inevitable result necessarily destroys the *polis* if men act with *hubris,* and the human sanctions of lawful *dikê* must be brought into agreement with natural *dikê* to prevent the destruction. *Dikê* in both senses is retributive, both in result and in process, and so far exclusively penal. The only principle for the *polis* here is that unjust actions spread inevitably, to the entire *polis* and thus to each one of us. This suggests that *dikê* is not an abstract principle or power *ruling* the *polis* but rather a guarantee of retribution which demands that people moderate their relations with one another *inside* the *polis*. To put it another way, an understanding of inevitable retribution in the *polis* need not require a philosophically idealistic interpretation of *dikê*, and if Solon has no such understanding it would not necessarily follow that his *dikê* is exclusively legal procedures used in particular disputes.

To understand *dikê* as something other than retribution we must return to fragment 12 (above), which describes the sea as remaining *dikaiotatê* unless disturbed by something. A sea in a 'most-just state' (or 'most calm condition') and a 'most just' *polis* are free from the kind of motivating cause that leads to storms and civil strife.[23] Solon's understanding of how *dikê* is manifested in the *polis* is suggested by his differentiation between retribution and *Dikê* at 4.14-16. *Dikê* says that if such a cause arises, strife (or a storm) results inevitably; Solon connects the inevitability of such consequences (and the process by which they occur) to proper conduct through *dikê*. At the level of human interactions, *Dikê* is the process (and result)

3. 'In time, retribution surely comes'

by which injustice is necessarily followed by retribution against the offending party; to give *dikê* is to render a decision and / or pay a penalty. Yet, should such unjust decisions occur throughout the *polis*, the *polis* as a whole becomes an offending party – and Solon describes the consequences as retribution brought by *Dikê* against the entire *polis*. Solon is applying to the *polis* as a whole the revenge actions he commonly saw between individual people. Conversely, the rejection of *hubris* in favour of *hêsuchia* creates a just condition in each man's *psychê*, and thereby removes the cause of strife in the *polis*, which becomes *dikaios*. *Dikê* is not a power imposed over the *polis*, but neither is it purely human procedures; it is how things work on individual and *polis*-wide levels. A *dikaios* condition is one in which *dikê* is distributed throughout the *polis*. It makes a world of difference whether *dikê* is seen as an imposed external power, with vengeance coming down from Zeus, or as an explanation for the inevitable interactions within the *polis-kosmos*. *Dikê* is still divine for Solon – and inescapable – but how he views her has changed since Hesiod.

In modern terms, to reify Solon's *Dikê* into a cosmic force or principle, formalized in the abstract and considered as if an archaic version of Hegel's dialectic, would fail to provide a suitable alternative to the divine interventions in Homer and Hesiod. Such a view would remove the personality from Zeus without challenging the despotism inherent in the authoritative relationship that remains. Further, this would ascribe an idealistic form of abstraction to Solon, improperly de-emphasizing the realism in his verses while failing to recognize his reliance on the real phenomena before his eyes. But to deny this idealistic conception does not necessitate a return to *Dikê* as nothing more than 'concrete legal procedures'. Solon's perspective on *dikê* in the *polis* presents *stasis* as neither the will of Zeus (a cosmic force) nor an unknowable power, but rather as what necessarily happens when men treat each other unjustly. Indeed, the whole problem in the *polis* may be to establish a humanly wrought *dikê* that brings the forcible necessity of human judgments in line with natural *dikê* through just decisions under written laws.

A similar recognition of two levels says much about the figure of *Eunomiê* at the climax of poem 4. Solon's perspective on the *polis* as a moral *kosmos* ordered by *dikê* allows him to stress that the roots of Good Order are also found in the minds and attitudes of his fellows. He describes the causal consequences of each person's adopting a proper disposition for the *polis*, which amounts to a normative programme for the education of the citizens:

ταῦτα διδάξαι θυμὸς Ἀθηναίους με κελεύει,
   ὡς κακὰ πλεῖστα πόλει Δυσνομίη παρέχει·
Εὐνομίη δ' εὔκοσμα καὶ ἄρτια πάντ' ἀποφαίνει,
   καὶ θαμὰ τοῖς ἀδίκοις ἀμφιτίθησι πέδας·
τραχέα λειαίνει, παύει κόρον, ὕβριν ἀμαυροῖ,

Solon the Thinker

αὑαίνει δ᾽ ἄτης ἄνθεα φυόμενα,
εὐθύνει δὲ δίκας σκολιάς, ὑπερήφανά τ᾽ ἔργα
πραΰνει· παύει δ᾽ ἔργα διχοστασίης,
παύει δ᾽ ἀργαλέης ἔριδος χόλον, ἔστι δ᾽ ὑπ᾽ αὐτῆς
πάντα κατ᾽ ἀνθρώπους ἄρτια καὶ πινυτά.

Solon 4.30-9

These things my heart prompts me to teach the Athenians:
   how Lawlessness (*Dusnomiê*) brings the worst evils to the city, and
Lawfulness (*Eunomiê*) manifests good order and everything perfect,
   and often puts fetters on the evil-doers.
It smoothes what is rough; quells anger, dims hubris
   and shrivels the flowering bud of arrogant destruction.
It straightens crooked judgments, calms
   overbearing deeds, stops the deeds of civil strife,
and stops the anger of grievous conflict. It is by this
   that all things to men are perfect and reach their peak.

In terms reminiscent of the two cities on Homer's Shield of Achilles in Book 18 of the *Iliad*, albeit in chiastic order, Solon has created two versions of the *polis*: the fragmented *polis* of *Dusnomiê*, destroyed by *hubris* and plunged into unjust conflict (lines 5-29), and the integrated *polis* of *Eunomiê* (lines 30-9), in which *hêsuchia* is distributed throughout the population.[24] *Dusnomiê* is a point of focus for the debased state of the *polis*; it means a condition in which *hubris* is distributed amongst the *polis*, and manifested as slavery and strife. The figure of *Eunomiê* – introduced by association with her opposite, *Dusnomiê* – arises at the darkest moment for each person in Solon's audience; the 'vision of a desirable ideal shown to them at the right moment'.[25] *Eunomiê* is an integrating symbol that stands for the *polis* that has reached its peak; such a *polis* is *eukosma* when *hêsuchia*, moderation and straight judgments are distributed throughout. The distributed nature of *hêsuchia* as 'peace' in the *polis* of *Eunomiê* is a goddess, but also a political condition that is dependent upon internal restraints from *hubris* in each man whose *noos* is healthy.[26]

For Solon the opposite of *Eunomiê* is *Dusnomiê*, not *anomia*; there was an order of a kind, but it was corrupted by the *hubris* in each one of them. Here we must distinguish the social and personal aspects of *Eunomiê*, which are akin to the external and internal perspectives on the *polis* that are implicit in Solon. In later Greek thought, *eunomia* for an individual person is the acceptance of the need for order in one's conduct, and the renunciation of violence, loot, etc. The opposite of *eunomia* is *anomia*, the lack of such order, and the policy of grabbing all one can at the moment. On a social level, however, the opposite to *eunomia* is *dusnomia*, or the acceptance of a bad form of order. The question hinges on what kind of order is to be accepted, meaning the nature of what one consideres to be *eu*. Jaeger observes the root of *eunomia* in ideas; 'It is found to be associated with the most varied ideas, always depending on what a person [or a

3. 'In time, retribution surely comes'

society] considers to be εὖ'. Andrewes saw that 'the virtue [of *Dikê*] attaches to the community as a whole because it is practised generally by the citizens, and *eunomia* is similarly the social result of the conduct of the individual citizens'.[27]

Challenges to values can lead to an overthrow of the present order and its replacement; what was once *eu* is now seen as bad. For example, Lycurgus *metestêse* 'changed' the early Spartan order, not *katestêse* 'established' it; they had an order, but it needed reform. The Cyclops, with no order, is distinguished from the Spartan form of *eunomia*, an order that is bad from the Athenian perspective but was nevertheless an order.[28] Social *eunomia* – a state of good order throughout the *polis* – is one in which the individuals have accepted the need for order in their lives, and express it in common values and institutions. *Dusnomia* is rather a state of the *polis* in which the individuals are *anomic*; they act without a sense of law in their dealings with each other. *Eunomia* and *dusnomia* are, on the social level, the results of individual conduct. In a sense, a man who acts with *anomia* is a greater threat than a tyrant, who at least accepts some form of order, and makes it possible to change the order (rather than having to establish order where it did not exist). It is easier to change the order associated with Sparta than to bring order to the Cyclops.[29]

The nature of the political order in Athens is a conceptual issue as well as a matter of social organization. A society is a group of individuals with some norms of interaction; it is neither an ontological entity nor an orderless mob. The terms of association between its members set the terms by which a society can even be discerned. Literal *anomia* among men would result in no society at all; with no relationships between people other than armed violence, the people would be a mob akin to Solon's pack of hounds. As Erasmus put it, under *anomia* 'there is no system or rule at all; all men seize what they can'.[30] A society cannot descend to a condition of pure *anomia* and remain a society. Thus the antonym for *eunomia* as 'good order in the community' is *dusnomia*, 'bad order', a normative opposition expressed in Solon as *Eunomiê* versus *Dusnomiê*. However, for an individual, the antonym of *eunomia* as 'good personal conduct' is *anomia* or 'lawlessness'. It is possible for an individual to act with no order at all, beyond the loot of the moment; he is a distinct being, and his 'order' is defined according to the terms by which he controls himself. Solon realizes that should the people in the *polis* act improperly, then the *polis* falls into *Dusnomiê*, and everyone in it suffers the consequences.

The *dusnomia* in the corrupted *polis* followed the order proper to Mafia families, with strict prerogatives, status levels, rituals and protocols, but based on a fundamentally unjust approach to life. Solon had to challenge such men by naming their actions for what they were, giving them a different way of understanding what is *eu*, and holding them responsible for the *stasis* in Athens – essentially the same action as the Spartan lawgiver Lycurgus', albeit with a different sense of what is *eu*. Solon's re-definition of the standards at the base of *polis* life separated his *polis* from the pre-Solonian norms that had motivated men to maintain their claims to traditional prerogatives by force – in Sparta, Lycurgus may have rather validated and strengthened their commitment to those norms. Solon's order for Athens must remain incomplete here, pending a reading of poem 36 (Chapter 7 below), in which *dikê* is solidified into the stone of written laws, connected to justice, and enforced alike for the base and the noble. Considered apart from the written laws of poem 36, however, Solon's *Eunomiê* 'implies not so much having good laws, as a condition in which the laws [founded on *Dikê*] are observed'.[31]

In the mind of a listener, Solon's *Eunomiê* is an integration of various aspects of good conduct in the *polis* into a single figure and a single point of focus. She has connections to every important aspect of the poem, as to the *polis*: the chains put on evil-doers, the calm actions of those at the ceremonial meal, the need to understand and to change one's willingness to destroy the *polis*, and the need to value the *polis* as necessary to secure the safety of the *oikos*.[32] A person who memorized the couplet in 4.34-5 would have an essentialized and unified synopsis of proper *polis* life that he could call up as a guide when he needed it. *Eunomiê* is what Solon urges his audience to recall when the righteous anger for revenge rises in one's *thumos*. Each man should think, right at the moment when *hubris* threatens to break out, that *Eunomiê d' eukosma kai artia pant' apophainei*, 'Lawfulness makes everything perfect', and then he should suppress the *hubris*. If this fails, he can remember *pantôs husteron êlthe dikê*, '*dikê* surely comes later' and contemplate the inevitable retribution that his *hubris* is inviting. Solon's poetry becomes an effective guide to conduct, an archaic *daimon* and a way of connecting the principles of the *polis* to the daily activities of each person. The *polis* in *Eunomiê* is one in which each person thinks and acts *en hêsuchiai*.

Solon's verses on *dikê* leave much to be desired. He never really says what it *is*; the gap in the literature between Hesiod's view of *dikê* as from Zeus and the sophist Protagoras' challenge that *dikê* is acquired and not endowed remains empty.[33] He remains thoroughly focused on consequences, and never really lays out the principle behind *dikê*; perhaps it seemed obvious to him. Although Solon does not speculate about *dikê* as a comprehensive order in the universe, he does speak of a necessity that is common to the sky, the sea and the *polis*. He is on the cusp of philosophical understanding, but not yet in its camp. Imagine a questioner pushing Solon's claim backwards, looking for the ultimate starting point: Q: 'Where does rain come from?' A: 'Clouds'. Q: 'Where do clouds come from?' A: 'Mist'. Q: 'Where does mist come from?' A: (nervously) 'Ah, Wind'. Q: 'Where does wind come from?' A: (visibly shaken) 'Zeus, dammit!' Solon's capacity to grasp the end of his own logical chain has its limits, but he is in some ways less mystical than those physicists today who accept the operation of natural law in the universe, but start from a 'Big Bang' that they claim

3. 'In time, retribution surely comes'

constitutes divine creation. Despite Solon's limited context when compared to the natural philosophers, he places the *polis* into a framework of necessity that transcends the *dikê* of the *polis* itself. A thinker with the intellectual range of Anaximander could expand the application of the ideas used by Solon further, into an account of the actions of all things in terms of justice. Similarly Anaximenes could expand upon Solon's idea that 'hail comes from clouds and thunder from lightning', finding an explicable sequence that extends from air, to clouds, to rain, to hail, to wind and to snow, now understood as cycles.[34] Others would argue against such cycles, calling them disorderly, and looking in other directions for explanations.[35] Each interpretation sees an order of a kind, although they disagree as to what constitutes order, and in this sense each agrees with Solon.

With respect to the moral ordering of the *polis* Solon stands between the military camp of Homer and the introspections of Democritus and Socrates, leading to Aristotle's 'philosophy of human affairs' that bridges from the *Ethics* into the *Politics*. Solon's need to bring the human dispute settlements into conformity with the retribution that occurs *pantôs* anticipates a later generalization by Heraclitus: 'Those speaking with sense must guard that which is common to all, as the *polis* guards its law and even more so; for all human laws are nourished by the one law of the divine'. Kirk, Raven and Schofield identify 'the real moral of Heraclitus' philosophy' as the belief that 'only by understanding the central pattern of things can a man become wise and fully effective'.[36] Solon establishes no central pattern for 'all things', but he lays its foundations in the necessity he finds underlying *polis* life, anchored in *dikê* and the values that he sees as necessary for life in a just *polis*.[37] In the *polis* – as in a sculpture such as the Sunium Kouros – it is not enough to say an order is present; the specific values it embodies distinguish it from others. Solon challenged those who saw value in outrage and thought that honour should come by seizing power and loot, and he offered an alternative. Whatever his own position in the archaic *polis*, and whatever use he made of it in his verses, this was the value that later Athenians saw in his ideas. Solon's perspective on the comprehensive necessity informs his views of the *polis* as a moral *kosmos* ordered by *dikê* – and doubtless his moral views affirm his grasp of necessity. It is impossible to know with certainty whether Solon influenced later philosophers directly; it is more fruitful to consider Solon and the later philosophers as participating in a common manner of thought.

4

'A *kosmos* of words'
Archaic logic and the organization of poem 4

> I have come as a herald from lovely Salamis,
> composing song, a *kosmos* of words, instead of speech
> Solon 1

Whether a speaker or a singer, Solon used his verses for a practical purpose: to exhort his fellows to think and to act as he wished. In this sense he is a proto-rhetor, an archaic practitioner of *rhetorikê*: public speaking with the aim of inducing a decision and an action from his audience. George Kennedy's definition of *rhetorikê* is important: '*Rhetorikê* in Greek specifically denotes the civic art of public speaking as it developed in deliberative assemblies, law courts, and other formal occasions under constitutional government in the Greek cities, especially the Athenian democracy'.[1] In Solon's time, 'government institutions', and indeed the very idea of 'formal occasions', were at best implicit, but this does not lessen the influential effect that groups – symposia, aristocratic get-togethers or spontaneous assemblies – could have on affairs in Athens. Solon's exhortations to such gatherings – in poetic metre – were his form of political oratory, and his way of changing the unwritten constitution of Athens. To call Solon a proto-rhetor is to affirm his status as a poet with a persuasive purpose, and to place that persuasive speech in a context that is prior to the deliberative, legal and constitutional institutions of the classical *polis*. His verses are embedded with their own subtle inventory of tropes and techniques, and doubtless he said what was appropriate to his audiences. Poem 4 in particular betrays a complex organization that is a direct portal into the mind of the poet, and the fulfilment of his own claim to have created a *kosmos epeôn*, a *kosmos* of words, ordered into a thing of beauty.[2]

Solon's concern for *noos* is evidence for a deeply rooted intellectualism in archaic thought, a conclusion that bids us to consider whether there is a logical structure present in his verses, and to what degree, if any, he thinks about how he thinks.[3] These issues come with many caveats. The evidence is fragmentary, and we must distinguish metric and poetic purposes. It is mandatory not to attempt to establish an epistemic position within Solon's own verses; for instance, he has no concept of 'knowledge'. Having considered issues such as *noos*, *koros* and *dikê* in poem 4, we can now step back for a broader view of its organization as a whole. Are there

4. 'A kosmos *of words*'

discernible, if not consistent, patterns of thought in his poems? This is not self-evidently so, and not only because he uses foreign terminology to direct his focus onto topics that may seem off-centre to political affairs. His very method of approach does not seem to make sense. To demonstrate that the townsmen are bringing Athens into conflict, he leads us from Athena to *hubris* at a meal, through *Dikê* into courtyards and bedrooms, to *Dusnomiê* and then *Eunomiê*. This series of images, metaphors and mythic symbols might be effective rhetorically – as much as the image of a 'Cross of Gold' could be convincing for the audience hearing William Jennings Bryan – but is it logical?[4]

In this poem Solon does present an archaic argument. It has a conclusion to be supported, and he gives reasons for it. But it is an oral declamation, and it is crucial to remember the oral delivery of such verses. Our examination is conditioned by *reading* what was earlier *spoken*, a point that bears upon how the poem will be understood, and our reading must not be allowed to overtake the listening. The aim of the poet was not to produce a work that could stand up to written analysis, but rather to produce an oral *kosmos* that could lead his listeners to a desired effect. The purpose of writing was to key the reader's mind to recreate the sounds, and therefore the ability to hear the words.[5]

The poem can be divided into three sections. The *polis* and its relationship to men and gods, lines 1 to 17, is arranged in a ring composition that begins and ends with the *polis* and centres on the sufferings of the citizens. When heard orally, the *polis* might become a character in the verses, undergoing an ordeal and in desperate need of help. The second section takes the destruction from the sufferings of the entire *polis* to the bedroom of every individual, 17 to 29; the general progression of the strife is from the *polis* as a whole through smaller groups to each one of us; this completes the picture of the *polis* corrupted by *hubris*. The third section is *Eunomiê*, 30-9, Solon's prescription for the troubles and an unmistakably distinct section in the poem.[6]

The verses move in a linear fashion, progressively shifting the focus: from the *polis* as a whole (lines 1 and 5), narrowing to the *dêmos* (7), the *dais* (10), and back to the *polis* (17). The poem then narrows its focus through levels of social organization, through smaller social groups to the home of each one of us: *phulai* (tribes, line 19), *sunodoi* (meetings, 22), the *oikos* (family homestead, 26), and *thalamos* (innermost bedroom, 29). Within these verses there is a series of lyrical resonances; for instance, in the first five lines alone we hear *oleitai / phtheirein* (destroyed / corrupted); *hêmeterê polis / megalên polin* (our *polis* / great *polis*); and *phrenas / aphradiêsin* (plans / foolishness).[7] Along the way Solon describes various men: some destroy the *polis* (5), others are killed (20), exiled (24), enslaved (25), and attacked in their bedroom (29). This poem progresses in a straight line from the *hubris* of the citizens in a public meal to the private recesses of each man's homestead, and demonstrates how the *polis* disin-

Solon the Thinker

tegrates into rival factions. With these sufferings fresh in the minds of the audience, the entrance of *Eunomiê* is very powerful.

There are also discernible ring formulations within the poem. The first section (lines 1-17) is a ring with four levels, beginning with *hêmeterê polis* (our *polis*, line 1), and returning to *pasê polei* (the entire *polis*, 17). The destruction of the *polis* is described as *algea polla pathein*, 'to suffer many pains' (8), the centre of the rings, which stresses the great sufferings of the citizens and positions those sufferings at the centre of the problems in the *polis*. The *polis* as the start and the end of the section strengthens the focus on Athens, in which the corruption runs its course.

The first seventeen lines of poem 4 can be represented diagrammatically:

Ring composition of Solon 4.1-17

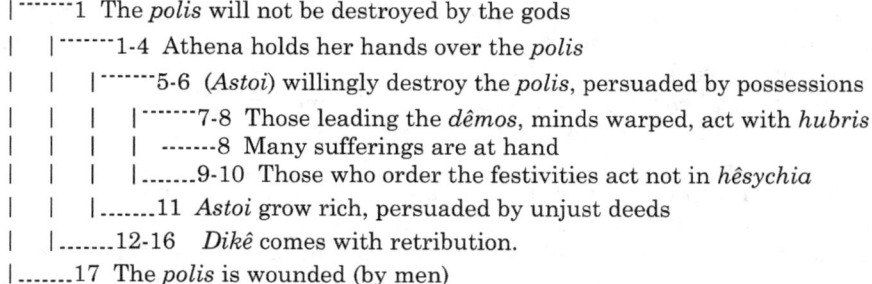

Beginning from the centre (line 8), the first ring has, at either end (7-8 and 9-10) someone taking public action (leading the *dêmos*, or ordering the festivities), with a noetic problem (an unjust *noos*, or lack of understanding), and a description of their condition (great *hubris*, or not in *hêsuchia*). The audience hears twice of immoderate men, acting improperly and without proper *noos*, bringing suffering between them. The *dêmos* errs in paying too much attention to the speaker's words; they would do better to pay attention to the disorder he creates, and Solon vivifies this in a scene that many of them might have experienced: a meal that turned into a confrontation. If living in the *polis* includes – or perhaps means – participating in such a meal, then leading the *dêmos* and ordering the festivities are poetically the same thing, and the rings are balanced.

Continuing out from the centre (8), the next ring, ended at 5-6 and 11, stresses an action performed by corrupted citizens, who are persuaded (*peithomenoi*) by *aphradiêsin*, 'by heartlessness', and *adikois ergmasi*, 'by unjust deeds'. In lines 5-6 the citizens *boulontai*, 'they are willing', to destroy the *polis*; they do this with a senselessness (*aphradiêsin*) that may recall the insensate dwellers of Hades, the *nekroi aphradees*, 'dimwitted dead', of *Odyssey* 11.475-6, but which does not contradict the ability of the Athenians to choose differently. At the other end of the ring (line 11), the

4. 'A kosmos of words'

citizens grow wealthy, motivated by their success at unjust deeds. The unjust ambitions of a *noos* as *adikos* (7) bring short-term success by the corresponding deeds, *adikois ergmasi*.

The next ring, ended at 1-4 and 12-16, contrasts the protections of Athena with the certainty of destruction by *Dikê*, should injustice prevail. The ring ends in a way that is qualitatively different from the way it begins. Athena's protections are not aimed against human assaults on the sacred roots of *Dikê*; to protect those foundations is the responsibility of human beings. The *themethla* of *Dikê* 4.14 may be related to the *horoi* of 36.6, originally marking straight lines between plots of land, thus calling upon the earliest establishment of *dikê* on earth and the very nature of human associations. Solon places himself as a *horos* in the middle of this at 37.10. The qualitative degradation of the *polis* between 4.1-4 and 4.12-16 is a foretaste of the effects of Solon's prescriptions in lines 30-9, by which the *polis* under *Dusnomiê* is qualitatively improved when *Eunomiê* replaces *hubris* with *hêsuchia*.

The central evidence for Solon's claim that the *polis* is being destroyed is in the verb *pathein*. This has a neutral meaning, 'to experience' as opposed to 'to do', both suffering and pleasure; context must establish whether the experience is of the good or the harmful. To experience something is to see, or feel, it directly; to experience (*pathein*) is distinguished from understanding something which we cannot see (*noein*). The centrality of *pathein* to Solon is illustrated elsewhere; in each case the experience is treated as if it demonstrated Solon's claim. In 24.4 *gastri te kai pleurais kai posin habra pathein*, 'to experience the good things in life, by feet, clothing and food', is equated with growing wealthy, and serves to bring Solon's views of wealth into the experiences of people who were less than rich. The lines may be sarcastic or ironic, depending on the audience; Solon may or may not be trying to convince the *kakoi* to accept their positions, or to assert the aristocratic status of a sumpotic audience.[8] In poem 13 line 35 the expectations of each one of us, base and noble, are challenged by the experiences of life; these experiences demonstrate the untrustworthiness of our expectations and set limits to our ability to understand the ends of all things. In poem 4 line 8, 'to suffer many pains' is a culmination of the unjust actions of the citizens and their leaders, which they have experienced or can recall, as a demonstration that Solon is right. Solon treats these experiences as validation of his position; in his hands, they are powerful tools of persuasion.[9]

But is such ring analysis valid for such an oral, archaic poem? John Keaney, in his discussion of Aristotle's *Athenaion Politeia*, notes that the basic purpose of ring composition 'is to focus on one segment of the narrative by isolating it from the rest of the narrative'.[10] Although ring analysis seems to shed light on the structure of poem 4 as we *read* it, such analysis does not explain the *oral* effects of the poem. It is vital that poems such as these be read *out loud*, preferably in an open area and with great force, in order to approach the original effect. Ideally one should hear it without having read it at all. The first level of rings does separate off the main sections of the verses, akin to the story of Niobe in the *Iliad* and the simile of the wind in Solon's poem 13, but such separation is not effective down to tertiary and quaternary levels.[11] Of course, there is no evidence that Solon was in any way consciously aware of this construction; it is evidence for how his mind works, whether he knows it or not.

Keaney's own analysis of Aristotle's *Politeia* often distinguishes rings in mid-sentence, which suggests their purpose to be something other than the separation of a section of narrative, even in written work.[12] In oral poetry, ring formulation may not always be a compositional technique but rather a form of later analysis. Such analysis may reveal a change in the direction of the poet's arguments that was intended to heighten the vividness of the narrative rather than to break it up. From this perspective, the arguments of Solon's poem 4 can rather be understood as beginning from a certain idea (e.g. Athena holds off the gods), progressing to a conclusion (the many sufferings) and then back to a restatement of the conclusion (*Dikê* brings retribution), done in a way that intends to drive home the danger to the *polis* and to each one of us. From this perspective, lines 1-8 approach the sufferings in line 8, and lines 9-17 move from those sufferings to a *de facto* restatement of these sufferings, the inescapable wound, in chiastic order of argumentation. This pattern continues, bringing the wound into the home of each person. This interpretation is simplified as:

  1-4   The *polis* will not be destroyed by fate or the gods, Athena raises her hands
      5-6   Citizens will to destroy the *polis*, persuaded by material goods
      7-8   Those leading the *dêmos* have warped minds, act with great *hubris*
  8   Consequently, the citizens suffer much
      9-10 The citizens do not understand; the festivities are not in *hêsuchiê*
      11   They grow rich, persuaded by unjust deeds
      12-16 They destroy the *polis* through larceny, *Dikê* comes with retribution

  17   Consequently, the wound comes to the *polis*
      18-20 Slavery awakens civil strife and war
      21   Many youths die
      21-2 Factional intrigues
      23-5 Slavery
  26-9: Consequently, the public evil comes into the bedroom of each person

4. 'A *kosmos of words*'

In poem 4, lines 1-8 approach the main point, the many sufferings that they will experience, by moving from the hand of Athena through the destructive actions of the citizens, their improper persuasions, their warped minds and their *hubris*. Once the poet reaches the sufferings he then sets off for the metaphorical restatement of the sufferings, the inescapable wound of line 17. But in doing so he restates the lack of understanding and the unrestrained *koros* of the unjust men, their improper persuasions, their destructive actions and their failure to guard the foundations of *Dikê*. *Dikê*, we then hear, silently knows all and brings retribution in time, and the wound comes to the *polis*. The result is analysable into a ring composition. But by considering the arguments not as centred on line 8, but rather as first approaching line 8, then line 17, and then line 28, we hear what is basically the same point, stated first as a generalization ('many sufferings'), then as a metaphor ('wound'), and then as a concretization ('public evil' in private homes). The progression from the tribulations at 4.8, to the wound at 4.17, to the bedroom at 4.29, is the series of images that Solon's audience could actually experience.

The reason for the poet's reversal of the order of delivery after line 8 may be associative thinking. Solon may continue with 'they do not understand how to restrain their excess' after line 8 because *hubris* is fresh in his mind; the last point in the first section may key the first point in the second section. In lines 9-17 he may approach the suffering in reverse order the second time because *hubris* brings to mind *koros* and *stasis*. If so, then the poem may be a loosely connected series of ideas, composed without clear plan by the poet, but based upon ideas that he had clarified in advance. However, in lieu of subconscious associative thinking on his part, he may be actively aware of the power of such associations for his audience, who would receive the impression of a powerful validation of his arguments. This of course would assume a strong control by Solon over his work.

Lines 17 to 29 may also be viewed from two perspectives. First, considered as a unit, the section is apposed to the sufferings of 8, and brings the wound of line 17 into each man's home. The *helkos aphukton*, 'inescapable wound', is everything that is happening to the *polis*, integrated into a single idea, and blamed on certain men. Solon's *polis* has been wounded by an attack, not damaged by a natural plague; *helkos* is a 'wound' and not 'disease'.[13] Solon, blaming certain men for the 'wound', is again isolating them, and accusing them of attacking 'our *polis*'. The lines detail the effects of the troubles on the individual members of the *polis* in order to demonstrate the effects on the *polis* as a whole. For those who had experienced – or might recall – the effects of civic strife, Solon's point is clear by direct experience.

Second, lines 17 to 29 may also be read as a progression that relates the public wound to the most private aspects of life, to 'each one of them', *hekastos autôn*. The verses progress through various levels of social organization; progressively narrowing from the *phulê*, the *sunodos*, the *oikos*, to the innermost *thalamos* of each person. This all implies the disintegration of *hêmeterê polis*; Athens is breaking up into warring groups and individual attacks. He stresses that the *polemos* is 'tribal', *emphulos*, an implication that dangerous regional groups based on clans or families are rising, and threatening the unity of the *polis*.[14] A precise definition of the *phulê* is not required here, only a recognition that there are groups with which a person identifies himself and places his loyalty. The *polis* divides further, worn out in unjust assemblies that destroy friendly relations. The 'unjust assemblies', *sunodois tois adikeousi*, could include the ceremonial meal (*dais*) and the symposium, which would have functioned not merely as a metaphor for the governance of the *polis* but as an actual institution in which an aristocracy ordered the affairs of the archaic *polis*. Many poor are sold in chains, a reference to the unseemly conditions of particular men and the effects of the 'wound' on them. But the division of the *polis* continues to the level of the family farm, into the bedroom. That lines 1-25 constitute the process by which the 'public evil' comes to each man is suggested by *houtô* in 26: *thus* the public evil comes to the home of each person. A contrast between Solon's values and those of a martial poet is revealed in a comparison with Callinus 1.14-15, who holds that the *oikos* is not a place of refuge for those who flee the battle.

To put it another way, the 'wound' is an integration of a series of unjust actions into a single term, which stands for everything that is happening to the *polis*. Upon reaching the wound at 4.17, Solon then takes it apart, describing it as slavery (*doulosunê*), civil strife (*stasis*) and war (*polemos*), which are themselves ideas that refer to myriad particular phenomena. But what exactly is *polemos*? It is lovely youth killed, 4.20, as *stasis* is the destruction of friendships in unjust assemblies, 21-2, and *doulosunê* is many poor sold in chains, 4.23-5. The 'wound' is no longer a metaphor; it is the real destruction of war, civil strife and slavery, which mean killing, factional fighting and chains. These are the observable consequences for each person.

Whichever reading of the poem we prefer – and it is not necessary to refute one to accept the other – the arrangement of Solon's work does suggest an ability to think on more than a simple linear level. But there are two overall trends revealed: the first, lines 5-17, is broadly one of synthesis, or integration, moving from the particular men who are destroying the *polis* to the integrated metaphor of the wound, which stands for everything bad happening to the *polis*. From 17 to 29 he deconstructs the wound, breaking it down and ending back at any particular man who tries to hide. The pattern here is broadly one of analysis. But in the process of analysis Solon creates a new integration, of *Dusnomiê*, civic strife breaking into each man's home, and a vivid picture not only of the *polis* but of an *oikos* under siege. This perspective on the poem reveals a constant shifting through levels of generalizations, narrowing and widen-

4. 'A kosmos *of words*'

ing in order to create an image that validates his point. There is an implicit organizational principle at work, which connects his unseen, abstract conclusions to perceptible consequences. Everything is about bringing the unseen into the range of human sight, through the poetic image.

In summary, the poem's order of presentation – which is how the audience hears the wound described – contrasts with an analysis of how Solon relates his abstractions to particular experiences:

Solon Poem 4

Order of presentation

    I.   the wounded (line 17)
    II.   the *polis* savaged by slavery, civil strife, war (lines 18-9)
    III.   youth killed, unjust friendships, men in chains (lines 20-25)

Analysis

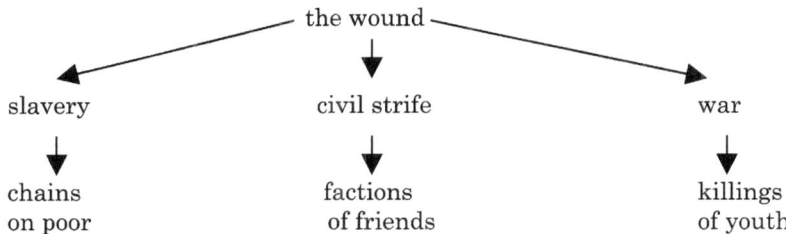

These patterns might have occurred by extemporaneous associations in the poet's mind, or might have been consciously designed to have maximum impact on the listener. In either case, only after the *oikos* has been made part of the *Dusnomiê* can *Eunomiê* enter, in a distinct section of the poem, lines 30-9. When Solon says, at line 4.30, that 'these things my heart prompts me to teach the Athenians', he is offering an alternative to those who acted *ou kata kosmon* due to their flawed understanding. A ring formulation, based on *eukosma / artia* in line 32, and *artia / pinuta* in line 39, sets the section off from the rest of the text, a point noted by Jaeger and Gerber among others.[15] (The poem may have continued, shifting its emphasis in ways lost to us, offering similar guideposts as it progressed.) A listener hears *artia* repeated, and understands that the focus is on what is appropriate – a distinct answer to the injustice of the preceding sections, caused by the *noos* that is not *artios*. The focus on proper conduct remains strong, in contrast to the rest of the poem.

That the *kosmos* consisted of particular men with certain psychic virtues is strengthened by *pinuta* and *artia*. In Homer these words are connected to persons, generally with respect to a prudent state of mind. Homer has Athena tell Telemachus that anyone who is *pinutos*, 'prudent', would be angered at the shameful acts of hubristic men at a meal; in a later passage Penelope is also *pinutê*.[16] The only occurrence in elegy and iambus apart from Solon is in Theognis, where discretion is contrasted with 'exceeding proper measure', *huper metron*, connected to drinking, and applicable to 'those who were formerly wise'.[17] *Artios* as 'appropriate' applies similarly to persons; the four Homeric uses are all found in context with *phrên*.[18] The only other occurrence in elegy and iambus is Theognis 946, which Bergk attributes to Solon; here it is right to know all proper things. In Solon *artia* at 4c.4 and 6.4 is also related to *noos*. Read in the light of these other passages, *pinuta* and *artia* might suggest that *Eunomiê* is directly connected to the state of mind of the citizens, and 4.32 and 39 refer to the effect of *Eunomiê* on that state of mind.[19]

Eunomiê's effects on *noos*, *koros*, *hubris* and *atê* are seen in lines 4.33-6. *Eunomiê* in line 33 often puts chains on the evildoers (*tois adikois*); this is a clear statement that *Eunomiê* physically restrains evil men, and is a pointed corrective to those with the *noos adikos* in line 7, who corrupted the *polis*, and those who put many poor into fetters, implied in lines 23-5. Since they failed to restrain themselves, but rather acted beyond the proper measure of justice, they will be restrained by *Eunomiê*, physically if necessary. Line 33 also reverberates in line 36; there *Eunomiê* straightens crooked judgments, a claim that depends upon the use of force to restrain the unjust and that will bear further discussion in context with Solon's laws.[20] Lines 33 and 36 thus may be read as a secondary ring within the primary ring framed by lines 30 and 39.

Lines 34 and 35 are indirect references to *koros*, *hubris* and *atê* (within the rings formed by lines 33-6, and 30-9). But what are the 'rough things' that are being smoothed? On the face of it Solon should mention *noos* here, given the relationships found elsewhere between *hubris* and *noos*. The verb *leiainô*, 'smooth', first appears in this form in Solon. Related forms elsewhere denote an active process of polishing or grinding down, suggesting that Solon's *Eunomiê* required active acceptance and practice by the citizens and that judgment may have to be physically enforced.[21] The general formulation *trachea leiainei* in 4.34 has a parallel in poem 34.3: [those who came at me expecting to find plunder also expected to find] 'me, babbling smoothly, and showing a rough *noos*', *trachun noon*. The rough things, *trachea*, in 4.34 that need smoothing may be an allusion to the hubristic feelings in each of the citizens, which follow from the *adikos noos*. It is their dispositions and their attitudes that are made smooth and turned from violence, through the unified figure of *Eunomiê*, a point of focus for all that is good and appropriate.

In the end, is there an overall organization in the poem, beyond the basic *Dusnomiê* and *Eunomiê* sections? Hermann Fränkel posited three methods within archaic poetic form: (1) passage from general rule to particular instance and back again, (2) circling around the subject matter, and (3) ring composition.[22] By the interpretation here, these may be

4. 'A kosmos of words'

variations on the same basic pattern: a poet's attempt to relate generalizations to observable particulars, by focusing his claims onto vivified scenarios that stand with the power of perceptible images. The ebb and flow between observable concretes and more abstract generalizations, including metaphors and mythic symbols, may demonstrate an archaic poet's reliance on the perceptual level of awareness, as a means to demonstrate the validity of his claims. The essence of his method is integration – using abstract concepts to build a scenario out of a multitude of disparate experiences – and vivification – demonstrating the validity of those abstractions by presenting them as if they were perceptible phenomena. There is no need for us to choose between ring versus linear analysis; each serves to demonstrate a different aspect of the poem's overall approach, its power and its richness.

The use of observable instances to illustrate abstract generalizations in Solon's thought must not be conflated with radical empiricism, in which only the results of direct observations can be known with certainty. Some scholars have maintained that Homeric knowledge is purely of personal experience, with no knowledge apart from direct perception.[23] This 'verified by event' interpretation locks knowledge into observation, disallowing any understanding of a situation beyond one's immediate awareness. A similar methodology has been postulated for Xenophanes, based upon a perceptual meaning of *oida* and *idein* words as opposed to *dokeô*, 'I have seen' vs 'I seem to know'.[24] On the face of it this distinction is analogous to Solon's *noeomen ... prin ti pathein*, 'we know ... until we suffer' in poem 13. However, had Solon thought that only that which is seen directly can be known, then there should be some evidence of such a perspective in the other verses. But only poems 13, 16 and 17 illustrate such an uncertainty directly, and only in 13 is a broader context preserved. There is no 'seeing versus seeming' dichotomy across the verses – which would have constituted an important step towards the explicit *alêtheia / doxa* distinction of Parmenides. Solon's political verses are better understood as attempts to expand his understanding – and that of his audience – beyond what is immediately observable while remaining true to what he does see. The *polis* remains a community of real men, understood in the terms of its order (or the breaks in that order), described by Solon using abstract ideas, metaphors and mythic symbols, but related back to scenes that would be vividly real to his audience. A 'wolf in the midst of a pack of hounds' can speak volumes about the situation in Athens, especially if one is beset by hordes of angry creditors.

Knowledge of the hidden, causal connections that integrate the *polis* is the wisdom that Solon seeks, and teaches. This point has been made by Emily Anhalt with respect to poem 13, which she interprets as an attempt to grasp those connections through a prayer to Memory.[25] But the lack of deductive arguments, and the preponderance of imagery and metaphors, have led some scholars to contend that the poet can have no such aims; the archaic mind, they claim, is like that of a child, preoccupied with what is directly before it and easily distracted from abstract formulations onto whatever seizes its attention. The poet works without plan or structure in creating his work; he goes where his ideas take him. In this interpretation the archaic mind is unable to assemble a logical argument because it remains 'concrete-bound', unable to deal with abstractions, and digressing easily; consequently the poems are a haphazard, rambling series of disconnected thoughts. For a 'concrete-bound' mentality, writes Leonard Peikoff, 'every issue is simply a new concrete, unrelated to what came before, to abstract principles, or to any context'.[26] The very idea of 'truth' may be foreign to such a mind; all that matters is the imagery, and each image stands alone, causally unconnected to other thoughts. In reaction to such views, some scholars have claimed that to look for causal connections, logical structures or organization in archaic poetry is misguided; they claim that parataxis, non-subordination or the 'strung-on style' (*lexis eiromenê*) do allow unity of composition and organization, albeit by means of associative relationships rather than syllogistic logic. In these terms to look for 'organic unity of composition' or to speak of 'illogicality' is to use improper criteria. The debate over these issues has been particularly energetic over Solon's poem 13 (see Chapter 5 below).

The issue of 'cause' and 'causation' is particularly pertinent in an interpretation of Solon. The concept of 'cause' is historically anachronistic and never more than implicit in Solon; he has not abstracted the idea of a neuter 'causal factor', and he shows no grasp of 'causal connections', beyond an understanding that 'if this, then that, necessarily', which explains the condition of the *polis* in relation to each one of us. But the nature of Solon's poetry – its paratactic arrangement, and its reliance on association rather than on syllogistic logic – has led some scholars to challenge any idea of 'cause' as existing in his thought, even implicitly. Some have challenged the very applicability of causation as an interpretative concept: given the general use of parataxis rather than subordination, archaic verses are, again, based upon associative rather than syllogistic thinking, and there is a lack of logical connection between ideas.[27] Without such logic, they claim, there is no basis for causal connections.

W.J. Henderson promoted this view, arguing that 'the scene [poem 4 line 17 f.] is synchronic, not historic', and the 'logic' of 'wound' exists 'not on the level of abstract causality as we see it', with one event following another inevitably, but rather in affective imagery and concreteness. 'The audience is not persuaded by the "logical chain" of inevitability, but by the truth of the total picture in which any one of the elements or phases implies the others'. A series of verbs is used 'to build up a graphic "reality" in the present'. Therefore, 'the "order" and "perfection" are presented in terms of real, particular situations without any necessary causal connection or sequence joining them'. Although conceding that there is 'causality' evident in the progression of the poem, ultimately Henderson opposes the

4. 'A *kosmos* of words'

use of causal terminology to interpret archaic thought, and argues against any causal principle in poem 4. By dichotomizing the issue into *either* a logical chain *or* a 'truth of the total picture', and then denying the existence of any causal consequences in the latter, Henderson claims, in essence, that a lack of deduction precludes any understanding by Solon that things happen causally.[28] In the end, Henderson links his concept of causation inextricably to two processes: temporal sequence, and deductive reasoning. He denies that any comprehensive view of the *polis*, even one that connects psychic factors to political conditions as explicitly as Solon did, can explain why political events occur as they do.

But Solon may see things in a different way. First off, an interval of time is not a determinant of causal necessity; 'if X then Y' is what Solon considers important, whether separated temporally or not.[29] Even so, Solon does say that 'in time, retribution surely comes', and 'justice surely comes later'; he is aware of this issue, and is deliberately projecting the consequences of noetic failure into the future. But, more important, Solon need not state his conclusions in syllogistic terms to demonstrate that he understands a necessary connection between things.

Further, Solon surely does not build his arguments around deductive, syllogistic reasoning, and any attempt to find such methods could only succeed by creating what is not there. But this may not mean that he does not support his case in a logical fashion. A different approach to Solon is possible, one that recognizes a way of demonstrating the truth in a way that is not deductive. 'Truth' – *alêtheia* – is literally the 'unhidden', or the 'unremembered', that which we do not see or have not remembered seeing directly, but that we know to be so.[30] For Solon, the problem is *noetic*: to bring the hidden aspects of the *polis* into the open. Possibly what we see as digressions – the use of vivid imagery and descriptive scenes – are Solon's ways of proving his point. Possibly he offers this 'proof' not by connecting abstract statements using syllogistic rules, but rather by showing that what he claims is undeniably true, given that it may be perceived directly, in the world around him. The poet's vivid examples, rather than indicating a digression by a 'concrete-bound' mentality, are his means of vivifying and explaining his generalizations by connecting them to that which is observable (or is remembered as such) by the audience. The validation of the claim is found by relating the abstract conclusion to the scene, not by drawing a deductive argument from propositions. To deny the conclusion would be to reject what is in front of one's face.

While Solon's perspective does not preclude an understanding that 'this leads to that, necessarily' it makes his conclusions vivid, by showing the individual factors (*noos, hubris, koros, atê*, etc.) that bring health or ruin to the *polis*. It is through an understanding that 'any one of the elements or phases necessitates the others' that Solon grasps causal necessity. This *is* archaic causality, grasped by understanding the elements of a situation relationally, as a vivid, integrated picture. To say that material resources, in the hands of a man with a weak mind, lead him to commit *hubris* against others, which leads to lawsuits, conflict and ultimately civil war, is a statement that a faulty *noos* causes *stasis*. To say that, if the faulty *noos* is not corrected, then the *stasis* will not be avoided, and then to point to a hubristic man who is committing an outrage, is to demonstrate that *noos* is a causal factor in the condition of the *polis*.

It is this continuous interaction between what can and cannot be seen, and between generalizations and particulars, that constitutes the basic structure of Solon's arguments.[31] Although this lacks the basic tools of syllogistic logic required to avoid contradictions and to evaluate the status of propositions, and it shows no evidence of systematic observation or the experimental method, it carries the important virtue of grounding its own arguments in evidence that every Athenian could validate for himself. Proof is found not in deductive chains of reasoning, but in reducing abstract claims to a plausible, integrated picture – to a vivid scene if not to real events. This interpretation avoids many of the problems inherent in reifying causality into a de-personalized cosmic force otherwise indistinguishable from Zeus, or in postulating an anachronistic understanding of a concept 'cause' in archaic thought. Yet it preserves Solon's stated claims about what it meant for something to be necessary in the *polis*, while remaining loyal to the general tenor of his verses and the vivid scenes he presents.[32]

All of this can take on a prescriptive force. Solon's use of such integrated imagery allows his verses to be memorized as units of sound, and recalled by his audience when they need his guidance. By claiming that *pantôs husteron êlthe dikê*, 'justice surely comes later', Solon creates a verse that can be held in the mind and applied to a multitude of concrete circumstances. The power of the verse is found in its ability to condense vast amounts of information into a single mental unit. Should a man face rising anger, and a desire for destructive vengeance, this verse may rise in his mind, reveal the hidden consequences of his response, and supplant the premises that gave rise to the anger. The couplet 6.3-4, 'excess breeds hubris whenever much wealth follows a man whose mind is not perfect', is a reminder that a man who is materially successful must be healthy in his *psuchê* else he becomes a brute. Once the flowering bud of calamity is withered, under the influence of *Eunomiê* in a man's mind, then the causal factor leading to civil strife will be eliminated, and *Eunomiê* will reign in the *polis*.

Near the start of Plato's dialogue bearing his name, the perfect youth Charmides enters, his unequalled body naked under the loving gaze of Chaerephon and many others. To Socrates, he would be perfect if he had just one thing more – a well-formed soul. Perhaps we can undress him, discuss things, and have a look at this part of him? Certainly, says Critias; he is not only a poet, but also a philosopher, and thus capable of such discussion. 'This is a gift, dear Critias, that has been in your family since

4. 'A kosmos *of words*'

the time of Solon'.[33] Plato's overt attribution, to Solon, of the genesis of the soul of the philosopher – which can be undressed and revealed – places Solon at the watershed of the greatest intellectual tradition in western thought. Solon, always anchored in an archaic mind-set, presages the abstract political understanding of later thinkers by placing man's soul into a rational civic framework, and revealing the unseen factors in its condition, through persuasive verses that possess their own mysterious structures. Plato, to serve his own purpose, credits Solon with deeply implanting, in the minds of the Athenians spanning generations, the ideas needed to plumb the depths of the soul and to grasp its unseen connections to the *polis*.

5

'Moira brings good and evil'
Bios and the failure of Dikê

> *Moira* brings good and evil to mortals,
> the gifts of the immortal gods may not be escaped
>
> Solon 13.63-4

There is a searing paradox evident in Solon's claims about the *polis*, wisdom and human life. On the one hand his verses proclaiming his ability to know the inevitable consequences of human actions in the *polis* are emboldened with the kind of unalloyed certainty once relegated to the gods alone. As lawgiver he takes over where *Dikê* dare not tread, seeing that which will be and claiming its inevitability in terms that are comprehensive and inescapable. Yet, the inability of any man to see the ultimate end of all things was a common tenet in early Greek thought, and Solon can claim no exception to this rule. Man's *noos* is ephemeral, and it is difficult or impossible to know the end of life itself. Solon's verses combine '*Dikê* surely comes later' with 'the mind of the immortals is hidden from men', claiming both the ability to know 'what will be', and that 'what will be' is hidden to us. Some readers have argued that a division, or split, exists in his thought, between his revolutionary view of political matters and his traditional view of fate, and that his poem 13, the *Hymn to the Muses*, expresses this split. But what is the mess here: is it in Solon's ideas, or our understanding of him?[1]

Gregory Vlastos highlighted this vital issue in his investigation of Solonian justice. Vlastos described a 'bifurcation of justice' in Solon's thought, a basic split between his 'justice of the *polis*' and 'justice of wealth'. 'In political justice he is a great innovator, for he thinks of it as an intelligible order of reparation. In acquisitive or distributive justice, he is a traditionalist'.[2] Beyond the *hubris* of unjust men and the 'inevitable' retribution that follows, the similarity between the two categories of justice ends. Vlastos here presents his first observation:

> 1. There is no suggestion that in the case of wealth the sequence of 'injustice' and 'reparation' is a natural, self-regulative process. There is no parallel here to the observable chain of consequences (injustice – bondage – strife) which we met in the account of political justice, hence no explanation as to *how* the original injustice leads to 'disaster' (*atê*)
>
> Vlastos 1995: 46

5. 'Moira brings good and evil'

The poet's own view of wealth pursuits can be found in passages such as:

> Μοῖρα δέ τοι θνητοῖσι κακὸν φέρει ἠδὲ καὶ ἐσθλόν,
>   δῶρα δ' ἄφυκτα θεῶν γίγνεται ἀθανάτων.
> πᾶσι δέ τοι κίνδυνος ἐπ' ἔργμασιν, οὐδέ τις οἶδεν
>   πῇ μέλλει σχήσειν χρήματος ἀρχομένου·
>
> Solon 13.63-6

> *Moira* brings good and evil to mortals,
>   and the gifts of the immortal gods may not be escaped.
> There is risk in all actions, and no one knows
>   how something, having started, will end up.

Such passages contrast utterly with Solon's view of the *polis*, as seen in his descriptions of *Dikê* and *Eunomiê*, which bring understandable consequences inevitably. But the problems involved in understanding matters of material values are wider than Vlastos brings out. Solon's problem is to explain not only how an 'original injustice' leads to ruin for any particular man, but also why men both just and unjust can fail or succeed. How is it that a man who thinks and acts properly can fall to ruin, while an evil man can end up successful? Is there an understandable pattern underlying the pursuit of material sustenance and wealth, or is it arbitrary and unknowable?

Vlastos lists a second reason why he claims that Solon's justice is 'bifurcated':

> 2. For all of Solon's initial assurance that unjustly got wealth will not last (13.11-13), he is promptly forced to admit that it may well outlast the life of the unjust man himself; the pursuing justice may only catch up 'with the innocents, their children or their seed after them' (13.31-2)
>
> Vlastos 1995: 46

The important passage in Solon's verses is:

> ἀλλ' ὁ μὲν αὐτίκ' ἔτεισεν, ὁ δ' ὕστερον· οἳ δὲ φύγωσιν
>   αὐτοί, μηδὲ θεῶν μοῖρ' ἐπιοῦσα κίχῃ,
> ἤλυθε πάντως αὖτις· ἀναίτιοι ἔργα τίνουσιν
>   ἢ παῖδες τούτων ἢ γένος ἐξοπίσω.
>
> Solon 13.29-32

> One man gets what he deserves right away, another later; others
>   flee, and if they escape the onrushing fate of the immortals,
> it comes surely sometime. The innocents pay for the deeds
>   or their children or their family thereafter.

Vlastos then notes that there is nothing 'so characteristic of the magical view of justice as the postulate that punishment descends biologically upon the sinner's posterity'.[3]

Solon the Thinker

An answer to Vlastos' second objection can be inferred by considering the nature of such retribution. In archaic Greece a creditor would certainly turn upon the children of those holding an obligation, and a pursuer would enforce his prerogatives upon an innocent son as upon his father. To use high-level legal distinctions from modern law, or even the Roman *ius ad personas, ad res* or *ad actiones*, to claim that a protagonist could pursue a debtor but not his land would be distinctly anachronistic. Land was the primary value, with implications far beyond its importance for growing crops – it is the anchor to one's ancestors and fatherland, as Solon's 'Black Earth' and 'roots' suggest.[4] That a family's land, livestock, material resources or forced labour might be taken to repay an informal barter loan is more plausible than writing off the debt because the debtor has died. The retribution of other men *did* fall on successors and other innocents, whether based on debts or other forms of obligation. This occurs in our own day; secured loans are not written off after death, but are pressed against the estate, and innocent children may be forced from their homes. Having observed similar actions, Solon would have been accurate to conclude that innocent persons were indeed at risk through no fault of their own. This is not magic.[5]

However, Vlastos' first objection is more fundamental and difficult. On the face of it Solon's world does not work the same way in matters of wealth attainment as he claims it does in political matters. A fundamental disconnect between the actions necessary to earn a living and the consequences of those actions would have been obvious to Solon. Good men do fall to evil and evil men to good. *Dikê* does not come *pantôs*. Solon's uses of *moira* to describe a man's mortal and material lot in life suggest that he may have understood these matters in a way that differs fundamentally from the ordering of the *polis*. This is the issue that this chapter must unpack.

At the outset, modern terminology must be distinguished from ancient, in order to differentiate the ideas involved. Solon did not have a concept of 'justice' at all; he thinks of *dikê, tisis, moira* and the like, and he may or may not think of these concepts in 'political' and 'distributive' senses. But Vlastos explains Solon by dichotomizing the single English term 'justice' in precisely this way, and then applying the narrower English ideas to Solon's verses. As Vlastos understands it, 'political justice' concerns itself with political and legal administration, and 'distributive justice' with the distribution of wealth. Vlastos' political and distributive *diaeresis* has affinities with Plato and Aristotle, but it may be wildly anachronistic for the early sixth century if not completely wrong. Does Solon have concepts of 'distributive justice' and 'political justice'? Is there one single, 'bifurcated' archaic Greek idea to express these ideas, or are there two distinct Greek terms and concepts explaining what are, to Solon, two different things? Would he see the distribution of wealth as a concern of *dikê* at all?

Solon's essential treatment of these issues is in poem 13, the *Hymn to*

5. 'Moira *brings good and evil*'

the Muses. Even a cursory look shows important thematic differences between this prayer and the more political poems, such as 4 and 36. Poem 13 begins asking for wealth (*olbos*) from the gods and renown (*doxa*) from men, and immediately distinguishes wealth which is proper and god-given from that which comes unnaturally (*ou kata kosmon*). Poems 4 and 36, along with fragments 9, 11, 32, 33, 34 and 37, rather focus on affairs in the *polis*: poem 4 begins 'our city ...', and poem 36 with Solon's own political action, 'on account of these things I brought the people together'. Poem 13 is thematically closer to fragments 14, 15, 23, 24 and 25, which address human affairs in terms that have wider application than political order, and poem 27, which is concerned with the stages of a person's life, than it is to the poems that are focused on the *polis*.

This division is supported by terminology. There is no mention of the *polis* in poem 13 at all, and no direct concern for either how a *polis* is to be ordered or the ramifications of ordering it improperly. Solon does not here use the language of the *polis*: missing are *hêsuchia*, *eleutheros*, *Eunomiê*, *astoi*, *dêmos* or *hêgemones* of the *dêmos*, *phulai*, and descriptors such as *dêmosion* and *pasei polei*. Nor is there any concern for *stasis*, *polemos*, *doulosunê* and similar ideas. The overriding concern is rather with the proper and improper ways to pursue and attain wealth, including the transmission of one man's obligations onto another, the alighting of wealth first on one man and then another, and the onset of *atê*.

The issue of wealth and its attainment is not limited to a *polis* context; it is a matter of a person's own *bios*, a general term denoting a person's maintenance of life and lifestyle.[6] This refers primarily to the processes necessary to maintaining one's life, especially the pursuit of material wealth, but it also embraces the lifestyle that results from successful living. Hesiod's *Works and Days* uses *bios* in both senses, as the lifestyle proper to obtaining vital material values, as well as the results, such as a barn full of grain.[7] Solon's two mentions of *bios*-words are both in poem 13: line 50 identifies *bioton* with specific artisanship skills, and line 72 speaks of *bios* as the broad 'life-style' in any particular manifestation, as well as the products of a successful way of life. As always, an explicit distinction between the process and the result is not in Solon's vocabulary; to act in a luxurious manner is to possess the material goods needed for a luxurious lifestyle. Solon also illustrates multiple ways that people can strive after a livelihood (lines 43-62), examples that apply to men *qua* men, not men *qua* citizens. Poem 13, in other words, passes the 'desert island test': its general principles would be applicable to a Philoctetes on a desert island, who would need to obtain material goods to stay alive and would face his allotted death, but would have no concern for the *polis* (other than to get back to it). On such an island questions of *bios* and of one's relationship to *moira* would be vitally important, but issues such as a communal banquet, slavery or civil strife could never arise. In contrast to poem 13, poems 4 and 36 are centrally concerned with the consequences of actions in the *polis*; poem 13 rather focuses on those actions as they affect a person *per se*. There are no *astoi* spoken of in poem 13 – and no crowds to influence our thinking – because the poem is not about the *polis*.

In poem 13 the relationship between biotic and political actions must be inferred; the *polis* context is not made explicit, and everything fits into an *oikos* (family homestead) context. In contrast, in poems 4 and 36 the *polis* is explicit (poem 4 denies outright that the *oikos* is a refuge from civic violence), and the specific actions by which wealth is attained must be inferred. In these verses Solon is more concerned with the problem of *hubris* in the community than he is with how *hubris* relates to human life in general. This difference in purposes makes it unsurprising if Solon's ultimate conclusions in poem 13 differ from the other fragments. We should respect Solon's ability to focus on different aspects of human life and to emphasize those aspects in relationship to each other. When he deals with the *polis* he deals with something that is conceptually distinct from a person's *bios*. This reveals a way that Solon's poems can be categorized: into political and non-political poems, based on whether its focus is primarily on the *polis* or on life in general. Use of such categories, of course, must not be allowed to overtake their purpose, which is as a means to understand the poems.

The difference in subject between *polis* and *bios* in poems 4 and 36 versus poem 13 is accompanied by a corresponding difference in normative terminology, between *dikê* and *moira*. *Dikê* and related words are almost always used in a context limited to the *polis*: twice in poem 4 and three times in 36: at 4.14; 4.36; 36.3; 36.16; 36.19. An exception is the sea in fragment 12, in which *dikaiotate* draws a parallel between the sea and the *polis*; an argument that *dikê* belongs to the *polis* and not to *bios* would strengthen this political interpretation of fragment 12. In poem 13, lines 7 and 8 are Solon's only attempts to apply the principle of *dikê* to the acquisition of wealth. When wealth is acquired unjustly, '*dikê* surely comes later', which establishes a parallel to the retribution that comes to the *polis* in poem 4 line 16. The only other *dikê* word in poem 13 is an adjective 'persuaded by unjust deeds' at line 12, also found in poem 4 line 11; in poem 4 it is men who are persuaded by unjust deeds; in poem 13 wealth itself is persuaded, to be taken in a way inconsistent with its proper nature. Possibly Solon, reciting poem 13, wanted the audience to recall poem 4, and his prior generalization that wealth acquired improperly follows against its nature and results in destruction; this might be the reason for his prayer to Memory at the start. Or, possibly poem 4 was intended to remind the audience of poem 13, to link the destruction of the *polis* more firmly to the unjust acquisition of wealth. In any case, *dikê* then vanishes from poem 13, which suggests that Solon drops *dikê* as an explanation and resolves the problems of wealth acquisition by means other than *dikê*. In contrast, poem 4 ends with *Eunomiê*'s commitment to *dikê*, by putting chains on the unjust (*tois adikois*) and straightening

5. 'Moira brings good and evil'

crooked judgments (*dikas*). In poem 13, Solon's attempt to use *dikê* to distinguish transitory, god-given wealth from unjust wealth has failed utterly.

The concept used in poem 13 to describe why things occur as they do in human life is not *dikê*, but *moira*. In all of Solon's fragments *moira* is never applied to the *polis*, but rather to matters of *bios* and to human life *per se*. Verses 13.30 and 13.63 relate *moira* to *bios*; fragments 20.4 and 27.18, concerned with human life, relate *moira* to death. Fragment 11.2 ('do not place the blame for your *moira* on the gods') is the closest to a political application of *moira*, although Solon addresses his audience in the second person; *moira* applies to the men, and he mentions neither *polis* nor *astoi*. They must not blame their lot on the gods; the *moira* they face here is akin to an end that they deserve due to past failings. (Perhaps *moira* here is a redistribution of lots, which Solon elsewhere condemns.) These terminological divisions suggest that *dikê* and *moira* are not a single concept dichotomized, but rather two concepts dealing with different aspects of human life. *Dikê* is conceptually very different from *moira*, as are the applications of the two terms, to the *polis* and to *bios*.[8]

The *polis* / *dikê* versus *bios* / *moira* distinction also coheres with Solon's perspectives on time, as they apply to the *polis* and more widely to human life. One vital difference is the existence of a *telos*, an ultimate end for every person's life, which has no counterpart in the *polis*. *Telos* is used thrice in poem 13. Lines 17 and 28 denote the ultimate end that comes to every man but that is knowable only by Zeus; line 58 indicates the limits to human foresight available to a physician, his inability to see to a patient's *telos*, ultimately his allotted death (*moira thanatou*). Poem 27 is Solon's attempt to find a coherent flow in each person's life, a further example of the systematic bent in his mind. But his organization of the seasons of a man's life starts from a beginning and progresses to an end in seven-year periods; it is a straight line to an end.[9] Zeus completes (*telesêi*) the first seven years of life in line 27.3, and if someone reaches the tenth stage in due order, then his allotted death (*moira thanatou*) is not unseasonable, in lines 17-18.[10]

That there is no *telos*, *moira* or death applicable to the *polis* suggests an important difference between Solon's views of individual life and of the *polis*. Solon's *polis* need not ever end, and neither the stages of life nor the *telos* of death have any counterpart in it. Stages or cycles of constitutional change are completely beyond his understanding; he has not conceptualized the idea of a *politeia* and does not consider it in the abstract. The order in the *polis* will be destroyed if the citizens fail to act justly, but this would be a chosen, foreseeable and avoidable development in Athens. In contrast to a person's life, time in the *polis* is referred to as *chronos* and is never associated with any *telos*. Solon wishes that the rule of Philocyprus over the Cypriot town of Soli be *polun chronon*, in fragment 19.1, and he predicts that, in the Court of Time (*en dikê Chronou*) his own reputation in Athens will be exonerated. These events can happen in the time of the *polis*, but there is no thought that the *polis* itself lives and dies within any wider conception of time.

Speaking metaphorically, human life is a straight-line progression towards an unknowable *telos* of death – a formulation that expresses Greek fatalism at its most explicit. The need here is to understand the end, a task that is fraught with difficulty if it is possible at all. The *polis* is rather like a circle, its buildings sprouting around a growing town centre, and with an order that can be disrupted by *hubris* but that has no *telos*. The need here is to understand its organizing principle, a problem that Solon claims to have solved. In poem 13, the dominant concern is rather with an unknowable *telos*. Sicking observes the importance of *telos* in the poem, 'the contrast between present behavior and its final results in the future'. But the *telos* in poem 13 is also the *final* end of life, towards which all things are ultimately pointed. This is the essence of fatalism.[11] Perhaps, for Solon, the *polis* is a natural thing, without the inevitable death reserved for human beings; the challenge is to maintain its order, not to consider its death.

The dichotomy in Solon's verses, between *polis / dikê / chronos*, and *bios / moira / telos*, is unbreached. These terminological and conceptual identifications suggest that Solon does not think the same way about the order in the *polis* as he does about each person's life. Closer consideration of poem 13 may reveal the reasons for this division in his thinking.

In shifting his focus, from the *polis* in poems such 4, 9 and 11 to matters of *bios* in a poem such as 13, Solon steps out of the *kosmos* of the *polis* and into human life as each one of us lives it. The basic focus of poem 13, Solon's *Hymn to the Muses*, is set in the first six lines: Solon prays for prosperity, *olbos*, from the gods, and *doxa*, 'reputation', from men:[12]

> Μνημοσύνης καὶ Ζηνὸς Ὀλυμπίου ἀγλαὰ τέκνα,
>   Μοῦσαι Πιερίδες, κλῦτέ μοι εὐχομένῳ·
> ὄλβόν μοι πρὸς θεῶν μακάρων δότε, καὶ πρὸς ἁπάντων
>   ἀνθρώπων αἰεὶ δόξαν ἔχειν ἀγαθήν·
> εἶναι δὲ γλυκὺν ὧδε φίλοις, ἐχθροῖσι δὲ πικρόν,
>   τοῖσι μὲν αἰδοῖον, τοῖσι δὲ δεινὸν ἰδεῖν.
>
> Solon 13.1-6

> Hear, O Muses, shining daughters of Olympian Zeus,
>   and Memory, my prayer.
> Grant me prosperity from the blessed gods, and always
>   to have a good reputation to all men.
> To be sweet to my friends, and bitter to my enemies,
>   Respected by one, and a terror to the others.

This immediately distinguishes Solon's intention here from the 'our *polis*' focus of poem 4, and his bringing together of the *dêmos* in 36.1-2.

5. 'Moira brings good and evil'

With *doxa* 'reputation' dropped after line 13.6 – it will re-appear as 'expectation' in line 34, an important change – the relationships between people are never again primary. For instance, from line 5 there is no further mention of *philoi* ('friends'). Poem 13 is from then on concerned almost exclusively with a person's attainment of material goods, and the consequences, in a context not limited to the *polis*.[13]

Solon then turns to matters directly applicable to wealth attainment:

> χρήματα δ' ἱμείρω μέν ἔχειν, ἀδίκως δὲ πεπᾶσθαι
> οὐκ ἐθέλω· πάντως ὕστερον ἦλθε δίκη.
> πλοῦτον δ' ὃν μὲν δῶσι θεοί, παραγίγνεται ἀνδρὶ
> ἔμπεδος ἐκ νεάτου πυθμένος ἐς κορυφήν·
> ὃν δ' ἄνδρες τιμῶσιν ὑφ' ὕβριος, οὐ κατὰ κόσμον
> ἔρχεται, ἀλλ' ἀδίκοις ἔργμασι πειθόμενος
> οὐκ ἐθέλων ἔπεται, ταχέως δ' ἀναμίσγεται ἄτῃ·
> ἀρχῆς δ' ἐξ ὀλίγης γίγνεται ὥστε πυρός,
> φλαύρη μὲν τὸ πρῶτον ἀνιηρὴ δὲ τελευτᾶι·
> οὐ γὰρ δὴ<ν> θνητοῖς ὕβριος ἔργα πέλει
>
> Solon 13.7-16

> I want to have money, but to get it unjustly
>   I am not willing; for *dikê* surely comes later.
> Wealth which the gods give remains with man,
>   steadfast from the deepest foundation to the top,
> but that which men honour (receive? gain?) by hubris comes not with
>   proper order,
>   but persuaded by unjust deeds
> does not follow willingly, but swiftly mixes with calamity.
>   It begins from small start, as a fire,
> at first it is minor, in the end devastating.
>   For the works of hubris do not abide for mortals

Solon begins with assumptions that may have been uncontroversial in Greek thought. He distinguishes wealth 'which the gods give and which abides', in line 9, from wealth which is gained 'not in good order' and is transient, line 11. The clear contrast between that which gods give, and that which men honour by hubris, differentiates two methods by which wealth is acquired, two mental states that accompany the pursuit of wealth, and two manifestly different results to follow. Björck sees wealth taken by *hubris* as an entirely other species ('une tout autre espèce') than god-given wealth – which means material wealth.[14] Solon states his basic expectation in terms of a generalization at 13.8, '*dikê* surely comes later'. This is a memorizable formula, a *kosmos* of words that may come to mind as a mental unit when a person thinks about the consequences of unjust actions. What occurs in human life, Solon claims, will be consistent; good results will follow good actions, and bad will follow bad. Solon begins poem 13, like poem 4, with the inevitable retribution of *dikê* as the guiding principle of each person's pursuit of wealth.

Solon the Thinker

It is of vital import that this is the first and only mention of *dikê* in the poem. Solon attempts to apply *dikê* to matters of *bios* as if it were a principle. A 'principle' here is a generalization that is applied to new particulars as a guide to understanding and evaluating those phenomena; it projects present understanding into the future. Solon may be praying for the memory of past events in order to establish the causal relationships in what he sees now; this depends upon Memory's providing the raw material needed to understand the connections to new phenomena. But what Solon says is more direct: '*dikê* surely comes later', a *kosmos* of words that is consistent with his views of the *polis*, and will apply to the pursuit of wealth across the board. He then sets out to illustrate this point, by drawing metaphors and bringing forth concrete examples. Unjust pursuits are followed by retribution, which grows until it lashes out like a wind:

> ἀλλὰ Ζεὺς πάντων ἐφορᾷ τέλος, ἐξαπίνης δὲ
>   ὥστ' ἄνεμος νεφέλας αἶψα διεσκέδασεν
> ἠρινός, ὅς πόντου πολυκύμονος ἀτρυγέτοιο
>   πυθμένα κινήσας, γῆν κάτα πυροφόρον
> δηιώσας καλὰ ἔργα θεῶν ἕδος αἰπὺν ἱκάνει
>   οὐρανόν, αἰθρίην δ' αὖτις ἔθηκεν ἰδεῖν,
> λάμπει δ' ἠελίοιο μένος κατὰ πίονα γαῖαν
>   καλόν, ἀτὰρ νεφέων οὐδ' ἕν ἔτ' ἐστὶν ἰδεῖν.
> τοιαύτη Ζηνὸς πέλεται τίσις·
>
> Solon 13.17-25

> But Zeus looks upon the end of all things, and suddenly
>   as a spring wind scatters the clouds
> which moves the depths of the swelling sea,
>   ravaging the lovely works of man
> along the wheat-bearing land, reaches the high seat
>   in the heavens and makes the sky clear.
> and the strength of the sun shines over the fair rich
>   land, and there is not a cloud to be seen.
> Such is the retribution of Zeus.

Richmond Lattimore thinks that the simile of the storm is 'pure illustration' and 'the projection of a sequence irrelevant to the original context'.[15] With this I cannot agree; the storm concretizes the generalization in line 13.8, vivifying the retribution for Solon's audience into an understandable scene that can be held in the mind as a single image. If '*dikê* surely comes later' is a maxim that has been conceived in the form of a mythic symbol, then the 'pure illustration' of it is no less relevant than the mythic figure itself. Tumult in the sky affects our ability to see and to understand; by ridding the sky of clouds a storm enhances natural phenomena, as social phenomena are enhanced in a chaotic *polis*.[16] In the *polis*, Solon's metaphor simplifies complex political phenomena – leader of the *dêmos* acting with *hubris* at a meal, the tyrant with his body-guards,

5. 'Moira brings good and evil'

men in chains, a missing neighbour who is in exile, a boundary stone set up to mark a claim, the shifty orator, a lawgiver with his shield – to a point of focus that is essential and clear. A disparate, seemingly fluctuant series of events is integrated into a single point of reference. But Solon also suggests a connection to natural philosophy, as Noussia demonstrates.[17]

The simile is expanded and clarified in lines 25-32, thus further suggesting that Solon has a deeper purpose than mere digressive illustration:

> οὐδ᾽ ἐφ᾽ ἑκάστῳ
> ὥσπερ θνητὸς ἀνὴρ γίγνεται ὀξύχολος,
> αἰεὶ δ᾽ οὔ ἑ λέληθε διαμπερές, ὅστις ἀλιτρὸν
> θυμὸν ἔχει, πάντως δ᾽ ἐς τέλος ἐξεφάνη·
> ἀλλ᾽ ὁ μὲν αὐτίκ᾽ ἔτεισεν, ὁ δ᾽ ὕστερον· οἳ δὲ φύγωσιν
> αὐτοί, μηδὲ θεῶν μοῖρ᾽ ἐπιοῦσα κίχῃ,
> ἤλυθε πάντως αὖτις· ἀναίτιοι ἔργα τίνουσιν
> ἢ παῖδες τούτων ἢ γένος ἐξοπίσω.
>
> Solon 13.25-32

> But not upon each thing
> as a mortal man does he [Zeus] become angry,
> it never escapes him when a man holds evil
> in his heart, and in the end he surely becomes visible.
> One man gets what he deserves right away, another later; some
> flee, and escape the onrushing fate of the immortals
> it comes surely sometime. The innocents pay for the deeds
> or their children or their family thereafter.

Zeus' retribution is a bit lenient given the range of his vision, but the promise of retribution is certain. The divide between the gods and men is fundamental and traditional: the retribution of Zeus is based not upon the sight of any particular thing – as Semonides' cattle view the grass – but rather upon his perfect view of the end and its cause in the *thumos* of a man. To this point the poem has vivified the meaning of '*dikê* surely comes later' for each one of us, in a naïve view of retribution that is couched in divine terms, visualized like the weather, and inevitable. But as Solon turns to particular examples, he – or his audience – discovers the inklings of a problem. Lines 29-32 provide the details of retribution in temporal terms: one man gets his comeuppance immediately (*autika*) another later (*husteron*). Another flees, not meeting the pursuing *moira* of the gods, but it comes sometime for sure, and innocents pay, either children or their descendants. This is a direct contradiction to the *dikê* that falls *pantôs* on the *polis* and everyone in it, not because innocents suffer due to others, but because the guilty can escape.

The conclusion is inescapable. *Dikê* does not explain what Solon sees. Her ability to know what is and was – the prelude to the inevitable retribution in poem 4 – is insufficient to explain what occurs across the span of a mortal's life. From this point on, *Dikê* is forced into the same silence that Solon decried for the *polis* in his *Hymn to the City*.

A key passage here is in line 30, 'nor does he [a man fleeing] meet the onrushing *moira* of the gods'. On the one hand a fugitive escapes his fate, on the other hand it comes with certainty, in unknowable time or circumstance. This reads similarly to fragment 20.4, where Solon argues with Mimnermus over the specific time that is proper to one's inevitable death.[18] The openness of the context leaves *moira* in 13.30 ambiguous: is it a material allotment, the onrushing threat of a creditor, or death which comes only Zeus knows when? One man, meeting his fated death, dies leaving an unresolved debt, obligation, or issue of revenge, which is taken out on his children or his family. Another, fleeing into foreign lands but avoiding the retribution of a debtor, leaves his innocent family destitute – one of Solon's *phugontes* (exiles) in 36.10-1, those fleeing in 4.23-5. Another simply dies, leaving his plans incomplete and his family without resources.[19] Solon makes the crucial observation that the connection between means and ends is broken; it is no longer possible for him to maintain that '*dikê* surely comes later'.[20] This severance of means from ends is more than an adjustment to his understanding of how we gain wealth; it is a profound challenge to the world-view anchored by *dikê*.

The pivotal phrase in the poem is line 35, *prin ti pathein*, 'until the experiencing', or 'until the suffering', personalized as 'until we suffer':

> θνητοὶ δ' ὧδε νοέομεν ὁμῶς ἀγαθός τε κακός τε,
> εὖ ῥεῖν ἣν αὐτὸς δόξαν ἕκαστος ἔχει,
> πρίν τι παθεῖν·
>
> Solon 13.33-5

> We mortals, both noble and base, think we understand (*noeomen*),
>   and each of us expects that things are going well;
> until experience hits us.

Pathein, 'the experiencing', or 'the suffering' that marked the many sufferings caused by *hubris* in Athens, offers a profound challenge to *noein*, 'the knowing' that we have of our present and future conditions. Until we experience the end we cannot know if we were correct about our earlier understanding. We may recognize the general point that 'the innocents suffer the consequences, and their children and their relatives thereafter', but we think things are well with ourselves only until we suffer, or experience, the opposite directly. Under the onslaught of experience, our expectations for the future become a 'seeming', an uncertain opinion of our actual situation and of the results to follow for us. By this point it has become unmistakably clear that there is an unsolvable problem with applying *dikê* as a principle to *bios*; it simply does not work. Experience negates the generalization, so Solon changes the generalization – certainly the mark of a person concerned for what is true.

5. 'Moira brings good and evil'

Solon's *doxa* in lines 4 and 34, and his use of *dokei*, demonstrate the collapse in his ability to understand the present and the future. *Doxa* in line 13.4, the first use of the word in Greek literary evidence to mean 'reputation' apart from glory in battle, denotes a positive evaluation of a person in the minds of others.[21] This usage goes back to Homer: how one 'seemed' to others was the index of a man's identity and worth as a warrior, and the possession of wealth was a measure of one's glory.[22] For Solon, *olbos* 'is a state of general well-being' and *doxa agathê* is 'the respect and honor which are its public recognition'.[23] In line 34, Solon shifts the meaning of *doxa* from a good 'reputation' now to an 'expectation' applied to our own future – only this is uncertain, given our inability to recognize the nature of our own position; it becomes an erroneous 'seeming' for the future that does not bear out. The verb *dokei* 'it seems' is used similarly, with a future infinitive to illustrate the erroneous seemings at lines 39 and 42. *Dokeô* plus the future infinitive is also untrue in fragment 34.2, 'and each one of them expected (*kadokeon*) to find much wealth'. To Solon, the reputation of one's self held by others and the expectations of a person with respect to his own future display a fundamental similarity: in each case the evaluation is uncertain and subject to error, a mere opinion we hold *prin ti pathein*, 'until we suffer'. Solon naturally exempts himself from such scepticism when he predicts the results of his own *polis* reforms in poem 32.4-5, 'for in this way I deem (*dokeô*) that I shall be superior to all men'.

This thunderbolt of experience leads us to wail, or to gape open-mouthed, grasping onto foolish expectations for the future, against the realization that we cannot know our ultimate ends:

τότε δ' αὖτις ὀδύρεται· ἄχρι δὲ τούτου
χάσκοντες κούφαις ἐλπίσι τερπόμεθα.

Solon 13.35-6

Then we wail forthwith, and until then
gaping open-mouthed we are entertained by foolish hopes.

In the four examples that follow the challenges to our self-understanding and to the inevitability of *dikê* are again made vivid in terms of particular situations we might directly identify with. Again, Solon concretizes his identification with examples that vividly illustrate the point:

χὥστις μὲν νούσοισιν ὑπ' ἀργαλέῃσι πιεσθῇ,
  ὡς ὑγιὴς ἔσται, τοῦτο κατεφράσατο·
ἄλλος δειλὸς ἐὼν ἀγαθὸς δοκεῖ ἔμμεναι ἀνήρ,
  καὶ καλὸς μορφὴν οὐ χαρίεσσαν ἔχων·
εἰ δέ τις ἀχρήμων, πενίης δέ μιν ἔργα βιᾶται,
  κτήσασθαι πάντως χρήματα πολλὰ δοκεῖ.

Solon 13.37-42

Solon the Thinker

One man, oppressed by miserable disease
  deems he will be healthy, he plans this.
Another man, being lowly, thinks himself high;
  and the ugly man thinks he is handsome.
If a man is poor, violated by poverty,
  he thinks he will surely possess great wealth.

The examples of lines 37-8 and 41-2 (which ring the passage) are future-oriented in that they project a misevaluation of what has yet to occur: the sick man is wrong to plan that he will become well; and a poor man is deluded if he looks ahead, and thinks he will surely possess much wealth.[24] In 39-40 the misevaluation is more closely set in the here and now: the mediocre man thinks he is and will remain a good man, and the ugly man handsome. In each case a misevaluation of what *will* occur is due to a failure to understand our present condition *now*. Solon's focus on what will be – what sneaks up on us from the rear – links the tenses in a way that extends beyond the capacity of *Dikê*, or us, to know.[25]

Solon follows the four examples of deception with the generalization in line 43 that 'men strive in different ways', followed by six concrete examples of earning a living, 43-62 – but these examples neither refute nor obscure his primary point, that there are limitations to the human ability to guide our actions to a predictable, successful end:

σπεύδει δ' ἄλλοθεν ἄλλος· ὁ μὲν κατὰ πόντον ἀλᾶται
  ἐν νηυσὶν χρήιζων οἴκαδε κέρδος ἄγειν
ἰχθυόεντ' ἀνέμοισι φορεόμενος ἀργαλέοισιν,
  φειδωλὴν ψυχῆς οὐδεμίαν θέμενος·
ἄλλος γῆν τέμνων πολυδένδρεον εἰς ἐνιαυτὸν
  λατρεύει, τοῖσιν καμπύλ' ἄροτρα μέλει·
ἄλλος Ἀθηναίης τε καὶ Ἡφαίστου πολυτέχνεω
  ἔργα δαεὶς χειροῖν ξυλλέγεται βίοτον,
ἄλλος Ὀλυμπιάδων Μουσέων πάρα δῶρα διδαχθείς,
  ἱμερτῆς σοφίης μέτρον ἐπιστάμενος·
ἄλλον μάντιν ἔθηκεν ἄναξ ἑκάεργος Ἀπόλλων,
  ἔγνω δ' ἀνδρὶ κακὸν τηλόθεν ἐρχόμενον,
ᾧ συνομαρτήσωσι θεοί· τὰ δὲ μόρσιμα πάντως
  οὔτέ τις οἰωνὸς ῥύσεται οὔθ' ἱερά·
ἄλλοι Παιῶνος πολυφαρμάκου ἔργον ἔχοντες
  ἰητροί· καὶ τοῖς οὐδὲν ἔπεστι τέλος·
πολλάκι δ' ἐξ ὀλίγης ὀδύνης μέγα γίγνεται ἄλγος,
  κοὐκ ἄν τις λύσαιτ' ἤπια φάρμακα δούς·
τὸν δὲ κακαῖς νούσοισι κυκώμενον ἀργαλέαις τε
  ἁψάμενος χειροῖν αἶψα τίθησ' ὑγιῆ.

Solon 13.43-62

Men pursue their livings in different ways. One fishes in the sea,
  using ships to bring home profit;
battered by the merciless winds,
  he places no regard upon life.

5. 'Moira brings good and evil'

Another man ploughs the many-treed land for a year,
  working the curved plough for hire.
Another man, having learned the works of Athena
  and Hephaestus of many crafts, gathers a livelihood with his hands.
Another one, taught the gifts of the Olympian Muses,
  is an expert at the metre of lovely poetic wisdom;
King Apollo far-shooter makes another man a seer,
  he knows the evil coming upon man from afar,
if the gods are witnesses. Surely neither augury
  nor sacred rites can protect against one's allotted fate.
Other men, holding the many potions of Paeon
  treat the sick; and there is no certain end to their efforts.
Often from a little pain comes a deep disease
  and he cannot be released from it by gentle remedies;
another one, in the grip of a deep debilitating disease,
  he cures by placing his hands on him.

Solon here recognizes a broad range of activities by which men pursue wealth, reputation and honour; he may be the first to describe various lifestyles akin to 'careers'.[26] The *speudein* here – the hustling to earn a living – is the pursuit of material goods and values needed for survival: food, crafts, poetry, avoidance of evil, health. In a charming little fragment 39, Solon tells us that 'Some hustle for kitchen-mortar, others *silphium*, others vinegar': *speudousi d' hoi men igdin, hoi de silphion, hoi de oxos*. These dainty treats are, in effect, the final causes that we think of and then struggle to obtain, all for the sake of making life better. No one wants to attain death; this is an end to be avoided as long as possible, but it is inescapable, in an unknowable time, place and manner, despite our best efforts. There is a massive disjunction between our goals and our inescapable *telos* as a human being, precisely because *dikê* cannot know the end, and guide us toward our goals, in the way she can guide us to preserve the *polis*. *Dikê* does not rule human life, and does not help us to succeed at matters of *bios*.

It is, of course, the seer and the physician who most need the ability to see ahead, and who are most explicitly unable to do it. Solon may be speaking self-referentially here, in placing a seer under the sanction of Apollo. For Solon to succeed, the gods must 'witness corroboratively', *sunmartêsôsi*, the same verb (*summarturoiê*) that Solon calls on in the third line of poem 36, when he proclaims his own vindication in the future: the Black Earth will be his corroborative witness in the Court of Time. In dealing with his own life he cannot have the kind of certainty that he has for the *polis*; he can claim a higher position only by virtue of a god's favour, precisely the position he took in poem 13. The importance of the divine has not been lessened here; human beings are even more dependent, in these areas of life, upon their help.

Solon unveils a *dikê*-centred perspective in lines 7-32 that is challenged by experiences in line 35. This perspective is negative in that it predicts with certainty the retribution for *improper* pursuits according to the

Solon the Thinker

principle of *dikê*. But *dikê* is hopeless for making predictions into the future; as in line 15 of poem 4, *Dikê* knows what was and is, but there is no mention of her knowing what will be. To answer the challenge posed by experience, Solon turns in poem 13 lines 33-70 from *Dikê* to *Moira*, the divine presence with authority to grant to each person his lot in life, leading to the end to which each person will come. In doing so Solon makes no claim to an ability to understand either the present or the future; the explanation he derives actually depends on the inability to do either.

To make this shift explicit, from the certain retribution of *dikê* to the uncertainties of human life, Solon replaces '*Dikê* surely comes later' in line 8 with '*Moira* brings good and evil to mortals' in line 63:[27]

Μοῖρα δέ τοι θνητοῖσι κακὸν φέρει ἠδὲ καὶ ἐσθλόν,
   δῶρα δ' ἄφυκτα θεῶν γίγνεται ἀθανάτων.
πᾶσι δέ τοι κίνδυνος ἐπ' ἔργμασιν, οὐδέ τις οἶδεν
   πῇ μέλλει σχήσειν χρήματος ἀρχομένου·

Solon 13.63-6

Moira brings good and evil to mortals,
   the gifts of the immortal gods may not be escaped.
There is risk in all actions, and no one knows
   how something, having started, will end up.

Maria Noussia has observed a difference in these two couplets: in lines 63-4, *Moira* 'Fate' now hands out the gifts once dispensed by Zeus, and those seers who have the help of the gods can see what is coming (although they cannot prevent it).[28] In the second couplet, 65-6, the element of risk, danger and luck adds to the inevitability of *Moira*; *kindunos*, found here perhaps for the first time, connects our actions indissolubly to uncertainties that are inherent in all affairs.[29] The first couplet, Noussia continues, is a divine perspective on the unforeseen and the inevitable; the second is a human point of view on the risk in events. There is also a distinction to be made in the forces operating in this passage: *Moira* (which she equates with *Tuchê*) must be distinguished from Zeus' will. Despite the ambiguity present in the relationship between *moira* and the gods, 'Solon does not explicitly involve Zeus, and deliberately chooses the word *moira* here to convey the idea that it is Fate or the gods generally who give good and bad, neither of which can be avoided'. Noussia makes the case that Solon is 'the first to speak in an archaic context about the dichotomy between the effectiveness of the medical profession and the power of *Moira = Tuchê*'.[30] Her important observation that the physician is a 'paradigm of the basic every-day situation of the human being', conveys the expanded scope of Solon's concerns, into every sphere of human life, with the same basic issue at stake: each of us, in any profession, can be effective only if *Moira* so allows it – as the physician and the seer are dependent upon the gods for success.

5. 'Moira *brings good and evil*'

Noussia is surely right that neither Homer nor Hesiod knows *Tuchê* as a force in the world, only *Moira*, and that, for Solon, *Moira* runs our lives. But Solon does not know *Tuchê* either – his verses, at least, do not present her as definitively as *Dikê* and *Moira* – and one must take care not to overstate the idea that Solon is introducing with his use of *kindunos*. *Tuchê* appears prior to Solon only rarely and as a personification linked, Noussia correctly notes, with *Moira*.[31] But the only place that *tuchê* appears in Solon's extant verses is the two hexameter lines in fragment 31, *tuchên agathên*; at 13.70 there is a compound in a related form, *suntuchiên agathên*. In each case *tuchê* is not the divinity, but rather that which the divinity brings; it is not an agent, but the agent's gift. Lines 14-15 had Zeus by simile as the power behind such events; Solon then tried *Dikê*, which did not work; so now the motor is *Moira* (lines 63-4), who serves to explain the arbitrary consequences that follow because there is danger in all things (lines 65-6). Lines 65-6 restate the idea in lines 14-15, in which a conflagration begins with a small spark, only now, in the absence of the justice of Zeus, there is uncertainty as to how the small beginning will end up. Solon certainly knows that much cannot be foreseen – this is fundamental to the poem – but without a concept of 'cause' he cannot think of something as happening 'without a cause'. He needs a real explanation for the actual risks he sees; and once *dikê* fails, and the split between our actions and our effectiveness is undeniable, he is forced to return to a divine power imposed over us. *Moira* fills in the vacuum of *Dikê*'s default, which may, as Noussia notes, be Solon's way of saying that 'it is Fate or the gods generally who give good and bad, neither of which can be avoided'.[32]

Under the influence of *Moira*, it is impossible to say even that a bad start will lead to a bad end; we no longer know what, if anything, must follow necessarily. The *noetic* errors that threaten the *polis* are understandable and preventable, and men are thus culpable, but this is not so for matters of *bios*:

ἀλλ' ὁ μὲν εὖ ἔρδειν πειρώμενος οὐ προνοήσας
ἐς μεγάλην ἄτην καὶ χαλεπὴν ἔπεσεν,
τῷ δὲ κακῶς ἔρδοντι θεὸς περὶ πάντα δίδωσιν
συντυχίην ἀγαθήν, ἔκλυσιν ἀφροσύνης.

Solon 13.67-70

But one man, attempting to do well, not seeing ahead
    falls into great and difficult calamity,
to another acting badly the god grants good luck in all things,
    releasing him from his folly.

This is true for everyone; not only does trying to do well not suffice to guarantee a good end, but failing to act well does not preclude a good outcome.[33] Lots of rotten people seem to get ahead. The problem was expressed in Theognis 373-80, in which Zeus is asked how equal *moira* can come to a man with a *noos* that turns to *hubris* as to *sôphrosunê*. But Solon demonstrates that evil can come just as readily to such a man as to one who looks for it consciously. The problem here is not an error, or even an unexpected fall, but rather an inherent inability to see ahead; *ou pronoêsas*, 'not knowing in advance', the lack of a capacity for effective insight – moral or otherwise – into our final end.[34] Man's ephemeral nature – the lot of a being that lives in the present day and cannot directly experience the future – returns him to the realm of incomprehensible circumstances, ultimately absolving him of culpability for his lot. Solon's poem is a comment not primarily on the corrupting nature of wealth, but on our inescapable inability to see beyond that which we directly experience, including proper limits to the pursuit of wealth. Richmond Lattimore writes that Zeus 'looks only in the large and toward the end'; the 'contrasted human way ... is to look at what is immediate and *not* to see the end'. Given this difference between men and the god, *ou pronoêsas* 'attaches no particular blame'.[35]

Considering the capabilities and limits of *dikê* and *moira* together reveals an important aspect of the fatalism that permeates early Greek thought. In the *polis* a single negative occurrence can wipe out any number of positives (thus, any *hubris* leads to destruction); in a matter of *bios*, no accumulation of positives can avert a fatal negative. Consequently, bad actions must lead to destruction in the *polis* (this is *dikê*) whereas good actions cannot guarantee good results in one's *bios* (this is *moira*). Solon's search for causal connections, if that is what it was, is dead; the presence of *moira* leads to a complete breakdown between means and ends. Failure here is of *to noein*, 'the knowing', which is simply too limited to solve the problem, and cannot survive an encounter with *to pathein*. Solon's central political injunction, 'now one ought to know all things', is simply useless – because in matters of *bios*, no one can know what is and will be.

The tensions in Solon's hymn emanate from the common Greek view that the ultimate measure by which the end of human life may be judged remains difficult, indeed impossible, to apprehend. Solon's fragment 16 universalizes this issue in terms of *noein*. The representation in poem 16 of 'the measure of wisdom' as 'hidden' is comparable to the hidden *noos* of the immortals of poem 17, symbolizing the opacity of the end of all knowing:

γνωμοσύνης δ' ἀφανὲς χαλεπώτατόν ἐστι νοῆσαι
μέτρον, ὃ δὴ πάντων πείρατα μοῦνον ἔχει.

Solon 16

πάντῃ δ' ἀθανάτων ἀφανὴς νόος ἀνθρώποισιν

Solon 17

5. 'Moira brings good and evil'

> It is most difficult to know the measure of wisdom, which
> alone holds the end of all things.

> The mind of the immortals is hidden in every way from men

It is impossible to distinguish securely the archaic meaning of Solon's fragments 16 and 17 from Clement's Christian purpose in citing them, and impossible to know the context in which Solon originally used them. Clement uses Solon 16 to support his Christian view that understanding transcends the body; he connects it to an Empedocles fragment that maintains the impossibility of bringing the divine into the reach of our eyes or our hands. Clement places fragment 17 in a series of fragments, from Hesiod (*noos* is off-limits to any seer), through Solon, Hesiod on toil, sorrow and perishing for the race of iron, the *Iliad* and the golden scales, to Menander's claim of a spirit as a guide beside us, ending with the goodness of God in all things. Such thematic connections are outside of Solon's cultural and historic context.[36]

Kirk, Raven and Schofield connect Solon's fragment 16 to a fragment from Heraclitus: 'The wise is one thing: to be acquainted with true judgment, how all things are steered through all'. Kirk, Raven and Schofield comment that this is

> the real nature of Heraclitus' philosophy ... the belief that every man's very life is indissociably bound up with his whole surroundings. Wisdom – and therefore, it might be inferred, satisfactory living – consists in understanding the Logos, the analogous structure or common element of arrangement in things.
>
> KRS comment to fr. 227

Solon's *gnômosunê* (first extant in this verse) may denote a special type of knowledge, concerned with the end, or limit, of all things.[37] But prior to, or concurrently with, the Ionian natural philosophers, Solon may have seen an order underlying all things that was similar to the order that properly underlies the *polis*, and he may have tried to direct his fellows into consistency with the order. This suggests another possible line of transmission from Solon to Heraclitus.[38] If so, the connections between early Greek philosophy and political thought may be stronger than we realize, and Solon may have begun to understand *dikê* as a *metron*, a truth 'in the middle', the common element of arrangement in the *polis* that he expressed in fragment 10. But to apply this to *gnômosunê* would have required him to know the end of life, and to bring this end into the middle. His failure to do so may mean that he could not relate the circle that is the *kosmos* of the *polis* to the linear progression that constitutes the stages of human life, leading to its *telos*. The integration of *dikê* with life in the community – through public exposure to the written word, the ordering of each person's time of life with activities in the *polis* through the festive calendar, and the practical use of straight legal judgments for each man's case – may be attempts to extend the roots of the *polis*-order into the earth beneath his feet, and thus to integrate the order of the *polis* with the order of life.

Hesiod's *Works and Days* had offered an alternative to violent contention: the Good Strife of honest striving that leads to prosperity. But Solon the *sophos* knows that Good Strife is based upon misidentifications and false pretences, and *hos speudei* 'whoever strives' is misled about his ability to attain a good end. Hesiod's inability to explain why he who works is given wealth, other than by the will of Zeus, left a vacuum when Solon removed divine will as a causal factor in human affairs. Solon understood the workings of that *polis* through the sight of his eyes, conditioned by the mythic context of his views of *noos*, *koros*, *atê*, et al. But in matters of *bios* he was buried under a barrage of observations in which results did not follow human actions as predicted, and he was left without an explanation for why. After all, no one knows the end except Zeus. In the face of unsolvable challenges to the 'justice follows with certainty' doctrine, Solon turned back to *Moira* and the unknowability of her particular effects.[39]

Solon cannot use *Dikê* with respect to *bios* because she understands the necessary connections between things and cannot explain the arbitrary. But the arbitrary is precisely *Moira*'s job. *Moira* parallels divine will in the pre-Solonian *polis* as an arbitrary factor used to explain arbitrary results; *Moira* fills the vacuum in human understanding brought about by the removal of the gods from control over human affairs. Without a natural explanation for how the ends of life will turn out, and with divine intervention crippled in the *polis*, Solon retreats into a position that both recalls the traditions of a far-seeing Zeus and anticipates the division between knowledge and opinion posited by Parmenides. In this sense Solon is a proto-sceptic; he knows that there are things that he cannot know. But it is important to distinguish an inability to know divine truth, the view represented in Xenophanes, from the view that there is no truth, represented by Heraclitus.[40] Solon is here distinctly Xenophanic, putting forth no opinion that can be construed as sceptical in the Heraclitian sense, but definitely setting whole areas of human life apart from that which we can know.

If the views of E.R. Dodds are correct, scepticism about what we know may have fed into an emotional response of helplessness, what Lloyd-Jones called a 'marked change in spiritual climate between the epic and the lyric age'. One consequence of reducing the scope of divine intervention was not a new set of beliefs, but rather, as Dodds puts it, 'a different emotional reaction to the old beliefs', echoed in personal *amêchania* – a sense of helplessness before divine hostility.[41] It might sound paradoxical that reducing the power of the gods led to increased fears of retribution among the poets, but an enhanced sense of mystery may have deepened their uncertainty and thus heightened their emotional response. There is

5. 'Moira brings good and evil'

a parallel in philosophy and the effects on people's attitudes towards customs and laws. Charles Kahn bases the negative views of *nomos* in the fifth century on 'an epistemological tradition going back to Parmenides, according to which the customary views of mortals can represent only falsehoods or at best mere appearances'.[42] Although Solon speaks with certainty about the nature of the *polis*, in broader areas of life he participates in the movement leading to Parmenides by positing a split between *to noein* and *to pathein*, 'understanding' and 'experience', that turns all understanding into 'foolish hopes'. Max Treu seems to misunderstand Solon and his time when, discussing 13.39-40, he states: 'but perhaps this is the time in Greek intellectual life, when the contentious separation of Appearance and Being first developed'.[43] Although Solon might agree that what he thinks he is differs from what he is, he would certainly not understand a reference to 'the being' (*to einai*) of a person; Treu's attribution of *Sein* 'being' is probably at least two generations early. Further, the distinction is not with *Schein* 'appearance' but with 'experience', the archaic *Erfahrung* that need recognize no dichotomy between outward appearance and being.

An inability to know the end of all things has been taken as the core of Solon's 'philosophy', exemplified in the Herodotean idea that no man can be judged *olbios* until he is dead. But Solonian philosophy, as understood and transmitted by Herodotus, may reflect fifth-century views of Solon's ideas, rather than Solon's own views, and may have been extended into areas beyond those preserved in the extant verses. Several recent studies have examined the role of religion and philosophy – especially the ideas expounded in Solon's meeting with Croesus – throughout Herodotus.[44] These studies have in general looked to understand the meaning of Herodotus' work in fifth-century terms, rather than to connect Herodotus to the evidence of Solon's poems.

What is the relationship between the Herodotean Solon and the Solon of the preserved verses? Susan Shapiro has observed three main points in Solon's speech at 1.32: first, that a jealous god makes trouble for men; second, that this jealousy makes human life ephemeral; and, third, that as a result human happiness cannot be determined until a man has ended his life well. The obvious point is that none of these ideas is explicit in Solon. Zeus is not the bringer of troubles to Solon's *polis*. In the areas of life covered in poem 13, his justice is wise, not anchored to particular circumstances, and inevitable in the long term. There is not a word of god's jealousy in any of the fragments, which may be an aspect of the decreased influence of divine will. For Solon, the troubles that may befall a man are associated with *Moira*, who operates by chance. The ephemeral nature of human life is part of what we are, not the immediate consequence of divine emotionalism.

The consequent idea, that one may not judge a man's happiness until his death, also has no expression in Solon's poems; it is among the constellation of ideas later associated with Solon. Thomas Harrison makes the point that 'the sentiment of death being preferable to life is first expressed by Solon through the story of Cleobis and Biton (1.31.3)'.[45] Divine interference as well as unknowable human fortune have ample precedents before Solon, and of course cannot be attributed to his invention. If it is possible to reason from Solon's words to the Herodotean view of death then this reasoning can be applied to works far earlier than Solon. But even if Herodotus is expressing the logical consequences of Solon's *Moira*, and 'Solonian' philosophy (created after Solon's death) is central to Herodotus, this remains only one aspect of Solon's own thought, and not the core of his ideas about the *polis*. Solon's *Moira* in poem 13 is rather a counter-revolutionary appeal to an ancient tradition to explain the plain truth that good actions do not lead necessarily to a good end for a man.[46] That a god is angry or jealous 'constitutes for Herodotus a deduction from the course of events'[47] is also true for Solon's view of *Moira*. In each case the conclusion is conditioned by a common heritage of fatalism stretching back to Homer and before. But Solon's 'deduction' may rather be broadly inductive: a movement from experience to a generalization that explains what he sees better than does *dikê*.

This leads to a particular interpretation of Solon's prayer to Memory, at the start of the poem. Plato speaks several times of Solon's position as a bringer of ancient – especially Egyptian – wisdom to Athens. In the *Critias*, Plato has Critias claim that Solon brought the names of the early founders of Athens from Egypt.[48] The passage evokes the story of the flood in the *Timaeus,* which Solon is said to have brought from Egypt, and which remained unfinished, given his need to turn from poetry to become a lawgiver in Athens. Solon takes on the aura of the man who brought Athens out of its own flood and led the shepherds into civilized life. But Critias had begun with a prayer to *Mnêmosune*, acknowledging the need for Memory to bring ancient wisdom forward.[49] Perhaps in his own time Solon was calling on Memory to bring him a solution to his own problem – the limitations of *dikê* – by returning himself and his audience to a proper understanding of *moira* as the defining principle of each man's life. This would again show Solon here to be a counter-revolutionary, turning away from the budding causal principles governing the *polis* and back to the arbitrary in human life. The world of *bios* remains incomprehensible, subject to whimsy and disobedient to anything remotely akin to the laws of causality.

Knowability and actionability are two conditions required for human responsibility. In fragments 4, 9 and 11 the denial of arbitrary divine disaster and the affirmation of human thought and action validated human responsibility for human affairs; the *polis* is both knowable and actionable. The sky in poem 9 is (in principle) understandable but it is not actionable; conversely, *bios* in poem 13 is actionable but its end is not knowable. The limitations placed on human action and understanding,

5. 'Moira *brings good and evil*'

and the reinstatement of the arbitrary, release men from culpability in either realm. Solon's rejection of an efficacious view of human knowledge and action is based on the uncertain results that fall across the span of a person's life and end in *moira thanatou*. Solon's turn to *Moira* is the re-establishment of the arbitrary as a causal explanation in human life, a precursor to the idea of *tuchê* as an explanation based on occurrences of a kind other than what is intended, and a premonition of Socrates' 'defence' that philosophy is preparation for death. Solon has an affinity with a broad tradition of later thinkers who would despair at their ability to understand and control their lives, and who would be left with only appeals to the gods to lead them as they will. Epictetus comes to mind here, who in the concluding section of his *Encheiridion* calls on Zeus and Fate to lead him as they will. To Solon *stasis* in the *polis* is the understandable result of corrupt human beings; calamity in a person's life is due to *Moira*, who brings good and evil, as she wishes.

6

'We will not exchange our excellence'
Moira and wealth

> Many evil men grow rich, and good men grow poor,
> But we will not exchange our excellence
> For their wealth ...
>
> Solon 15.1-3

Solon's prayer to Memory in poem 13 has been answered, which is not to say that Solon (like Croesus) got the answer he wanted. *Moira* brings good and evil *pantôs*, but the when, where and how are beyond our capacity to know – a matter of grave practical consequence to a subsistence farmer who might not understand the issue abstractly, but would recognize his own vulnerability before a powerful enemy. The intellectual chasm between the *moira* of each man's life and *dikê* of the *polis* is unbridged. But human beings do not earn their livings in a vacuum, and the non-political poems, especially those concerned with wealth, had importance to the *polis*.[1] Solon does not mention the *polis* in poem 27, on the periods of life. Yet the issues in the poem applied to the *polis*, if for no other reason than that young men had to be of age prior to becoming citizens, and thus had to apply Solon's stages of life to *polis* activities. As archaic Athens coalesced into the political capital of Attica, the unjust pursuit of honour, prestige and material wealth – acquired by what was in effect the Homeric standard of the *agathos* – could lead directly to the dangers that Hesiod had said the Good Strife of benevolent competition was supposed to prevent. The motivations to pursue wealth *perforce* could include complex psychological and social values that might warp a man's disposition and fuel his desire for further outrage. The limits that Solon places to the pursuit of material wealth are surely related to his view that no limits to wealth are revealed to us – a matter of *noos* – but also to the fact that wealth itself has little value if its pursuit is not restrained by *dikê*.

Solon's view of each man's inability to recognize a limit, or *terma*, to wealth itself, is central to the pursuit of wealth, and how it relates to the *polis*. Continuing poem 13, Solon says:

> πλούτου δ' οὐδὲν τέρμα πεφασμένον ἀνδράσι κεῖται·
> οἳ γὰρ νῦν ἡμέων πλεῖστον ἔχουσι βίον,
> διπλάσιον σπεύδουσι· τίς ἂν κορέσειεν ἅπαντας;
>
> Solon 13.71-3[2]

6. 'We will not exchange our excellence'

> Of wealth no limit lies revealed to men,
>   for those of us who have the greatest standard of living
> work twice as hard. Who can be satisfied in every way?

Solon makes no attempt to ask, as Aristotle would, whether there is an actual physical limit to the wealth a person can possess, which for Aristotle is a matter of the finite nature of all things.[3] He rather says that no limit is revealed, *pephasmenon*, which makes the issue, again, firmly a matter of our ability (or inability) to see beyond the goods of the present moment to their *terma* – to the limits proper to wealth or the striving for it. Probably the cattle, without *noos*, also see no end to the grass, which they munch with thoughtless abandon. The limited capacity of *noos* to bring about material success was established by the context of the previous four lines: one person, attempting to do well but *ou pronoêsas* ('not seeing ahead') falls into ruin, while another has his blindness lifted by a god and succeeds. Ivan Linforth translates line 71 as 'In the pursuit of wealth there is no fixed goal visible from the start'; he then interprets: 'the distant object of one's effort constantly recedes while one gives chase'. Perhaps we can never reach the point of satisfaction *hapantas* 'in every respect' because we keep reaching the goal – the amount of wealth we need to flourish – but can neither recognize the goal when we have reached it nor project it into the future.[4]

The identity of wealth is ambiguous in Solon's fragments; the terms he uses – such as *aphenos, ploutos, chrêmata, kteanon, agatha,* and *olbos* – span from physical goods to complex ideas associated with necessity, moral standards, social status and political authority. The complexity and ambiguity is wider than Solon, of course; the scholiast to Homer *Iliad* 1.171 distinguishes *aphenos* and *ploutos* in terms of time. In Solon such terms can refer to material values (one's lot in life, a plot of land, precious metals or a walled homestead), as well as psychological values (glory, respect, reputation). In many cases Solon has not left us enough of the context to establish their precise meanings; for instance, the only reference to debts in Solon, *chreious*, at 36.10-11, is ambiguous, and bound up in the forcible necessity of a pursuing enemy. Solon's rapacious critic in fragment 33 is after both power (*kratêsas*) and vast wealth (*plouton aphthon*), and he associates both to his being a tyrant (*turanneusas*) for a single day.

Nevertheless, Solon does leave fragments that describe his values with some specificity; his words here have a personal focus that is closer to the *bios*-perspective in poem 13 than to the *polis*. His values are derived from certain fundamental aspects of human existence:

> πολλοὶ γὰρ πλουτέουσι κακοί, ἀγαθοὶ δὲ πένονται·
>   ἀλλ' ἡμεῖς τούτοις οὐ διαμειψόμεθα
> τῆς ἀρετῆς τὸν πλοῦτον, ἐπεὶ τὸ μὲν ἔμπεδον αἰεί,
>   χρήματα δ' ἀνθρώπων ἄλλοτε ἄλλος ἔχει.
>
>   Solon 15

Solon the Thinker

ἴσόν τοι πλουτέουσιν, ὅτῳ πολὺς ἄργυρός ἐστι
 καὶ χρυσὸς καὶ γῆς πυροφόρου πεδία
ἵπποί θ' ἡμίονοί τε, καὶ ᾧ μόνα ταῦτα πάρεστι,
 γαστρί τε καὶ πλευραῖς καὶ ποσὶν ἁβρὰ παθεῖν,
παιδός τ' ἠδὲ γυναικός, ἐπὴν καὶ ταῦτ' ἀφίκηται,
 ὥρη, σὺν δ' ἥβη γίνεται ἁρμοδίη.
ταῦτ' ἄφενος θνητοῖσι· τὰ γὰρ περιώσια πάντα
 χρήματ' ἔχων οὐδεὶς ἔρχεται εἰς Ἀΐδεω,
οὐδ' ἂν ἄποινα διδοὺς θάνατον φύγοι, οὐδὲ βαρείας
 νούσους, οὐδὲ κακὸν γῆρας ἐπερχόμενον.

Solon 24

ἔσθ' ἥβης ἐρατοῖσιν ἐπ' ἄνθεσι παιδοφιλήσῃ,
 μηρῶν ἱμείρων καὶ γλυκεροῦ στόματος.

Solon 25

Many evil men grow rich, and good men grow poor,
 but we will not exchange our excellence (*aretê*)
for their wealth, since the one abides forever,
 but possessions jump from one man to another.

He is equally rich is he who has much silver
 and gold, and wheat-bearing plains
and horses and mules, and he who has this alone,
 to live pleasantly in stomach and sides and feet,
and when this comes, a season for woman and child
 with proper youthful vigour.
This is wealth to mortals; for no one
 carries to Hades all their surplus possessions,
nor can he pay a ransom and escape death,
 deep disease, or encroaching evil old age.

(until?) he falls in love with a boy in the flower of youth,
 of desiring thighs and sweet lips.

The goods associated with living well are revealed in stomach, sides and feet, parts of the body that denote the basics of food, clothing and footwear. Land and precious metals round out the material possessions of a man rich in goods, although a good but poor man should not wish to change places with a bad but rich man. Solon repeatedly separates excellence from the possession of wealth, undoubtedly a slap at any *nouveau riche* who was claiming the status associated with aristocratic birth based on his wealth. Personal well-being, family and vigour – the essentials of a pleasant lifestyle – are the most important values a man can possess. More sensuous values include the enjoyment of the blooming charms of a youth. But the fundamental limits to the value of material goods are stated starkly, in wealth's inability to ward off the three main enemies of man: death, old age and disease. Limits to the value of material goods are set by their

6. 'We will not exchange our excellence'

transitory and temporary nature, their failure to reflect the characters of men, and their lack of power against man's unconquerable enemies. They are worthless once man reaches his ultimate *telos*; you can't take it with you. This becomes all the more pointed once contextualized with his feelings for the *polis* – which he clearly sees as a value above all others, a value so deep that he never actually identifies it as such.

Taken together, Solon's claims here amount to a simple hierarchy of personal values: the basics of a luxurious life, personal vitality and family are of a higher order than money, land and horses. These rankings – never made explicit, but implicit in any statement that places one value over another – are combined with his recognition of many ways to pursue one's means of life; they bring an order to his understanding. All of this is, in effect if not in intention, a system of values based upon traditional normative ideals as well as new moral standards, which are justified or condemned in terms of the practical consequences that follow by necessity. It is surely important to Solon's view of wealth that its value ends at the hidden *telos* of life – the *terma* of death that we cannot know and over which wealth has no effect.[5]

There are many reasons why Solon might have pushed these views. As a political operator, perhaps he was trying to keep an affluent crowd, bent on power, from pledging its wealth towards the aggrandizement of tyrants. His target might rather have been a mob of farmers, goaded by an eminent man (*prostatês*) into redistributing the land of the rich. His attitude might have been ironic or condescending, a cynical attempt to talk the poor into accepting their positions in order to maintain elite control of the shrines or public displays.[6] Perhaps he was waxing philosophically, presaging Plato and others who would ask whether a tyrant can really be happy, or a rich man better off than a pauper. But, considering the thrust of his other verses, there is good reason to think that he genuinely saw material riches as valuable only in a context determined by the proper condition of a man's *noos*. The *agathos*, who is no longer defined by the values of the Homeric warrior, will not be found in the man of material success.

Solon's views of wealth may be considered from psychic and physical perspectives, of which the former dominate his verses. In terms of the *psuchê*, Solon remains concerned primarily with the central noetic problem in knowing the end of all things, and in avoiding the threat to Athens that follows such ignorance. The effects of wealth on a person's physical situation – the extent to which it can actually improve a person's life – must be inferred; Solon's own silence here carries an implication about his view of wealth's efficacy and importance. From either perspective the improper pursuit of wealth is caused by a misunderstanding of its value-significance to the person pursuing it. The danger is not the possession of wealth *per se* – Solon never says 'wealth is bad'; the danger is rather in an inversion of the proper hierarchy of values, including any claims that conspicuous displays of wealth or the power associated with it indicate

Solon the Thinker

personal excellence. This occurs when a person elevates the pursuit of wealth above health, enjoyment of a rational pleasure, a good reputation, and a harmonious existence. In the *polis* such a person has a noetic deficiency; he fails to recognize the need to act *in hêsuchia* or under the terms proper to *Eunomiê*. He may think that wealth obtained unjustly is a value, but he is mistaken, since he does not see the full measure of the consequences to flow from his actions – a serious problem, given that those consequences are ultimately hidden to man.

As a result, Solon rates certain political values – which are proper to all Attic-speakers – on a higher level than wealth. It is good to live in Attica as a free man (*eleutheros*), and unseemly to be trembling (*tromeomenos*) before the whims of another. The traditional values of *timê*, *doxa*, and *aretê* must be redefined and subordinated to the values of the *polis*, lest a man of defective *noos* be misled by them. Solon might have been forcing these values into conflict with emerging (or re-emerging) values of the *polis*, for which those 'traditional' standards are a danger. 'Traditional' here belongs in scare quotes; what may seem to be ancient to one party might actually represent a relatively recent collapse of older values. Solon might have been looking to return to the *polis* ideal that had existed a few generations earlier.[7] In either case, a man who was *agathos* in the heroic sense, taking loot perforce from a man perceived as an enemy, would be unjust and hubristic in the *polis*.[8] Similarly, a man who used his intelligence in a cunning way, especially against those in his own *polis*, would be thinking in a way akin to the conniving *dêmos* that Solon criticizes, or to the potential tyrant in fragment 33.[9] According to a fragment reconstructed from the Aristotelian *Constitution of the Athenians*, psychic states such as love of lucre and arrogance may create hateful actions that lead Athens to ruin.[10] The political result is the first inklings of what would one day become a democratic revolution; for example, in Homer *geras* ('gifts', 'offices' or 'honours') always flow to the leaders; in Solon they may accrue to the people, albeit in moderation appropriate to them (fragment 5).

Solon's break with the heroic past – and a parallel to his own meal scene in poem 4 – is mirrored in Xenophanes poem 1, set in a symposium that is deeply opposed to the Homeric concepts of *arête* and the *agathos*.[11] It is better to invoke Memory for a new excellence that is something other than the deeds represented by the ancient battles, and to avoid dangerous emotions and the strife they engender. The poet conveys a sense of joyous celebration and good will, tied to reverence for the divine and a clean, sensual purity. The 'clean' (*katharon*) floor, hands and cups, the 'sacred smells' (*hagnên odmên*) which are 'holy' (*libanôtos*), the 'altar of blooms' (*bômos anthesin*) and 'reverent' (*gegarê*) table – all serve to legitimate the new sense of *arête* by uniting the physical and the divine with reverent stories and clean talk (*euphêmois muthois kai katharoisi logois*). The 'clean hands' in particular are free of the pollution so destructive of conviviality.[12] Such cleanliness fosters the dispositions necessary for the *euphronas*

6. 'We will not exchange our excellence'

andras, 'men of good cheer' to offer prayers and libations to do right ('just things', *ta dikaia*). The danger here – that which can undercut the *euphrosunê* as it was undercut in Solon's poem 4 – is in the man who lingers around the wine, bringing forth violent sentiments with tales of battles between Giants and Titans. Nothing useful can come from old battle stories, except the kind of outburst that Solon decried. Solon, like Xenophanes, was using a post-Homeric standard of *arête* to isolate and condemn anyone who was persuaded to destroy the conviviality of the *polis*.

Also like Xenophanes, Solon's appeal to moderation is not only negative – in his desire to prevent destruction – and not only based on observations that those with wealth were often the most hubristic in their pursuit of it. There were real, physical limits to the efficacy of material wealth in Solon's day that foreshortened the *terma* of its pursuit. Solon's denigration of material goods as incapable of staving off death, disease or old age is not an abstract philosophical conclusion, but rather an accurate reflection of the value of material goods in the ancient world. The non-technological state of Solon's era bears strong emphasis, for wealth was pursued in ways, and for purposes, that may differ fundamentally from those of our own day. It is easy to think anachronistically about Solon if this is not kept in mind. Apart from land and agricultural resources needed for survival, objects of beauty, variations in diet, and the escape from backbreaking labour to a non-farming lifestyle, the greatest value of material wealth was probably psychological: the attainment of reputation and prestige through conspicuous display of the products of success.

The material goods that allowed one to live above subsistence level remained *fundamentally* unable to affect one's health, to influence one's span of life, or to stave off old age and death. The author of the Hippocratic treatise *Epidemics* describes as hopeless a whole range of cases that would be routinely cured today.[13] *The Science of Medicine* holds that 'the refusal to undertake to cure cases in which disease has already won the mastery' is a simple recognition that 'deep disease' is beyond the reach of a physician, and of money. Apart from outright starvation or slavery perforce, a rich man would be little more able to save a sick child than would a poor man. In such conditions there would be no reason to associate wealth with an extension of one's life-span; a sick man of means might avail himself of elixirs and rituals that would give him no advantage over a poor man, and would attain the same results for both. This could have fed into Solon's view that knowledge and control of our ultimate ends is impossible, and that material goods are of no fundamental import in such matters. Only in the modern world, with capital markets, mass transportation and communication, prescription drugs, intensive care units and MRI scans, can the possession of material wealth be so closely linked to good health – but our time is not his.

Solon actually goes further than this, linking good bodily health to the absence of wealth. Those possessing only stomach, sides and feet experience a certain luxury (*habra pathein*) not open to a rich man, who was presumably burdened with responsibilities and the pressing need to avoid a fall. Herodotus states the thought directly, in the Solon–Croesus encounter, giving a poor man an actual advantage over a rich man. The former, if he is lucky, is better able to avoid great ruin (*atên megalên*), to be free of disease (*anousos*), to be blessed with good children (*eupais*), and to avoid experiencing evils (*apathês kakôn*). The rich man may be better equipped to bear ruin, bane or calamities (*atê*), but the poor can (somehow?) avoid them. The Herodotean Croesus epitomizes the person who cannot see to the end and has no desire to try; the wealth before his eyes is sufficient to claim blessedness. But his wealth did not avert his fate; it was no good to him at the point of death, and he only narrowly escaped annihilation – by his opponent's recognition of his own ephemeral state – before he collapsed into misery. He lost his power, and many of his poor subjects moved into the Persian army. He had no great reputation; Croesus did not impress Solon, and was pitied by the Persian king. It took the intervention of Apollo – who sees the end – to reverse Croesus' fate. That a man of means has further to fall than a poor man – and thus suffers more, given his wealth – fits a tragic sense of rise and fall.

Solon's own thought reflects the fundamental uncertainties of a world where sickness, crop failure or storm could wipe out the labour of years in a few moments. These uncertainties were omnipresent, and accepted without arguments for or against. From Solon's point of view the excessive pursuit of wealth could lead to the destruction of a man's character, and his community, without any serious benefit beyond social recognition. And, if the social approbation were to be removed from such actions by linking them to *hubris*, then wealth could lead to a social stigma or even expropriation. This could have greatly strengthened the idea that the most important things in life were outside of human control, thus further stoking the idea that the ends of life are not open to man's understanding. *Moira* brings good and evil to man, and, for Solon, attempts to redistribute wealth will not alter this fact.

It is significant, in Solon's examples of various deluded men in poem 13 lines 37-42, that a man's ability to become wealthy is equated with his ability to become healthy, courageous and handsome: he can do neither. Solon's equation of these characteristics may indicate that social and economic status (e.g. *agathos* / *kakos*, or *deilos* / *agathos*), were not considered open to human effort, and that he could not envisage a society in which men could become wealthy by legitimate means. Without a concept of production, with little sight of economic prosperity attained without slave labour, and with the *polis* under the control of wealthy but unjust men, he drew the obvious conclusion: that great wealth was necessarily linked to tyranny and taken perforce. The distinctions we draw between *moira qua* 'allotted economic share', *moira qua* 'fate', and *moira qua* 'death' may be anachronistic to the archaic age, masking the essential

6. 'We will not exchange our excellence'

similarity betrayed by the use of one word: that these aspects of human life are beyond human understanding or control, and that for each only Zeus knows the end. Solon's refusal to embrace *isomoiriê* may be more than an attempt to maintain an elite control of the *polis*; it may also express his conviction that such a redistribution is not properly within human powers. Far from conceiving an idea such as 'distributive justice' as a species of a wider genus of 'justice', fragment 34.7-8 explicitly links the idea of equal shares to the injustice of violence and tyranny, which would constitute stepping beyond one's station in Solon's world as fully as Thersites stepped beyond his in the world of Homer. Of course the question who is to be *isos* and to what degree is patently unclear. But Solon's basic opposition to the redistribution of wealth is not affected if *isomoiria* is limited to the wealthy or newly wealthy.[14]

Consequently, those who usurped the *moira* ('material allotment') of a person – by planting a stone on another farmer's land, on a common sanctuary, or on the estate of a landed aristocrat – could be guilty of an egregious effrontery and violent *hubris* against the gods as well as men. To move a boundary stone was a violation of the ancient laws, as serious as stealing a man's horse in the nineteenth-century American West. Such an attack on *Moira* would be an invitation to the retribution of *Dikê*, a retribution that Solon could avert by stigmatizing the aggressors and enacting statutes that made their claims unenforceable. If a judge is precluded from settling a dispute by ordering the enslavement of another or taking his land, then the *dikê* of dispute settlement cannot be used against the foundations of natural *dikê*, and the *polis* will not be subject to the destruction it brings. Solon may think that to protect a person's *moira* against violent expropriation also protects the sacred roots of *Dikê* in their fundamental sense, through the earth on which the lot is anchored.

What then constitutes the just pursuit of wealth for Solon? Or, is every pursuit of wealth inherently harmful? Poem 13 offers some clues, while leaving much ambiguous and open to interpretation. Solon's differentiation of justly from unjustly acquired wealth in lines 9-11 includes the disputed word *timôsin*, which I translate as 'they honour' and which Solon relates to *hubris*.[15] To 'honour' wealth by *hubris* is not merely to covet it above its proper status; it is to get it by arrogant action – arrogance as determined under the new standard of moderation. This is transitory wealth, the *erga* of *hubris* that do not abide for mortals. Indications of a normative shift in the meaning of *timê* (roughly 'honour', also 'recompense' or 'present', depending on the context) are implied in these passages. If *timê* was traditionally based on the achievement of the visible signs of aristocratic success – a socially elevated position and the attendant material wealth – then Solon may be redefining the terms of *timê* towards an ideal of moderation, which he aligns with *dikê*, and which would later become a guiding principle of democratic Athens. However, by the end of the poem Solon is claiming that all wealth is transitory, and necessarily

103

flits from man to man. As *dikê* had to retreat into silence before the whims of *Moira*, so the justice afforded to some wealth at the start of the poem must retreat, leaving all wealth outside the bounds of justice. *Moira* rules all. All wealth is at least potentially harmful, since no man can know its proper limit, and no one carries it past one's own unknown *moira thanatou*.

Improper possession of wealth – 'improper' meaning beyond a limit that is unknowable to us, which may mean all wealth beyond subsistence – leads to *atê*, the psychic bewilderment or blindness that can lead a man to go berserk, and the physical calamity, ruin or bane that follows. Like so many archaic ideas, it embraces both a process and a result, a psychic cause and a physical consequent, of course undistinguished in Solon's mind. Earlier identified with the active, physical involvement of a deity, for Solon it may have become a natural characteristic of human beings, even if divinely conceived.[16] Further, *atê* can apply to an individual apart from a *polis* context, as *stasis* cannot; an individual can fall into *atê*, but only multiple individuals can be in *stasis*. But where does *atê* come from? Solon's verse in line 75 says that *atê* comes *ex autôn*, 'from these things', but from which things? Scholars have argued that *atê* in line 75 must come from either the material gains, mortal men, or the immortals.[17] Richard Hamilton's argument for the gods as the source of *atê* is based on his reading of lines 74-6. But if the passage is extended to include three couplets, and is considered in context with other relevant passages and the remainder of the poem, a different conclusion is possible.

> πλούτου δ' οὐδὲν τέρμα πεφασμένον ἀνδράσι κεῖται·
> οἵ γὰρ νῦν ἡμέων πλεῖστον ἔχουσι βίον,
> διπλάσιον σπεύδουσι. τίς ἂν κορέσειεν ἅπαντας;
> κέρδεά τοι θνητοῖς ὤπασαν ἀθάνατοι,
> ἄτη δ' ἐξ αὐτῶν ἀναφαίνεται, ἥν ὁπότε Ζεὺς
> πέμψῃ τεισομένην, ἄλλοτε ἄλλος ἔχει.
>
> Solon 13.71-6

Of wealth there is no limit revealed to man,
   for those of us who have the greatest standard of living
work twice as hard. Who can be satisfied in every way?
   The immortals bring profit to mortals,
but calamity arises from these things (*ex autôn*), [calamity] which
   when Zeus sends retribution, passes from one man to another.

The hypothesis that Solon always looks for the underlying organization of things lends itself to a particular source of *atê*. The way in which men can be overcome by *hubris* provides grounds for taking neither the gods, mortals nor gain alone as the referent of *ex autôn*. The cause of man's troubles is elsewhere described by Solon as arising from an unjust *noos*, a failure to restrain *koros* and *hubris*, and a willingness to destroy the *polis*;

6. 'We will not exchange our excellence'

an imperfect *noos*, great wealth and *koros* lead to *hubris* and stasis. In such passages the combination of a faulty *noos*, *koros* and *hubris* is the source of calamity. A person can control the state of his mind, as the demands for moderation and the claims that unjust men do not understand imply, but if he fails to do so then *hubris* follows, which are the conditions under which wealth 'mixes with *atê*' (*anamisgetai atê*, 13.13). In poem 4 a man can control *atê* by stepping further back in the sequence and restraining his *noos* and his *koros*, by adopting *Eunomiê*.

A similar combination of factors explains the *ex autôn* of line 75. Neither the gods nor man nor the gifts alone cause such a reaction; the issue is the relationship between *noos*, *ploutos*, *hubris* and *atê* in a man's *psuchê*. *Atê* comes from 'those things'.[18] There is a parallel of a sort to Indra Kagis McEwen's discussion of the Anaximander fragment. She observes that the generation and destruction of all things is not in any particular things in the *kosmos*, but neither is it in the Boundless. The *kosmoi*, 'these 'orders' ... regulate and guide the ebb and flow of elements'. Similarly, in Solon, *atê* arises from the combination of psychic and material factors – not from any single factor. Given that we are inherently unable to see to the end, Solon sees no way to prevent the Good Strife of Hesiod from blowing up into Bad Strife. But is wealth *necessarily* corrupting? Can wealth cause the *noos* to become empty, which allows *atê* to bloom? To this, Solon seems to be saying yes, at least, to the audience of poem 13, and possibly to the crowd in fragment 11. What is common to both contexts – the immoderate pursuit of wealth and the illegitimate pursuit of public honours – is a dependent standard of evaluation, the desire for social status gained through loot or power, and motivated by the presence of others. Ultimately this desire is under the control of his audience, if the *noos* is corrected, but to do so is difficult; Solon is not hopeful that this will happen soon.

Solon's appeal to moderation helped establish the background for an institutional revolution in the fifth century, when public forums, properly used, could restrain any one person from acting beyond the limits appropriate to the *polis*. Rather than eliminating competitions by a shift from 'competitive' to 'cooperative values', the competitions were transferred into the law-courts and political institutions, which mirrored the tragic festivals and athletic contests and battlefield, but under limits set by laws and the challenges of political opponents.[19] When the institutions themselves – especially the assembly – began to exceed those limits, the people of Athens set out to re-inscribe the laws of Solon, and to subordinate the decrees of the assembly (*psêphismata*) to the law (*nomos*). The key here is limits – setting a *terma* for pursuit of an enemy that precludes the kind of revenge actions that wracked the *polis* of *Dusnomiê*, and maintaining laws against land redistribution for the farmer who works his *oikos*.

Solon's *Hymn to the Muses* undergoes a double reversal. It begins with the claim that wealth blessed by the gods abides forever and is good, while wealth obtained unjustly leads to ruin. In a ring composition, it ends with

105

the unqualified claim that wealth is transitory and leads to the corruption of *atê*.[20] The prayer begins with claims that are consistent with the *polis*, and ends in the very terms that Solon has disavowed for the *polis*. In more abstract terms it begins with man as subject to the consistent effects of *dikê*, a cosmetic principle of organization; it ends with the assertion that *moira* brings good and evil as she wishes, without rhyme or reason. Even more deeply, it begins with the assumption that we can understand the patterns of life and avoid calamity; it ends with a denial that this knowledge is possible. An unbridgeable divide remains between the knowable consequences of *dikê* and the unknowable *telos* that is *moira*. To put it another way, the fact that Hesiod's 'the gods keep hidden from men the means of life' leaves Solon's 'those of us who now hold the greatest means of life work doubly hard' without any means of understanding why. This places the responsibility for work in each man's hands, but places the ends of that work into the hands of *Moira*.[21]

But why does Solon adopt this poetic structure, and this argumentative strategy, in poem 13? Why does he begin with a conclusion – that *dikê* comes with certainty, and unjust wealth alone is bad – that he repudiates in the end? Several explanations are possible. Perhaps archaic thought moves from particulars to particulars without logical structure, the poet changing his mind as topics strike him, distracted from his abstractions by concrete items of interest.[22] If he begins by asserting the power of *Dikê*, and ends by supporting *Moira*'s incomprehensible whims, then this is the direction in which his mind moves, unbound by the rigours of logic and unconcerned with contradictions. But, if so, then any question of an underlying order in the poems becomes hopelessly arbitrary. If Solon is at the mercy of his own whims then so are we, and all we can do is experience, but never understand, the poem. However, Solon's use of terminology, even given his ambiguity, supports an explanation that is less arbitrary than this.

A second possibility assumes associative / linear thinking, loosely directed by a leitmotif but without a coherent goal, purpose or unified structure. One version of this is championed by Richmond Lattimore, who sees the poem as a 'self-generating series of connected ideas'.[23] Solon is basically thinking out loud, trying to solve a problem in a way that had not been tried before. He begins with a commonplace idea – that *dikê* is inevitable, and unjust wealth is bad – but in the face of intractable problems, literally thinking on his feet, he changes his mind. The changes in direction are not aimless drifting, but rather a glimpse into the mind of a man devising a new approach to his problem. This would be evidence for his intellectual honesty, and for the improvisational nature of the verses. In this view he at least roughly knows what he is after, but has not thought through his own position before composing.

Other interpretations have assumed an organic unity to the poem, and have supported this with analyses of certain structures, or connected

6. 'We will not exchange our excellence'

sections, based on a coherent theme and purpose. Allen claims that the search for wisdom is the theme, and thereby rejects any thematic breaks in the poem; Sicking rather concludes that the poem is not unified, but 'is the consistent development of the implications of the ideas it starts with'.[24] Another possibility is offered by Kate Stoddard, who maintains that Solon's strategy is ironic.[25] Solon draws his audience in with ideas about justly acquired wealth that his audience, who are well-to-do, would accept as vindications of their positions. According to the persuasions they have accepted, justly acquired wealth is unflawed, and Solon bolsters their positions. He first hooks his audience using the authority of *Dikê*, and then reverses his stance, dropping the bombshell that all wealth necessarily corrupts. They are not exempt from the consequences of *ploutos*, which corrupts no matter how it is pursued. Solon here has thought out his strategy very well, is in firm control of his poem, and understands how to lead the audience through their own misconceptions to his own view. Solon's self-conscious didactic purpose, to challenge existing standards of honour, empowers this ironic strategy and allows him to undercut claims that run counter to his own terms of political excellence. His prayer to Memory, again, is a prayer to return *Moira* to her proper place, because wealth and justice do not mix.

These questions of interpretation may come down to the degree to which Solon had a firm grasp on the issues, and a coherent strategy to present them. If my interpretation is correct, Solon understands the basic problem – the incompatibility of *dikê* and matters of individual *bios* – so he makes a strong differentiation between *dikê* and *moira*, allowing each its own sphere of influence, a different standard of action, and a unique normative force. With *dikê* taken out of the picture there is no way to judge the consequences of wealth of any kind; there is only *Moira*, who acts arbitrarily. The best intentions, and even the best use of one's own knowledge to gain wealth properly, will not avert destruction, if *Moira* so chooses. The question of Solon's strategy for poem 13 turns on whether Solon had this all worked out in advance, or came to understand it only while composing the poem. We will never know, for it would require us to see into his mind, and to do that, all we have is the fragments. Whatever the truth of the poem's composition and delivery, two concepts, causal *dikê*, which applies to the *kosmos* that is Solon's *polis*, and arbitrary *moira*, which relates to the progression of each man's life, do dichotomize human life into two realms, which cannot be reconciled. To do the best they can the Athenians must try to understand the straight line that constitutes their own lives as a means to controlling the circle that is the *polis*, and they must do it without knowing the end of that line.

7

'I set them free'
Tyranny, slavery and freedom

> *Eunomiê* manifests good order and everything perfect,
> and often puts fetters on the evil-doers
>
> Solon 4.30-1

To turn to tyranny, slavery and freedom in Solon's verses appears to place us on more secure ground than we have trodden so far. Rather than images of Athena, flawed psychic qualities, hubris at meals followed by retribution, and good and evil brought by *Moira*, the topics are now manifestly political, as understandable by post-Enlightenment students of political thought. Even the later Greeks placed their emphasis in this direction, giving Solon the greatest fame for his 'shaking off of burdens' (*seisachtheia*), reforms of political offices, written laws and jury courts. According to Aristotle or his student, the 'most democratic' (*dêmotikôtata*) aspects of Solon's programme were the elimination of debt slavery, his allowing anyone who wishes (*ho boulomenos*) to sue (not only the aggrieved party), and the establishment of jury appeals.[1] But the security of such anachronistic terminology is tenuous. Solon is dealing not with modern nations and Lockean concepts, but with small towns and pre-Aristotelian ideas, built upon traditional prerogatives, religious veneration and only the earliest philosophical identifications. In his eyes, the fundamental alternatives facing the men of Athens were not oligarchy versus democracy, or kingship versus republicanism, but rather *hubris* versus *hêsuchia*, *dikê* versus *stasis*, and *Dusnomiê* versus *Eunomiê*. He does not write the *Federalist Papers* to defend a constitutional plan of government; he sings a song about a wound in his beloved fatherland in order to return it to justice. It is a mark of innovation that he connected the condition of a free man to the protections of written laws, under a proper understanding of *dikê*, enforced alike for all – a first rank development in political thought.

To call on tyranny and slavery en route to freedom is to be loyal to Solon's own approach. Once setting his fundamental terms – the role of the gods in poem 4 and his own position in poem 36 – he vivifies the twin evils of tyranny and slavery before displaying his positive programme of Good Order and written laws. There is a parallel to the American *Declaration of Independence*, which first states the principles by which a nation may demand its independence, then presents a litany of grievances against the

7. 'I set them free'

powers that be, prior to declaring the terms of independence. Working under very different circumstances, Solon and the American Founders each saw a serious breach of the proper political order, and to condemn it they each pointedly condemned the particular malfeasants (the leaders of the people, and the king and Parliament) prior to proposing a positive alternative. As the Americans had to radically re-order their constitution, adapting the language of John Locke et al. to their own needs, so Solon needed to re-order his world, using existing poetic forms in new ways. In each case tyranny and slavery had to be demonized in the political rhetoric, and freedom enshrined, if the changes were to be accepted. This chapter will take their lead, and approach freedom through tyranny and slavery.[2]

What makes someone a tyrant in Solon's world? An intractable problem of sources confronts anyone addressing this question.

The earliest source in which tyranny is solidly differentiated from other forms of rule is Herodotus, writing c. 440 BC. But he was a child of the fifth century, who is especially prone to apply fifth-century concepts to earlier events, a point made manifest in his Persian 'constitutional debate', which he framed using political terminology and principles of deliberation from fifth-century Athens, and resolved with a rigged contest of neighing horses. The archaic poets Archilochus and Alcaeus leave us the earliest references to a tyrant, but their failure to distinguish him from a king provides little solid ground on which to evaluate tyranny as apart from proper rule. Theognis carries his own problems of dating and tradition, as well as of understanding the social conditions in Megara. Pindar, who had dealings with tyrants as athletic victors, also warrants scepticism; even apart from his fifth-century dates, his encomiastic odes are not objective guides to the archaic concept of tyranny.[3]

Despite his early position, and myriad problems of interpretation – the non-existent chronology, the unanswered questions of Solon's own relationship with tyrants (which ones?), the dearth of information about clans and families, even Solon's possible use of tyrannical power himself, to name but four – Solon's identification and evaluation of tyranny is unprecedented in archaic evidence. He is the first extant thinker to describe tyranny as unqualifiably bad, to identify its essential error in psychic-intellectual terms, to equate it with slavery and distinguish it from proper rule under written laws. Tyranny is the mark of a city that has fallen into injustice, a leitmotif that runs throughout his political verses as a point of contrast that cuts to the heart of the *polis* as a moral *kosmos*. To Solon, the tyrant is an anathema to the *polis* not simply because of his hubristic power-seeking, but owing to the very nature of the power he seeks.

Poems 9 and 11 set the stage for his explanations of tyranny in the *polis*:

ἐκ νεφέλης πέλεται χιόνος μένος ἠδὲ χαλάζης,
βροντὴ δ' ἐκ λαμπρῆς γίγνεται ἀστεροπῆς·

ἀνδρῶν δ' ἐκ μεγάλων πόλις ὄλλυται, ἐς δὲ τυράννου
δῆμος ἀϊδρίῃ δουλοσύνην ἔπεσεν.
λίην δ' ἐξάραντ' <οὐ> ῥάιδιόν ἐστι κατασχεῖν
ὕστερον, ἀλλ' ἤδη χρὴ <καλὰ> πάντα νοεῖν.[4]

Solon 9

εἰ δὲ πεπόνθατε λυγρὰ δι' ὑμετέρην κακότητα,
μὴ θεοῖσιν τούτων μοῖραν ἐπαμφέρετε·
αὐτοὶ γὰρ τούτους ηὐξήσατε ῥύματα δόντες,
καὶ διὰ ταῦτα κακὴν ἔσχετε δουλοσύνην.
ὑμέων δ' εἷς μὲν ἕκαστος ἀλώπεκος ἴχνεσι βαίνει,
σύμπασιν δ' ὑμῖν χαῦνος ἔνεστι νόος·
ἐς γὰρ γλῶσσαν ὁρᾶτε καὶ εἰς ἔπη αἱμύλου ἀνδρός,
εἰς ἔργον δ' οὐδὲν γιγνόμενον βλέπετε.

Solon 11

The force of snow and hail comes from a cloud,
   and thunder from a flash of lightning.
But the ruin of the city comes from unjust men
   and the people fall into the slavery of a tyrant by ignorance.
Having raised these men up it is <not> easy
   to restrain them later. Now it is right to know all things <well>.[5]

If by your own actions you have suffered these most grievous calamities
   do not place the blame for your lot (*moira*) on the gods.
You yourselves increased [the power of] these men, providing them with arms,
   and this is why you have dreadful slavery.
Each one of you walks in the steps of a fox,
   but all together your *noos* is empty.
For you look to the tongue and words of a wily man,
   and fail to see the things he does.

In this, the second discussion of poem 9, I am favouring *turannou* over *monarchou* in line 3. This goes against every editor I know of and every manuscript source save one.[6] First off, forms of *monarchos* are rare in archaic evidence, and the abstract term *monarchia* is not securely attested before the fifth century.[7] The lack of contextualized attestations of *monarchia*, *oligarchia* or *dêmokratia* prior to the fifth century – and of *politeia* prior to the development of the Athenian democracy – strengthens the possibility that a concept of *monarchia,* as distinguished from other forms of political constitution, was at best implicit in the early sixth century. Possibly the Greeks did not distinguish the various forms of political rule until they had the experience of democracy in the fifth century, and did not before then understand those forms within the wider idea of *politeia*, '*polis*-ness'. It is important to resist connotations of *forms* of constitutions in Solon, including 'constitutional reforms' on his part; this runs the risk of overstating the conceptual differentiations made in archaic Athens. Solon's own concern may lie not with single rule versus rule by the few or the many, but rather with proper versus improper rule regardless of

7. 'I set them free'

numbers. This would be consistent with his condemnation of evil men in the *polis* in terms of their *hubris*, not by which faction they support or its size. It is the nature of the power they use that matters here, not the numbers of those using it.

Given Solon's scathing admonishments, slavery under a tyrant – the lot (*moira*) that befalls the townsmen, the precise meaning of which remains opaque in Solon – is not caused by *Moira* or the divine, but by the unjust actions of the people themselves. The *polis* is destroyed (*ollutai*) by overbearing men (*andrôn d' ek megalôn*) who are associated with slavery and misfortune (*doulosunê* and *lugra* or *deina*); the crowd acts by ignorance (*aidriê*), ambitious men with arms (*rhumata*) are easier to restrain (*kataschein*) up front than to reverse later (*husteron*). In other words, tyrants rise through noetic failures – ignorance, *hubris* and excess – in both themselves and the crowd that elevates them, and they maintain their positions by force. Each of these fragments starts with a wide statement about the issue; each then narrows to the specific physical and noetic causes. In lines 9.1-2 (as in fragment 12) Solon establishes his view that an uproar in the *polis* (as in the sky) occurs for a reason. In lines 9.3-4 he then points to the source of upheaval in the *polis*: men of unrestrained and unjust ambitions and an ignorant crowd. Lines 9.5-6 vivify the result – powerful men who cannot easily be overthrown – and the cure: to comprehend the situation properly. Fragment 11 follows a similar general direction: lines 11.1-2 exhort the Athenians not to blame the gods for these problems but to look to their own actions; lines 11.3-4 shows how they allowed the tyrants to sustain their power; lines 11.5-8 then deal with the noetic reasons for these errors, in a group context.

The physical means by which a tyrant gains and guards his power is found in the disputed *rhumata dontes*, 11.3. This is read as *rhusia dontes* by Ivan Linforth, which he translates as ' "giving pledges or hostages," thereby putting yourselves in their power'. Scholarship over the passage has been contentious.[8] Liddell, Scott and Jones gloss *rhusia* as 'property held or seized as a pledge or compensation', which depends upon a prior seizure of a value, some existing power to which pledges must be made, or an existing claim for which the *rhusia* is reciprocal.[9] *Rhusia* is thus a form of compensation. However, the possession of prior power, or material claims, by the leaders is not consistent with Solon's explanation in 11.7-8, especially with his description of the orator as *aimulos* 'wily' and the audience as falling into slavery *aidriê*, 'by ignorance'. In short, what is the prior value or power for which the *rhusia* are compensation?[10] Should we not prefer *rhumata*, 'defence, protection'?

T.E. Rihll accepts *rhusia* as part of a challenge to the accepted dating of fragments 9, 10 and 11. Dating the fragments to Solon's youth, she concludes that the tyrant was not Pisistratus, who was grafted onto the legend during its transmission, but rather Draco, who 'gave security in the form of land or hostages'.[11] Rihll offers five reasons for rejecting Pisistratus; the important one here is based on fragment 11: 'The people *had* the means to resist Pisistratus, which is inconsistent with the tone and content of the fragment'. Rihll notes that in the fifth and fourth centuries individuals and groups could demand 'sureties' on a loan; default led to an *atimos* status, including fines, confiscation and prison. In the archaic period the exiles were those who defaulted on similar sureties, granted for the use of the 'public' land; they would be unable to resist such power, and this is the position that the people of fragment 11 found themselves in.[12]

However, this whole construct depends upon the leaders already possessing power, with some institutionalized control over 'public' land, and is less than compatible with the *attainment* of power through cunning persuasion – which is Solon's whole point. This begs the question as to how the archaic leaders had achieved such power over the land, why the people had granted those particular men the 'sureties' they did, and why Solon makes no mention of any of this as a reason for the rise of tyranny in poems 9 and 11. What is the reason for importing ideas such as 'public land', 'hostages', 'securities' or 'legal claims' to explain Solon's verses?[13]

Rihll may be right to reject Pisistratus in favour of Draco (although Solon's purported visit to King Amasis of Egypt, who took power c. 570 BC, would remain a problem), but her reasoning does not explain Solon's verses. In Solon's own words, at an earlier point in time the people of fragment 11 had had the means to resist these men; but their ability to do so existed only prior to the appointment of club-bearers or their equivalent. The force granted to the tyrants was turned against the people and used for the tyrants' ends. Rihll's argument leaves open the difference between the *fact* of an established ruler ('it is not easy to restrain him later') and the *words* of a speaker seeking power ('you look to his tongue'). Solon, appreciating the difference between the thing he does (*to ergon, to gignomenon*) and what he says (*hê glôssa*), recognizes a potential for mischief in the tongue that was made real only with the acquiescence of the people. The people could not resist a tyrant once he had a bodyguard; this was, of course, precisely his aim. Once his arbitrary will was imposed *over* the *polis*, like a wound, *Dikê inside* the *polis* was silenced.

In contrast to this 'granting securities' interpretation, a 'granting resources' (*rhumata dontes*) interpretation acknowledges that the support of at least some of the people, assembled as a group, was how a relatively powerless but verbally wily man attained physical power. Gagarin and Woodruff translate 11.3-4 as 'For you increased the strength of these men yourselves when you gave them guards'.[14] This interpretation allows an emphasis to be placed where Solon placed it: on a defect in *noos* by which an audience is deceived, empowers a gang and falls under its rule. Solon 11.3-4, read in context with other passages that describe why people act as they do, strongly implies that the *dêmos* gave those men resources with the expectation of later favours; these favours were of the kind that Solon refused to grant in fragment 34, and which he rejected and parodied in

7. 'I set them free'

fragments 32 and 33. This reading favours the widest interpretation of *rhumata* as 'defensive resources' without identification as to their specific forms. The resources could have been a bodyguard, some form of allegiance from a group backed by arms, physical refuge (possibly, but not likely, the Acropolis) or other sacred areas, from which the tyrants could not be easily removed.[15] The Athenians followed a fox, seeking gain from it. In doing so their *noos* was empty, since they failed to understand the consequences of their actions. When they approached the leaders for the pay-off they were disappointed indeed, for tyrants are not easily restrained.

There is at least one scenario that could support the 'granting securities' interpretation: that certain members of the aristocracy had divided off sacred areas for private use by setting up stone markers (*horoi*), an injustice that Solon corrects by his own authority:

ἐγὼ δὲ τούτων ὥσπερ ἐν μεταιχμίῳ
ὅρος κατέστην.

Solon 37.9-10

But I, on account of these things, as in a no-man's land,
stood, a boundary stone.

This could provide a framework for securities, but it might also pose a challenge to Solon's own claims to virtue, since he tore up the stones only to become one himself. But this criticism would be misplaced. The *horoi* are legitimate, beneficial tools; injustice arises only from their improper use. Solon might claim to have corrected such injustices by re-aligning the boundaries inside the *polis* into agreement with *dikê*, perhaps as he had marked the boundary between the human and the divine. In any case, the use of the stones to expropriate public and sacred areas would provide an interpretation for the *horoi* passages that is not economic, and does not depend upon anachronistic 'mortgages' or sophisticated terms of sale. This would be consistent with the archaic boundary stones that have been found, which suggest that they were used to set limits to areas reserved for the *polis*.[16] The complex relationships between the noble families and the *dêmos*, reflected in the opaque metaphor of 'stirring up the cream' that precedes the *horos* passage in fragment 37, could now be understood in terms of struggles between noble families, involving the *dêmos*, for control of the shrines. This interpretation is also consistent with lines 12-13 in poem 4, in which the leaders of the people, or the *astoi*, rob and steal from public and sacred treasuries. Whatever the truth here, there were usurpations by both sides against established boundaries and prerogatives – given that Solon does stress the need to restrain the *dêmos* in fragment 37 – and these outrages fuelled the conflicts that allowed certain strongmen to cement their power.

Solon remains firm that, although physical defences allow tyrants to keep their power, the reason for their rise is the flawed expectation of gain that corrupts their *noos* and that of their audience. He vivifies this noetic failure and then admonishes a solution, in fragment 9, that the people must 'know all things', by recognizing the situation with the connotation of 'intending' that all things be well. This parallels the general direction in fragment 11, which places each person into the context of an assembly, and draws a solid parallel between animals and the failure of *noos*, which is 'empty' when men in a group resort to cunning. The *alôpêx* ('fox') may be the *aimulos anêr* ('wily man') himself, or perhaps a metaphor for the crowd's walking with the *noos*-less cunning of a fox.[17] In either case, lines 11.7-8 abandon the metaphor and make the specific error in the audience explicit: their concern for words rather than deeds leads them to misapprise the situation and to support wily men. Without its foundation in a proper *noos*, the internal energy of the *polis* collapses, usurped by the force imposed by tyrants. The people here have actually usurped the gods, who prior to Solon always had the sole right to 'raise someone up'. This is *hubris* in the first degree, and it leads necessarily to the retribution of *dikê* – the slavery of tyranny.[18]

Slavery, also a term with a complex set of referents, is caused by the same noetic failure. Despite myriad cultural variations, it has one essential meaning: a slave is subject to the unconditional command of another man. Solon's own concern is with Attic-speaking men, for whom slavery is unseemly and shameful; women and foreigners have no voice in the fragments. On the one hand, Solon's claim to virtue by freeing the enslaved Attic-speakers differentiates archaic Greece from a slave society such as the antebellum American south, where an open condemnation of slavery would probably have meant political suicide. Many people in Athens must have recognized that Solon was right. On the other hand, Attic speakers were in fact being enslaved, which implies that not everyone saw this as wrong. Some might have seen Solon's stance against slavery as an attack on their proper prerogatives; their version of the sacred roots anchoring Athens to the earth could not coexist with Solon's *dikê*. In such a conflict of values, Solon himself denied any intention of bringing shame to those who possessed glory through power and wealth; in fragment 5.3-4 – which may be sarcastic – he would make the 'better sort' his friends, thus recognizing existing status levels as proper. To end slavery, then, those aristocratic prerogatives would have to be preserved, all the while being limited so as not to include the right to enslave. Whatever his rhetorical purpose in poem 36, he extends the unseemliness of slavery to all Attic-speakers – an issue of which *Dikê* would take notice, as she returns to her proper place in Athens – and sets a precedent for this principle in later Athenian culture and law.[19]

Solon has two passages of primary concern for slavery. The first is at the end of his description of the strife-ridden *polis* in poem 4. As a result of the unjust *noos* of the people, and their abandonment of justice, many poor are put in chains and sold.

7. 'I set them free'

ταῦτα μὲν ἐν δήμῳ στρέφεται κακά· τῶν δὲ πενιχρῶν
  ἱκνέονται πολλοὶ γαῖαν ἐς ἀλλοδαπὴν
πραθέντες δεσμοῖσί τ' ἀεικελίοισι δεθέντες
  ....

                                          Solon 4.23-5

These evils turn on the people: and of the poor
  many are going into foreign lands,
sold and bound in shameful fetters
  ....

A second, somewhat more lengthy passage on slavery is in Solon's poem 36, his *apologia* that begins:

ἐγὼ δὲ τῶν μὲν οὕνεκα ξυνήγαγον
δῆμον, τί τούτων πρὶν τυχεῖν ἐπαυσάμην;
συμμαρτυροίη ταῦτ' ἂν ἐν δίκη χρόνου
μήτηρ μεγίστη δαιμόνων Ὀλυμπίων
ἄριστα, Γῆ μέλαινα, τῆς ἐγώ ποτε
ὅρους ἀνεῖλον πολλαχῇ πεπηγότας,
πρόσθεν δὲ δουλεύουσα, νῦν ἐλευθέρη.
πολλοὺς δ' Ἀθήνας πατρίδ' ἐς θεόκτιτον
ἀνήγαγον πραθέντας, ἄλλον ἐκδίκως,
ἄλλον δικαίως, τοὺς δ' ἀναγκαίης ὑπὸ
χρειοῦς φυγόντας, γλῶσσαν οὐκέτ' Ἀττικὴν
ἱέντας, ὡς δὴ πολλαχῇ πλανωμένους·
τοὺς δ' ἐνθάδ' αὐτοῦ δουλίην ἀεικέα
ἔχοντας, ἤθη δεσποτέων τρομεομένους·
ἐλευθέρους ἔθηκα.

                                          Solon 36.1-15

I brought the people together for these reasons,
How did I stop before I accomplished them?
In the Court of Time these things will be witnessed
by the testimony of the great mother of the Olympian
gods, the Black Earth, from whom I drew
up the boundary stones stuck in everywhere;
earlier she was enslaved, now she is free.
Many men I brought up to their divinely founded
fatherland, men sold, one illegally,
another legally, and others fleeing their debts
by forcible necessity, no longer speaking an Attic-tongue,
as men wandering everywhere;
and others holding a shameful slavery,
now trembling before their masters,
I set them free.

First, some general comments are in order about the longest of Solon's extant iambic trimeter verses. Echoes, repetitions, contrasts and parallels are used to connect the values Solon espouses to the *polis* and to his audience. Rhythmically, *pollachêi pepêgotas ... pollachêi planômenous* presents a parallel between the earth, stuck in with the *horoi* everywhere, and those slaves wandering everywhere; the 'everywhere' corresponds to the *Gê melaina* and *Athênas* (and probably the *gaian es allodapên* of fragment 4.24). *Planômenous ... tromeomenous* associates the wanderers abroad with the tremblers at home, linking the *prathentes* 'those sold' with the *phugontes* 'the exiles' and their separation from their native land. To contrast the different standards accepted by foreign lands and their negative effects upon exiled Attic men Solon juxtaposes *Athênas* with *Attikên*, confirming language as a key to one's identity. The participles *douleuousa* and *tromeomenous* would vivify slavery for a poor Greek farmer, drawing that farmer into Solon's moral orbit and differentiating that farmer from the destroyers of Athens. *Erexa* and *egrapsa* juxtapose his deeds with the writing required to put his plan in place, substituting written *thesmoi* for the *glôssa* of the orator. The passage is a powerful claim to Solon's own value to the *polis*, to be vindicated across time: the slavery that Athens faced prior to Solon's appointment is ended by his actions, asserted concisely as 'I set men free'. In Lesky's words, 'Justifiable pride, deep piety and a vigilant determination to repulse the enemy give these verses a stormy tempo unparalleled in archaic poetry'.[20]

Given his fervent claim to future vindication 'in the Court of Time', one might again wonder whether Solon had been put on trial – akin to Pisistratus, a tyrant who allowed himself to be 'tried', or more like Pericles, who was fined by the people of Athens, removed from office and then restored – and perhaps even convicted. This would tie the metaphor to real events, demonstrate his sense of independent judgment, explain his exile, and express a deep optimism for the ultimate triumph of *dikê*. There is no need to assume anachronistic legal institutions, or that the term '*dikê*' referred to a 'trial', only that Solon was calling on *dikê* to reverse an unjust judgment. Was he charged with improperly releasing men from debt-slavery judgments and giving them back their land, or limiting the encroachments of powerful families or cliques? Did he call on the gods as witnesses, since allies had deserted him despite his attempts to make them his friends – a point consistent with his claims that many were angry at him after he failed to bend the laws to their immediate desires?[21] His focus on statutes and judgments alike to each man's case might have reminded the people that written laws applied alike were relevant to their own cases, as to his. Did he go into exile neither on the Herodotean *prophasis* ('pretext') that he was engaged in *theoria* ('sightseeing'), nor to allow the Athenians to live under the laws, but rather to escape harsher judgment, onto which other motives were later attached?[22] Did he leave Athens after his archonship, and then return to write his legislation under personal authority rather than formal office? Speculation remains all we have – and the silence of later commentators is deafening – but this solution would anchor the abstract 'Court of Time' to a real case, and would have set a powerful context for poem 36 as the first extant legal speech from Athens.

7. 'I set them free'

Whatever the context, Solon's views of slavery in poem 36 – like his views of tyranny – imply physical and psychic aspects. Slavery is caused by a flawed *noos* and the *hubris* this engenders, but is maintained by physical force. Some men are enslaved at home, others overseas; some are taken legally and sold, others illegally; for some it is immediate, for others later; some are put in chains, and others flee into exile. The enslaved tremble before the whims of their master and fear his onrush. To live without physical constraint or fear of such constraint is the mark of a free man.

Solon demonstrates a sophisticated view of individual slavery, with several different forms and at least three different terms for it (*doulosunê, douniê,* and *douleuousa,* from *douleuô*). In lines 36.8-15, Solon describes slavery as occurring in three general ways: *ekdikôs* ('illegally'), *dikaiôs* ('legally'), and *anagkaiês hupo chreious* ('from forcible necessity').[23] This is not a dichotomy, but a trichotomy of illegal, legal or extra-legal actions. It is a series of coercions by those who might appeal to a judge or other person of repute, properly or improperly, to support their claims, or who might then ignore his decision or not even bother with such a formality. Solon is stating explicitly that slavery can occur without the sanction of a formal decision; he describes some slavery as neither legal nor illegal.

These three legal descriptions subsume three conditions for the enslaved. First, many Athenians have been sold (*pollous prathentas*), some illegally and others legally, at home or abroad. A key term here is *prathentes*, nominally 'those having been sold'. In Solon's time, *prathentes,* a participle of *pernêmi,* need not have implied sale overseas, as implied by the contrast he makes with the *phugontes* 'exiles'. At a far earlier stage, the verbs *paraô* ('passing over, esp. water') and *pernêmi* ('sell') had been confused, and often only the context can determine whether a man has been 'sold' or simply been sent overseas by force.[24] What then would 'being sold' mean? 'Ownership' is problematic in archaic society; the idea is based on a sanctioned right under law to use and dispose, and a sale involves a transfer as part of an exchange.[25] Ownership is much more than simple possession. The 'ownership' of a chattel slave gives the master an unconditional, unlimited right to command and dispose of the slave, to transfer him without any say by the slave, with neither time nor terms of manumission attached. Whether by custom or a deviance in the practice, no enforceable decision of a magistrate was available to release the slave from the command of his master. This must be distinguished from debt-bondage, in which the servitude is enforced for a period or until the debt is paid. It is probable that Solon eliminated debt slavery, but not debt bondage.[26]

The *phugontes* are a second category, those who may not have been sold, but have simply fled from forcible necessity (*anagkaiês hupo chreious*), without reference to laws and judges. They were not literally in chains, else they could not escape, but the threat of chains was real; they lived in constant fear of enslavement. Many might have become outlaws, if not

Solon the Thinker

because there were no legal standards by which to judge their cases, then because the officials or institutions necessary for a remedy were also not available to them. The exiles overseas no longer speak Attic, which, Solon must think, cuts them off from a vital aspect of being Athenian.[27] Those fleeing a late night knock on the door from a gang seeking vengeance are as much coerced as those physically hauled before a magistrate and judged – only they are forced underground or outside Attica, *personae non gratae*, without protections and in a state of legal non-existence. Solon had to bring justice to their victims, not only by correcting the laws, but by providing some means to enforce them. This would set limits to what could be done; when Solon claims that he brought back those enslaved overseas and led up those enslaved at home, he may have meant that slavery was now unenforceable under law inside Attica, and those Attic-speakers who could make it back would enjoy the result.[28]

Solon also speaks of those inside Attica holding a shameful slavery (*tous douliên aeikea echontas*), who are 'tremblers' (*tromeomenous*) before the whims of their masters (36.14). Their palpable fear of hands-on, physical force is a psychological attack on their freedom through a threat of force, and may hearken back to the fear that a soldier has of the enemy, now become fear of the masters of slaves.[29] This has important implications for the nature of the forcible necessity. Both *anagkê* and *chreios* are terms with wide meanings. Tandy and Neale, discussing Hesiod's *Works and Days*, refer to Louis Gernet for four basic ideas related to *chreios*: constraint of a debtor; obligation in which default is punishable; the thing that obligates; and matters of propriety, duty or religious observation.[30] In these terms, the obligation in Solon's passage could refer to a debt that is understood beforehand; a disputed obligation that was improperly imposed on the victim; or an obligation claimed under a prerogative that is derived from customs. In fragment 13.29, Solon describes one, presumably a debtor, who receives justice now, another who gets it later, and others who flee.[31] But the fundamental issue here, for an unprotected farmer facing true chattel slavery, is not 'debts', but rather his vulnerability to the use of physical force, against his person and the persons of his family. The threat is the 'forcible necessity' created by the capacity of a pursuer to enslave his target by force.

In her study of *hekôn*- words, Gail Ann Rickert has properly classified *anagkê* ('necessity') passages that do not expressly include the term *bia* ('physical force') with passages involving the direct use of force, if it can be shown that force underlies the necessity. Rickert shows three categories in which actions occur under *anagkê*: first, circumstances of *bia*, meaning force or the threat of hands-on physical coercion; second, 'compelling social practices'; and third, 'unavoidable prevailing circumstances'.[32] *Bia* and threats of *bia* are instances of force that are more specific than *anagkê*. Solon knows that threats of force can underlie the necessity that compels a man, even when not sanctioned by a decision of an official or an

7. 'I set them free'

institution. Those who suffer such extra-legal attacks – those exiled, in hiding or taken perforce – are in a state of servitude that had neither legal status nor name; they are simply in fear or in flight from the forcible necessity of others. The essence of slavery is hands-on force (or threat of force) from other men, without regard for the laws or legal judgment. A trembler (*tromeomenos*) before a master is in a nightmare world without escape; for Solon's laws to have any meaning for him, he would need a means to enforce them in his own case.

Solon's concern for those exiled or enslaved by forcible necessity is evidence that he recognized an unrestrained lawlessness throughout Attica, a lawlessness that was derived from traditional mores that had been twisted into unjust forms, and that created crushing pressures upon powerless men. Local strongmen, aligned in familial and territorial terms, enforced their versions of justice in Attica in terms consistent with their traditional claims to authority, acting outside of legal institutions as we know them. They might fill a power vacuum, dividing up Attica, acting as benefactors akin to Mafia godfathers and creating an atmosphere of fear, all the while claiming to be the protectors of those in cut off from the laws, a bizarre inversion that is common to Godfather figures.[33] Each one of them acted to gain some advantage, forming friendships and ad hoc gangs to get something from someone else. Bribing a magistrate or a local bigshot to get a desired judgment, knocking down an opponent's door in the middle of the night, and pursuing a debtor running for his life were the paths to an unseemly slavery. Small raiding parties or gangs, sometimes led by a local person with power (*dunamis*), might have terrorized the countryside.

It is vital to recognize the presence of non-institutionalized slavery in wild and woolly Attica. Any analysis that considers slavery only in legal terms is suspect, as is any overly formalized view of institutional authorities in Attica. Solon needed to bring new ideals and institutions into a countryside where only customary prerogatives existed. This would have led to some very unpleasant encounters, when the *polis* began to impose (or re-impose) its authority over Attica, and to make the idea of law real outside of Athens. The establishment of circuit courts throughout Attica by Pisistratus comes to mind.[34] Not everyone would have accepted this new understanding of *dikê*. Solon and his adversaries could have approached this issue from different moral assumptions, and, as in any such clash, each side would proclaim the other to be unjust. To the enslavers, Solon might have represented the overthrow of legal order and thus an improper challenge to existing prerogatives; they could claim that the slavery was just and that refusing to enforce it threatened the foundations of justice. An exemplar here is Athena in Aeschylus' *Eumenides* 731, lambasted by the Furies as a 'younger god' who is overturning the ancient order in favour of a new tribunal of deliberation. But to Solon the Furies have it wrong. The foundations of *dikê* must be guarded against the threats of *hubris* from any age, and slavery is the greatest threat of all.

Solon also describes slavery in two other ways, each fraught with unclarity: the slavery of the *polis*, and the slavery of the earth. Solon condemns the slavery (*doulosunê*) that befalls the *polis* when hubristic men take over and become tyrants. The only secure precedent for *doulosunê* is *Odyssey* 22.423, where the nurse Eurycleia tells Odysseus that she has trained the women to bear the yoke of service (*doulosunên anexesthai*). The phrase may mean 'to abstain from bed slavery'.[35] The slavery of the *polis* at 4.18 is an aspect of the 'inescapable wound' that comes to the entire *polis*, which includes the literal 'many were poor sold in chains' (in lines 23-5). That Solon sees slavery and tyranny as closely connected is clear from other fragments; the *dêmos* falls into the slavery of tyranny by its ignorance at 9.4; and he lambastes his audience at 11.4 that 'you yourselves' hold a dreadful slavery because 'each one of you' granted arms to the tyrants. Although Solon's audience was not physically in chains, they were subject to the force wielded by the bodyguards they had granted to the tyrants. The end result of the slavery of tyranny is also hands-on physical coercion by an armed group, which controls public areas and defends the tyrant(s) from enemies. It is difficult to get more specific about the slavery of the *polis* in Solon, but force – and the fear that follows – are central. Once he attains the ability (*dunamis*) to do so, the tyrant imposes his will over the public areas of the *polis* unconditionally, by force.[36] Taking the *polis–oikos* distinction seriously, for Solon perhaps slavery in a narrow sense refers to the coercion of other men with respect to their land and homes, while tyranny over the *polis* places public discourse, *polis* rituals and citizen interactions – the internal energy of the *polis* – under a tyrant's club.

To end the slavery of the earth on Attica, Solon tore up the boundary stones, and expressed the result as 'Black Earth ... earlier enslaved, now free', using a participle of *douleuô* at 36.7. Solon's is the first use of any form of this verb; the passage remains without definitive interpretation, but it must relate, either literally or metaphorically, to claims against land.[37] Taken literally, the boundary stones – whether inscribed markers or simply pieces of rock – could have been claims against people farming in the marked areas, showing that they owed crops to another (although 'mortgage' or conditional sale remains highly anachronistic). The stones could represent attempts by the *dêmos* to redistribute the land of the aristocracy; claims by the aristocrats against small plot-holders or even sacred areas; or (dubiously) conflicts over border lands between Megara and Athens.[38] Solon would have had to tear up the boundary stones that divided off the territories and ended someone's freedom. A metaphorical interpretation would be no less strong if considered in relation to the sacred roots of *Dikê* spoken in poem 4. To draw a straight boundary on the ground and re-establish the foundations of *dikê* would be precisely the kind of claim that Solon might make at a trial, or in response to a trial: to bond his laws with *dikê* and the ancestral land. Whatever he intended, the

7. 'I set them free'

slavery of the *polis* and the slavery of the earth must refer, ultimately, to the kind of hands-on physical coercion (or credible threat of coercion) that is opposed to *dikê*, and the fear this engenders for a man who should be free.

This brings us to the opposite of all this: freedom, Solon's vastly under-discussed but sublimely important political innovation. Solon's own claim is succinct: 'I set them free', a proclamation of his own goodness and his future victory. Such a claim in and of itself may not refer to political freedom; how many times in history have tyrants proclaimed the freedom of their peoples in order to establish a dictatorship? But as a political idea, and apart from a historical reconstruction of Solon's own actions, Solon's thought can be understood only in relation to his other ideas, especially the foil of slavery. The issue of Greek freedom is co-extensive with the strong value placed by Greek men on being able to act for their own purposes, within the limits of necessity, the avoidance of *hubris* and the honours due to the gods.[39] Solon's views of freedom reflect the fundamental distinction between a man whose person is subject to the forcible necessity of another, and one who is not under such compulsion. 'I set them free' is centred upon Attic-speaking men, who must be protected against those who act with *hubris*, through *polis*-wide written laws that are enforced alike. Solon's claim – in context with a *polis* under *Eunomiê*, centred on *dikê* and written laws, enforced alike for the purpose of ending hands-on slavery – is a statement of *political* freedom, unattested before him in extant evidence, and a matter of the highest importance.

The first question is whether Solon has an explicit concept of 'freedom' at all. No use of the abstract *eleutheria* is attested in Solon's fragments. Direct references to freedom are expressed adjectively, as *Gê eleutherê*, 'free earth', and *eleutherous*, 'free men'. Men who are now *eleutherous* are contrasted with the earlier (*enthade*) slaves of 36.13-15 (*douliên ... echontas*), and those who are *eleutherous* must be those who are neither among the *pollous prathentas*, 'many sold', in 4.23-4 and 36.9, nor fleeing from forcible necessity. All of this suggests that an *eleutheros* state was understood in opposition to enslavement, as 'not enslaved' or literally 'set loose'. By virtue of Solon's two uses of adjective forms of *eleutheros*, the contrasts with 'slavery', and his portraits of men sold in chains, it is valid to infer that Solon had an implicit idea of *eleutheria* in the sense of personal freedom from the forcible necessity of other men. His implicit idea is one that has not been fully conceptualized; he speaks explicitly of 'free men' but never says 'freedom'. But they are free men in a special, heretofore unprecedented sense: they are free politically.

It is a serious matter for political thought that Solon's first use of these terms as *political* freedom should get so little emphasis. This point cannot be overstressed: Solon's is the first statement of political freedom in all of western thought.[40] His special sense of freedom is its political nature. The word *eleutheria* exists in texts prior to Solon, but is not understood in distinction from political despotism. The four 'day of freedom' and 'cup of freedom' phrases in the *Iliad* exhaust Homer's uses of *eleuther-* forms. The Trojans who cry for *eleutheria* want to drive off foreign armies, in order to return to despotic rule under their king. Freedom means living under Priam's rule, and slavery means being taken in personal bondage to work in a far-off land. This is not political freedom; it is independence from foreign takeover.[41] *Eleuther-* terms are otherwise used only rarely in poets before Solon. In Alcaeus and Theognis the term is intended to distinguish those with birth and / or wealth from others, and must be understood in the context of the aristocratic *ethos* they are defending.[42]

For Solon a free man is an Attic-speaking male whose personal autonomy *inside* the *polis* is protected from attacks by his fellows. Solon's poem 36 is the first statement in western thought to base a political order on a distinct idea of justice under enforced written laws, promoted by persuasion rather than divine commandment, and legitimated by a claim to have set its inhabitants free. Paradoxically – but consistent with the historical development of the concept of freedom after that of slavery – Solon says virtually nothing about what freedom actually is; his goal is to end its opposites, slavery and tyranny. The physical restraint of those, both *agathoi* and *kakoi*, who would use hands-on force against Attic-speakers to separate them from their land is of central importance. Poem 36 continues:

> ταῦτα μὲν κράτει
> ὁμοῦ βίην τε καὶ δίκην ξυναρμόσας
> ἔρεξα᾽ καὶ διῆλθον ὡς ὑπεσχόμην·
> θεσμοὺς δ᾽ ὁμοίως τῷ κακῷ τε κἀγαθῷ
> εὐθεῖαν εἰς ἕκαστον ἁρμόσας δίκην
> ἔγραψα.
>
> Solon 36.15-20

> By my own power,
> fitting together force with justice,
> these things I did, and I came through as I promised.
> And statutes alike to the base man and to the noble
> fitting straight justice onto each man's case
> these I wrote.

The slavery and civil strife in poem 4 are the violence that follows the silence of *Dikê*, when the *bia* of individual *hubris* is unleashed without the restraining power of *dikê*. To end the conflicts, Solon in poem 36 empowers *dikê* to defend herself, by harmoniously joining *bia* together with *dikê* (*biên te kai dikên xunharmosas*). This depends upon reading *homou* in line 16, 'merging together both justice and force'.[43] Solon unites two mythological houses, two estranged sides of Zeus' family that are distinguished in Hesiod but not directly allied.[44] Solon's implicit sense of *harmonia*, a later

7. 'I set them free'

term derived from *harmozô*, respects the integrity of the two parts being joined. Force and justice remain distinct, but the merger creates a new whole in the 'straight justice' that is *dikê* enforced in particular cases. But like the joining of discrete pieces of wood together into a single ship, each piece remains unique, and each joint has its own requirements.[45] On the one hand, Solon's *dikê* is no longer impotent in particular judgments, but is physically protected – her own foundations are guarded – through the *bia* of the magistrates. The days of negotiated, voluntary decisions as the end-all of justice are passing away. Conversely, people cannot use *bia* in any way they wish; the *stasis* is ended when the force wielded by a human being in any particular case will be guided by *dikê*, not his own interpretation of his prerogatives.

It is Solon's claim to be guided by *dikê* – meaning *dikê* as he understands it – that distinguishes his own use of force from that of the tyrant, who elevates *bia* into the dominant fact of his rule and uses *dikê* as a rhetorical tool of deception while claiming to 'straighten' the *hubris* in the *polis*. Every explicit reference to a tyrant in Solon, and every implicit reference to a tyranny, is connected to *bia*.[46] In fragments 32.2 and 34.8, Solon rejects 'tyranny by force'. In the former he proclaims that by rejecting tyranny perforce he will seem to be superior to others; in the latter he rejects both tyranny perforce and 'equal lots' for the base men and the good Athens. In 9.3 the slavery (*doulosunê*) of a tyrant would have strengthened the idea of force, especially as connected to the *menos* 'force' of a cloud in the previous lines, and at 13.23.[47] Solon's claim to have restrained the people properly – his use of his own *kratos* to write *thesmoi* means that he has imposed them on Athens – means that force is not the factor that distinguishes a tyrant from a legitimate ruler, but rather how and for what purpose each uses force. Martin Ostwald notes: 'in the case of θεσμός ['statute'] the etymological relation to τίθημι ['I place'] supports what we find in actual usage: it is a thing imposed by a higher power' that makes the statute an obligation. The lawgiver is thus 'standing apart from and above the persons upon whom his law is binding'.[48] A tyrant also stands above, but uses force for his own short-term aggrandizement, while in Solon's conception the lawgiver merges force with *dikê* and protects the sacred foundations of *Dikê*. The tyrant usurps the internal power of the *polis*; Solon affirms and strengthens it, by re-ordering it according to *dikê*. The central problem with the tyrant is the noetic flaws in both him and his followers, and their conceptions of what needs straightening and why: their failure to recognize the inevitability of natural *dikê* and the consequences for the *polis*.

The empowerment of *dikê* requires a second 'joining'; his 'statutes (*thesmous*) written alike to the base man and to the noble' are used in 'fitting (*harmosas*) straight justice onto each man's case'. The *polis* becomes *dikaiê* when *dikê* is protected through a double harmonization brought to bear on each case; *dikê* as revealed in the statutes is the intermediary between force and particular judgments. The differences between Solon's views of *dikê* in poems 4 and 36 demonstrate different aspects of his thinking about *dikê* and the *polis*. In poem 4 *Eunomiê* is central; in a dispute, an official's judgment will be straight or not based on his acceptance of the moderation that is the essence of *Eunomiê*, and the outcome will depend primarily upon the state of mind of the parties. A magistrate's point of reference is unwritten customs, either his own view of the case or the pressure of those around him. The relevance of the laws to every situation might not have been obvious, but *justice* was probably an ever-present issue, and a certain general sense of justice could have guided the proceedings. Greek laws were not, strictly speaking, codes, but rather lists of particular rules. If a rule was not listed or not known, then the applicability of the laws to a given situation would not be obvious.[49] The two sides would come to agreement because they remember the verse about *Eunomiê*; the roughness of their dispute is smoothed by their considered moderation, enhanced by recall of Solon's maxims, and implemented by the straight decision of the official. *Eunomiê* is distributed among the population, and the dispute is resolved because the judge and the litigants act as *Dikê* requires. But this is not a situation in which the judgments of officials have the guidance of laws.

In poem 36, the specific factor that keeps *bia* and *dikê* joined to 'each man's case' is the written *thesmoi*, the new point of focus for the magistrate or the assembled jurors. It is in the written laws that the general dictates of *Dikê* receive particular expression, and she becomes relevant to each man's life. Solon offers a generalized idea of justice in line 36.16 – he *did* merge *dikê* with *bia* – and then, in line 19, shows how this is to be applied to particular cases – he *wrote* statutes alike to each. Solon wrote 'impartial justice' in poem 36, not 'straight judgments' (as the officials provide in poem 4), and the change in language reflects a fundamental difference in approach between the *dikê* that is written into laws and the customary *dikê* of officials.[50] In poem 36 Solon is in effect reducing the general principles of *dikê* to the variations in each particular case – as he had reduced the inescapable wound on the *polis* to each one of us in poem 4 – all the while preserving the foundations of *Dikê*. As a causal chain reaches from our psychic states through the overt condition of the *polis* back to each one of us in poem 4, so in poem 36 *Dikê* reaches each of us through written laws, applied alike to the base and the noble. *Eunomiê* is still a precondition of *polis* life – she constitutes the sacred roots of *dikê* in each man's mind, which will dispose him to follow the laws – but she no longer disposes men to follow the sense of justice or customs found in each man's own mind, but rather the *dikê* inscribed in the statutes. The new integration of the *polis* is centred on the written laws, enshrined in public view. Athens as a *kosmos* takes on a particular shape given the laws that govern individual cases and the general commitment to follow them; the nature of the *kosmos* is in the nature of its parts.

7. 'I set them free'

Completing what we have of poem 36, Solon's own use of the goad, *to kentron*, as a restraint demonstrates the proper use of power that Solon claimed, which must not waver with the winds of any particular case:

κέντρον δ' ἄλλος ὡς ἐγὼ λαβών,
κακοφραδής τε καὶ φιλοκτήμων ἀνήρ,
οὐκ ἂν κατέσχε δῆμον· εἰ γὰρ ἤθελον
ἃ τοῖς ἐναντίοισιν ἥνδανεν τότε,
αὖτις δ' ἃ τοῖσιν οὕτεροι φρασαίατο,
πολλῶν ἂν ἀνδρῶν ἥδ' ἐχηρώθη πόλις.
τῶν οὕνεκ' ἀλκὴν πάντοθεν ποιεόμενος
ὡς ἐν κυσὶν πολλῇσιν ἐστράφην λύκος.

Solon 36.20-7

But had another man than I taken the goad,
an evil-thinking and power-hungry man,
he would not have restrained the people.
For if I acquiesced to whatever things were pleasing to my enemies,
and then shifted to what the other side thought,
this city would be widowed of many men.
On account of these things, making a defence in all directions,
I stood, as a wolf among many hounds.

The bad-thinking, loot-loving man of poem 36 cannot restrain the people precisely because he himself is unrestrained. When he caters first to one party and then to the other, he gives up the general strictures of the written statutes and relies upon his own free-floating interpretation of any particular case. This is how he implements the short-range view of his own actions that Solon caricatured in fragment 33. The tyrant is in the *dusnomic* world of poem 4 – prior to *Eunomiê* – in which each man's decision was limited only by his own whims. But Solon is now in the world of poem 36, in which the goad is merged harmoniously with justice through written laws, and in which even the rulers must be restrained from stepping outside its bounds, as they wield the goad to restrain others.

To understand *kentron*, Sandys and Linforth agree on a cross-reference to Sophocles: 'having taken the goad in his hands he compelled the city'. Sandys notes that it is a 'symbol of strong control'.[51] The Homeric use of the *kentron* is as a physical means of compulsion, as in the horse-goad of *Iliad* 23.387. This use carried over into the classical period, as the might of Zeus and an incentive in Aeschylus, and an instrument of torture in Herodotus. The goad became the sting of bees in Aristophanes; of scorpions in Aristotle's biology; of people in Euripides; and of Socrates according to Plato. Sophocles spoke of the chariot goad and the smart of a gadfly's sting. In the fifth century Eupolis had attributed a *kentron* to Pericles, indicating that the speaker has a lasting effect upon the audience. Euripides portrayed the reverse in a democracy: the poor enviously hurling their stings at the rich, deceived by their leaders. The man who stings opportunisti-

Solon the Thinker

cally may be read in Demosthenes, who has his fourth-century opponent 'carrying himself through the market, like a serpent or a scorpion with his stinger erect'. By the mid-fifth century, the portrayal of orators and democrats as using goads was well established.[52]

Solon's use of the *kentron* in his verse as a means of restraining the people may be a double metaphorical innovation. In addition to using the goad to symbolize physical restraint rather than compulsion forward, a development related to the growth of conscience as an internal voice of restraint, he may also imply the use of a stinger (a 'persuasion') in his speech, which goads an audience onto the correct path. Solon may be a bridge between Homer and Plato, from the physical horse-goad to the sting of a drone as oral persuasion. Solon knows that a wily use of the tongue can lead to the elevation and enrichment of a tyrannical ruler, who gains power by the deceitful word but maintains it by force (fragment 11). 'An evil-thinking and power-hungry man' in line 21, can be compared to *Iliad* 23.483 as an imputation of 'bad in counsel' through malice rather than folly.[53] To avoid this, the goad must become an agent of restraint that is limited to speech, wielded under just laws, and used to prevent the unjust thoughts and actions that threaten the *polis*.

There have been many Near Eastern and Hebraic examples of positive restraints, and nearly all such laws were written in the form of 'if ... then ...' statements, often with complex logical relationships between qualifying statements.[54] All laws purport to project in the future, to say what will result if something happens now. It is possible that such laws were first used to restrain accusers in order to prevent the rise of feuds and to subordinate vengeance to an outside controls, a view that assumes there is seldom a lack of energy towards vengeance.[55] But Hebraic tribal laws were legitimated by a single transcendant God, and Mesopotamian laws pointed to the figure of the warlord. One searches in vain for the kind of approach that bases the laws on freedom in the political sense, proclaims in writing the evil of taking one's fellows into slavery, purports to extend its restraints to the rulers themselves, and justifies this not by divine commandment, but rather by the natural consequences of improper actions.

Solon's fitting together harmoniously *bia* with *dikê* can be read pessimistically, as his appropriation of tyrannical discourse for the purpose of maintaining his own rule. Fragment 30, the injunction to obey the magistrate whether just or unjust, is even more explicit; it demands obedience even if one thinks that a specific judgment is wrong:

ἀρχῶν ἄκουε καὶ δίκαια κἄδικα

Solon 30

Hearken to the officials, both right and wrong[56]

7. 'I set them free'

But the willingness to acquiesce, in a political context, to a judgment that one thinks is wrong, is vital to accepting the rule of law. The alternative is to get one's spear – or a gang – and take care of the issue by private force – to return to city to *dusnomia*. Newly created laws may go against accepted prerogatives – and the values at their base – that have been accorded the legitimacy of tradition and a sense of righteous propriety. A losing party may genuinely feel that he has been the victim of an injustice – an understandable response in a society in which privileged positions and important values are under attack – and he may think that his freedom is at stake. The verse recognizes the need to put aside one's demands for vengeance, to quell the anger that rises in one's *thumos*, and to forgo private vengeance, even if one disagrees with the decision. A person must accept the judgments of a magistrate, even if he thinks them wrong, because the alternative is to turn revenge actions back over to each one of us, to return to the inevitable contests of force that plague a city under *Dusnomiê*, to drive *Dikê* into silent retribution, and to invite the return of slavery perforce.

The *thesmoi* were imposed, of course; in the archaic period the term meant a written law, and contrasted with an unwritten *nomos*.[57] Solon imposed the *thesmoi* by his own *kratos*, 'power' or 'authority', a term that a tyrant might also use.[58] The seeming paradox of his having 'imposed' laws over the *polis* may be resolved by stressing their legitimacy according to *dikê*, the human responsibility for the order in the *polis*, and the restraint that Solon accepts for himself under those laws. Solon's *kratos* becomes 'authority' – 'power' that is not only legally proper, but also consistent with a deeper sense of right and wrong – to which even the lawgiver must defer.[59] For Solon in poem 36, the legitimacy is clearly focused on his setting enslaved men free. Aristotle commented on the early development of the *polis*, that it exists 'by nature' (*phusei*) because it arises out of the natural union of males and females, yet 'the first man to construct a *polis* deserves credit for conferring very great benefits. For as man is the best of all animals when he has reached his full development, so he is worst of all when divorced from law and justice'.[60] A *polis* that develops naturally, from the coalescence of families in a geographic place, yet without a shared sense of justice, will fall into conflict. It is only when the lawgiver brings a single form of *dikê* that accords with life in the *polis*, and the people make it a part of their lives, that the lawgiver's conception of justice becomes the order by which the *polis* functions. A sculptor forms the Sunium Kouros, but once he leaves the scene the product stands of its own power. So it is when the lawgiver goes into exile, and swears his people to follow the laws.[61]

The need for restraint before the laws in a political *kosmos* is offered in a later explanation of the status of revenge killings, stated by Democritus and showing the relevance of this issue into the fifth century:

Solon the Thinker

κατὰ νόμους τοὺς πατρίους κτείνειν πολέμιον ἐν παντὶ κόσμῳ, ἐν ᾧ μὴ νόμους ἀπείργει

Deomocritus B259 = Taylor D123 excerpt

According to the ancient laws (*kata nomous*) it is right to kill an enemy in every political order (*en panti kosmôi*), unless the law (*nomous*) forbids it

This passage counterpoises the wide traditional norms with the narrower constraints of a particular law. The traditional sense is closer to Hesiod's *nomos* of animals – who do not have *dikê* in them – than the order proper to human beings; it leaves vengeance to one's individual decision.[62] By prescribing a law to forbid such a killing, the passage presumes a subordination of individual prerogatives to laws, an idea that might not have been as omnipresent in archaic Attica as Democritus implies. This is the meaning of Solon's merger of *dikê* with *bia*: the wide ancient *nomos* must be narrowed to a new normative standard that subsumes traditionally accepted revenge actions and is given physical form. If every one of us is free to kill an enemy as we wish, there can be neither freedom nor peace. Solon takes early steps in this direction, narrowing the terms by which *hubris* is understood, implanting the ideal of moderation in Athenian thought, and writing laws that preclude slavery as means to maintain traditional prerogatives.

Solon's merging of *dikê* together harmoniously with *bia* relates directly to his claims to have 'brought the people together', into 'our *polis*, we', and to the idea of *sunoikism* that would capture the Athenian mind in later centuries. Solon's first use of *summartureô* 'witness corroboratively' may expand the range of *polis*-unification into a reconciliation with the divine, and establish a claim to legitimacy with enormous import for later history. But the centre of the political integration has become the written laws – the power of the wily orator has been made subservient to the stone, and the literary has been unified with the legal – which objectifies the order and provides an external, immutable point of focus for all to see. The order now is not longer merely traditional, the subject of memory or a subjective interpretation of *dikê*, although later Athenians will have to make their own entreaties to Memory when their democracy loses its sense of restraint, and they need to re-inscribe their laws. Solon's laws will eventually become a legitimizing point of focus for a very resilient, yet highly mutable, tradition.

But has this reading of Solon's poetry as archaic political ideas been too lenient in its judgment of Solon the ruler? Is it not possible that all of this has been rhetoric – and nothing but rhetoric – to legitimate his place as a tyrant over Athens? Don't all tyrants – from Hammurabi to Pol Pot – call upon 'justice' to legitimate their positions? Of course. A historical reconstruction of Solon's actions is outside the scope of this book. But the important point is that to judge Solon as a tyrant – a man who wielded

7. 'I set them free'

power for his own sake, maintaining order and his own position by force and deception – one must use some version of Solon's identifications of what a tyrant is. One will need to use Solon's intellectual achievements – his descriptions of *dikê*, and the tyrant – to defeat him. It is only by accepting Solon's differentiation of a tyrant from a legitimate, just, moderate ruler that we can develop the very idea of a tyrant, and then ask whether his words could be rhetorical ploys to establish just such rule. Should we do so, then let us give credit to Solon the Thinker for the first firm description of a tyrant – and the first picture of a lawful alternative – that we have.

In the end, it is not likely that Solon introduced the idea of freedom to Athens. In his verses he expresses no need to justify his freeing the slaves, but rather claims self-evident virtue in having done so. Freedom was valued in Athens, and it is the value that the Athenians saw in freedom that would allow a tyrant to hijack the term and use it to gain popularity and power. The lack of arguments *for* freedom is telling; people do not argue for that which is already accepted.[63] (It is possible that Solon's verses justifying *eleutheria* were not saved by later writers, but this is unlikely given the importance those writers placed on *eleutheria*.) In contrast, *hêsuchia* and its beneficial effects required conscious justification by Solon. If accidents of preservation have not misled us, Solon established a new ideal of moderation as a personal virtue in the *polis* by disavowing the violent prerogatives of the past. *Hêsuchia* was not yet a hurrah word; it required a certain understanding and practice if it was to lose its connotations of shame, and become a value to the people of Athens. If this is so, then it is in moderation – a sense of restraint especially before the laws – that Solon was the true cultural creator. In terms of freedom, he may have given voice to that which people already knew, and longed to regain. In connecting free men to a lawful political order he made a first-rank identification in the history of political thinking.

Solon's moral exhortations and his descriptions of how the laws connected justice to the *polis* were premonitions of how the later Athenians would view their *polis* and themselves. Solon does not connect his idea of freedom to participation in civic governance – so I have not discussed it – but it is an implication of his ideas. It is no accident that Solon came back into vogue, at the end of the fifth and the middle of the fourth centuries BC, precisely at those times when the Athenians needed to restrain their democracy by rejuvenating their laws. Solon's verses provided an ideal by which the Athenians could address not only those laws and customs that threatened the *polis*, but also the attitudes and practices that allowed powerful men to take matters into their own hands. In doing so they twisted his words, fabricated his positions, called on him out of context and used him in unseemly ways – but they did it in a political context that maintained the most stable, freedom-conscious city that the world had yet seen, until conquered from without. If it is true that vital aspects of his poems are lost – perhaps evidence that he thought Zeus was directly involved in administering justice in poem 4, or claims that Athens might be fated for destruction – the historical importance of Solon for the later Greeks is in what they preserved. In the end, that is, of course, all we have. We have what was important to them.

Solon's final legacy embraces a dichotomy. On the one hand, he tells us, we are beings of the moment, unable to see to the end of all things, subject to *Moira*. Given such fatalism, the great may become small, and the small great, as Herodotus would say – and there is not much any one of us can do about it. On the other hand, the *polis* is a *kosmos* that functions by its own internal power – the energy in its citizens – and, as Aeschylus would have Athena say in his *Eumenides*, Athens will not be destroyed, as long as its people remain loyal to the laws. The *polis* is man's to control, and he has the freedom to do so, within the limits of *Dikê;* this is how the gods may be honoured, and Athens preserved. I can make no claim to have penetrated into the form that Solon holds his ideas – his mythic context and pre-scientific view of the world are too foreign – but there is a meaning to his verses that is available to us, and that takes on a greater power when we consider what Athens later became. Solon, the self-styled anti-tyrant, whose specific actions are forever hidden, merges force with justice in his laws, the new centre of the *polis-kosmos*, a haven for men otherwise trapped in a world they cannot control.

Appendix
Glossary of terms used by Solon

Greek	Transliteration	Description
ἀγών	agôn	Contest, competition. Athens was agonistic, i.e. competitive.
αἶσα	aisa	Dispensation, from the gods. Related to *moira*. Fate in the sense of one's lot in life, inevitable but not deterministic.
ἀνομία	anomia	Without order. See *Eunomiê* and *Dusnomiê*.
ἀστός	astos	Citizen, meaning no more than a townsman or a member of the community. Always plural in Solon: *astoi*.
ἄτη	atê	Has two primary senses: either blindness (a psychic condition), or calamity (a physical condition) that results from a psychic flaw. Solon has not distinguished psychic calamity from material calamity with a specific term. Context is the guide.
βίος	bios	In particular, earning a living; more widely, the means of life, course of life, or lifestyle. In Solon it is the pursuit of material values to maintain one's life.
γῆ	gê	When capitalized, the personified 'Earth' as goddess. In lower case, the earth as the soil.
δίκη	dikê	Justice. *Dikê* has 3 basic meanings for Solon. First, the retribution that results from improper actions. Second, the procedures by which such retribution is decided. Third, a calm state, as in the sea (analogous to the *polis*).
δόξα	doxa	Two meanings: Expectation, the Homeric meaning, 13.34. Good reputation, 13.4.

Appendix

Greek	Transliteration	Description
δουλίη	*douliê*	Slavery, primarily of the *polis*. Ionic form of *douleia*. The slavery of the earth is referred to by *douleuousa*, from the verb *douleuô*.
δουλοσύνη	*doulosunê*	Slavery, of men. Linked to *polemos* and *stasis*.
Δυσνομίη	*Dusnomiê*	Disorder, or Bad Order. Ionic form of Δυσνομία. Opposed to Εὐνομίη. The single citation in Solon is personified.
ἐλεύθερος	*eleutheros*	Free (adjective), used of men and the earth.
Εὐνομίη	*Eunomiê*	'Good Order' in the *polis*. The Ionic form of Εὐνομία. Opposed to Δυσνομίη. The single use in Solon is personified.
ἡσυχίη	*hêsuchiê*	Calmness, or stillness. Ionic form of ἡσυχία. Opposed to *hubris*.
θεσμός	*thesmos*	Written statute.
θυμός	*thumos*	A psychic quality: heart, chest, seat of emotions rather than rational deliberation. See *psuchê*.
κόρος	*koros*	Excess, both psychically and materially. Excess is satiety that exceeds the state of one's *noos*, leading to the action of *hubris*.
κόσμος	*kosmos*	An arrangement of aspects of reality, fit for a purpose, and understood in terms of an underlying order. For the Presocratic philosophers, all of reality was a *kosmos*.
κῦδος	*kudos*	Glory, renown. For the ruler of Solioi, 19.2.
μοῖρα	*moira*	One's lot in life: one's material allotment, an onrushing fate, or one's allotted death.
νόος	*noos*	A psychic quality: mind. An insight into a situation that is deeper than perception; or, a mental disposition. A flawed or imperfect *noos* is an improper understanding that leads to *hubris, stasis*.
οἶκος	*oikos*	The family farm, or home. Solon uses it only once, in the form of *oikade*, meaning 'to the *oikos*'.

Glossary of terms used by Solon

Greek	Transliteration	Description
ὄλβος	olbos	Prosperity, or wealth. Related to *ploutos* and *chrêmata*.
πλοῦτος	ploutos	Material wealth or riches. Related to *olbos* and *chrêmata*.
πόλεμος	polemos	War. Solon distinguishes it, in a single citation, from *stasis* by a reference to the tribes, *phulai*. Linked with *stasis* and *doulosunê*.
πόλις	polis	The Greek city-state, i.e. the politically autonomous Greek community. In Solon it always refers to a specific community, usually Athens. Poem 19 refers to Solioi, on Cyprus. Poem 4, line one begins with a possible reference to the high city, the Acropolis, of Athens, where Athena held her hand over Athens. All other passages refer to Athens.
στάσις	stasis	Civil strife, viewed as a conflict between men or as a disease coming over the *polis*. Linked with *doulosunê* and *polemos*.
τυραννίς	turannis	Tyranny, rule for short-range gain by force. *Turannou* is disputed in 9.3, possibly equated with monarchy by force. Linked with *doulosunê* and *bia*.
τύχη	tuchê	Luck. *Tuchên agathên* is in fragment 31; and *suntuchiên agathên* in 13.70, good luck, given by the gods. 'Chance' may evolve as a secular explanation related to *moira*. The verb form *tuchein*, 'to accomplish,' is at 36.2.
ὕβρις	hubris	Arrogant assault. Psychically, an overbearing attitude. In action, an egregious assault on another.
φρήν	phrên	A psychic quality, *phrên* is linked to counsels, and to action, thus serving loosely as a will to act.
χρήματα	chrêmata	Material goods or (anachronistically) money. Related to *ploutos* and *olbos*.

Appendix

Greek	Transliteration	Description
ψυχή	*psuchê*	Life, or life-force. The English 'psychic' is used in this book with reference to intellectual, emotional, and psychological factors, such as *noos, thumos,* and *phrên*. All such factors are only loosely differentiated in archaic thought. It can also mean 'life,' which is what one risks when going to sea in pursuit of *kerdos* 'profit'.

Notes

Introduction

1. 594/3 is the nominal date of his archonship; see Wallace 1983, but Miller 1969. Podlecki 1975 exposes the problems in dating his travels and laws. Perhaps Case 1888 has been right all along: Solon's archonship of 594 must be distinguished from post-570 his legislation. A separation of thirty years between the 'Good Order' of poem 4 and the written statutes of poem 36 would add an important line of development to his ideas – but the chronology is lost.

2. For the *hepta sophoi*, Pl. *Prt.* 343a, *Letter* II to Dionysius, 311a; Plu. *Sol.* 3; 12.3-4; *Ath.* 463c, 781d. Martin 1993 on the Seven Sages as singers. Burn 1960: 207-9. Zeller 1931: 18-19. Cicero *De Leg.* 2.64. For Madison, see Hamilton, Madison and Jay, *Federalist* #38. Wilson 1994 5: 27. Modern veneration for the Seven Sages borders on the religious; Cavarnos 1996.

3. Commentaries by Noussia 2001a, and Mülke 2002, in Italian and German respectively, should be consulted at every step. Noussia's inclusion of later iconographical material says much about Solon's reception. But for the state of the art in sculpture for his own time, I look at the Sunium Kouros. Earlier commentaries: Linforth 1919; Masaracchia 1958 (in Italian). Other full-length works include Freeman 1926, Woodhouse 1938 and Anhalt 1993. Almeida 2003 connects Solon to classical archaeology. Irwin 2005a mines the influences of 'martial exhortation elegy' in poem 4. Published too late to be considered here is a volume from a conference organized by Josine Blok and André Lardinois: 'Solon: New Historical and Philological Perspectives', in Soeterbeeck, the Netherlands, 11-15 Dec. 2003 (E.J. Brill, 2006). Gerber 1991 offers a bibliography.

4. Lattimore 1947: 175 n. 38; Parker 1998. Parker 1983: 14 and n. 60 connects Solon 4 and 11.1-2 to Old Comedy: the gods are 'decent sorts' and Solon 4 is an 'influential text'.

5. Balot 2001: 76-7 infers competitiveness from the archaeological record.

6. Henderson 1982: 21, n. 4, n. 7. Rudberg 1952; Linforth 1919: 28 for Solon as the first user for literary purposes of the Attic language.

7. Almeida 2003: 1 n. 1 evaluates the poems against archaeological material. Linforth 1919 holds that historical narratives must be validated against the poems.

8. The scepticism of Roebuck 2001: 38, that there is 'no conclusive evidence that there ever was a Solon', becomes even less credible when he states as a matter of fact, three pages later, that the rise of Pisistratus was amidst a 'many-faceted and long-lasting political contest in Athens between the democratic and the oligarchic factions'.

9. Raaflaub 2004: 45.

10. Martina 1968 for collected testimonia. On Solon's laws: Ruschenbusch 1966; Gagarin 1986; Stroud 1979; Parker 1983: 35; Longo 1988; Carawan 1998. Calhoun 1927.

11. Economic treatments: Lehmann-Haupt 1912; Laistner 1923; Milne 1930, 1945; French 1956, 1963; Andrewes in *CAH* III^2.3.380f.; Rihll 1991.

12. See Murray 1993: 181-200; Manville 1990: 55-69; Osborne 1996: 217-19; van Wees 1999b. Almeida 2003 uses a class-warfare interpretation of classical archaeology to understand Solon, based on Morris 2000, 1994, 1987. Also, Snodgrass 1977, 1981, 1991; and Coldstream 1977, 1984.

13. Havelock 1978: 259.

14. Irwin 2005a: 96, 105. Kurke 1992 sees an 'aristocratic lifestyle' as in opposition to the *polis*. Similarly, Morris 1987. Hammer 2004 challenges such claims. In Xenoph. 1, the poet rejects poetry that would lead to assertions of martial excellence, and set his verses in a symposium.

15. Bowra 1938: 73-4; and Lesky 1996: 127 see no sharp thematic distinction between elegy and iambus in Solon. Anhalt 1993: 7 cautions: 'metre never fully determined subject matter', citing Gentili 1988: 33-4 and 109, and West 1974: 4, 7 and 22-4.

16. Irwin 2005a: 235 n. 85.

17. A guiding assumption of Irwin 2005a.

18. Parker 1998.

19. Griffith 1990, similar to Bowie 1993, followed by Irwin 2005a. Solmsen 1949: 82 sees contradictions in the verses as perhaps indicating complexity or a struggle by the poet.

20. Fränkel 1975: 105, 519: 3.3-2. Von Fritz 1943: 81 n. 14 uses a spiral analogy to express this point.

21. Reinhardt 1916; Stier 1928; Andrewes 1938; Abel 1943; Will 1958; Jaeger 1966; Vlastos 1995. Emlyn-Jones 1980: 107-8. Fränkel 1975: 220 for responsibility as 'imposed upon men'. In contrast, Williams 1993: 150: Solon sees humans as powerless before 'mysterious' forces. For Solon's thought as close to Homer and Hesiod, see Adkins 1985: 117; Havelock 1978: 262; Lloyd-Jones 1971: 45, 185 n. 7. Harrison 2002: 31-63 finds 'Solonian philosophy' permeating Herodotus. Croiset 1903 and Matthiessen 1994, among others, have looked to Solon for developments in law or legal thought.

22. Solmsen 1949: 113f.; Ostwald 1969: 66f.; Meier 1990 40f, 126. Ehrhardt 1959: 22-3 sees a 'politische Metaphysik' in which Solon established a *nomos*. Havelock 1957: 125-54 on Solon and Democritus. Havelock 1978: 236, building on his pre-literate assumptions, sees neither true poet nor philosopher in Solon.

23. Also Lesher 1983: 6-7. Kahn 1979: 9 for two traditions in early thought: the 'popular tradition of wisdom' represented by Solon and Bias; and the 'scientific culture' centred on Thales and Anaximander. Lloyd 1970: 14-15 compares him to Thales. On Solon and *phusis*: Myres 1927: 168-9. Solon and necessity: Guthrie 1969: 3.125-6. Snell 1982: 212 sees Solon 'on the threshold of philosophy'.

24. For instance, Hussey 1972, not mentioning Solon, states: 'The aim of this book is to introduce the reader ... to the history of ancient Greek thought between approx. 600 and 400 BC'.

25. von Fritz 1993.

26. Long 1999: 13. Hussey 1995: 530-2 on 'all things'; 542 n. 4 for ancient citations.

27. Adkins 1985: 123.

1. 'I brought the people together': Solon's *polis* as *kosmos*

1. Arist. *Ath. Pol.* 41, the summary paragraph, grants Draco no constitutional status. Perhaps the passage is a later insertion. Sealey 1976: 104, invoking K.J. Beloch, thinks he represented a snake.

Notes to pages 12-16

2. *OED* 'World' 26 has 'world-view [G. *weltanschauung*], contemplation of the world, view of life'. Lloyd 2000: 20 prefers to equate a world-view with cosmology: 'Although we speak loosely of the "worldview" of great literary figures of antiquity ... most of the authors in question were not presenting cosmological theories at all'.

3. Lloyd 1987: 178. In Solmsen 1949: 83 the children of Night beset men because 'Zeus has willed their presence'. For *hekôn* in epic see Hes. *Op.* 282 and *Th.* 232; and West's comment to *Th.* 232. Rickert 1989 for a study of *hekôn* words. This must be distinguished from Judeo-Christian conceptions: Dihle 1982: 1-25 argues against any individuated faculty of 'will' in classical Greek thought.

4. von Fritz 1943, and 1993. Sullivan 1988b: 2 n. 9 for Homeric psychic activities as individuated functions.

5. Xenoph. KRS fr. 171; tr. von Fritz 1993: 30-3. The KRS comment to fr. 173 considers A. *Supp.* 96-103, in which Zeus accomplishes things by his thought, then connects it to Solon: 'In some ways this reminds one of Solon; we cannot be quite sure that Xenophanes' view of deity was as original as it now seems to be'. Hes. *Th.* 554, 889 for deceptions followed by emotion in the *phrên* followed by action; *Op.* 455 for a man deceived and acting wrongly as *aphrênas aphneios*.

6. Hes. *Th.* 226-32 for divine woes to fall on a deceitful man. For natural rewards, see, e.g. *Op.* 280-1. M.L. West's comment on Hes. *Th.* 465 demonstrates the straitjacket shackling Hesiod's understanding: 'Kronos was not told "Zeus has a mind to overthrow you", only "you will be overthrown by your own son". It is from Hesiod's viewpoint that the overthrow occurred *dios dia boulas* ["by the counsel of Zeus"], and the phrase naturally comes to mind when he thinks of that event.' West 1997.

7. Arist. *Ath. Pol.* 1 associates Epimenides with the aftermath of the Cylon affair. Plu. *Sol.* 12.4 puts him with Solon. Pl. *Lg.* 642d places him later. Solon and Egyptian priests: e.g. Pl. *Crit.* 108d, 113a; *Tim.* 22a f.

8. Fragments 36.3-5 (divine Earth) poem 38 (earth beneath one's feet). Adkins 1972a: 49 notes that Solon can hold *Gê*, Earth, as a 'divine person' and 'dark earth' in his mind 'with no feeling of contradiction'.

9. Fränkel 1975: 220 and Henderson 1982: 27 translate *phrên* here as 'will'. Campbell 1982: 240 and Gerber 1970: 132 see 'purpose'; Adkins 1985: 109 and Gerber 1999 'intentions'. Solon's fragment 33 links *phrên* to counsels.

10. Leaf [1900]1960 comments on 16.780, distinguishing 'beyond measure' from 17.321 'contrary to destiny'.

11. Men wrongly blame the gods: *Od.* 1.33-4, cited by Adkins 1985: 113, who recalls Jaeger 1926: 73 (repr. in Jaeger 1966). Lloyd-Jones 1971: 28. The gods' failures follow their withdrawal, e.g. *Il.* 9.420, 685-7; 22.296-303. For Solon's poem 4 and Homer: Anhalt 1993: 75; Campbell 1982: 240, 1983: 92; Fowler 1987: 46; Irwin 2005a.

12. Anhalt 1993: 76, citing *Il.* 22.254-5. Jaeger 1947: 119: for Heraclitus as first extant use of *harmonia* 'agreement' as a fitting-together of opposites. Linforth 1919: 195 sees a partnership between the divine and the human, with Athena as a champion. But where are the attacks by Athena's divine opponents?

13. Murray 1990: 12-16; 1991: 10-11.

14. Kahn 1960: 193; similarly Jaeger 1966: 89-90.

15. Jaeger 1966: 83 sees *aisa* and *moira* as equivalent; similarly Adkins 1960: 17. Campbell 1982: 240 reads *Dios ... aisa* as 'the portion sent by Zeus'. However, *moira* in Solon is never elsewhere explicitly directed towards the *polis*.

16. As Hes. *Op.* 173d, 180.

Notes to pages 16-19

17. E.g. Hes. *Op.* 256-62. *Dikê* also sits next to Zeus at A. fr. 282. Also, Orph. fr. 23 (Kern).
18. Cf. *Il.* 24.729 for *episkopos* and Hector; 10.38, 342 a spy; *Od.* 8.163 a cargo. Snodgrass 1980: 39; de Polignac 1995: 84 for Athena's procession towards Athens as unique. Parker 1983: 69 on Athena's traces in Athens as post-Solonian. Parker 1995: 69 discusses lines 4.1-4 and building in Athens.
19. Noussia 2001a: 379-80 for the tradition of Solon's laws as written in epic metre. The phrase *agathê tuchê* does not again appear until Aeschylus, *Ag.* 755. The fragment may resound in Pl. *Smp.* 209d: 'For you, the honour (*timios*) goes to Solon, on account of his creation of the laws (*tên tôn nomôn gennêsin*)'.
20. 13.1, 17, 25 and 75. Chapters 5 and 6 below on poem 13.
21. Cartledge 1998a for discussion of the *kosmos* in the political realm.
22. Treu 1968: 270. Kahn 1985: 193. Wheelwright 1999: 4. *Hekêti* 'by the will of' takes on neuter meanings, 'for the sake of' things. In Homer *hekêti* is only in the *Odyssey*, of the gods, e.g. *Od.* 15.319; 19.86; 20.42, and of people: *Od.* 11.384. In lyric-tragic poets it is of gods, e.g. B. 1.6; A. *Eu.* 759; *Ch.* 214; of men, as Sim. 11.15, but also things, in the sense of 'on account of, for the sake of, by reason of', e.g. A. *Pers.* 'on account of numbers'; Pi. *N.* 8.47; A. *Ch.* 701; S. *Ph.* 669; *Tr.* 274, 353; E. *Med.* 1235; *Cyc.* 365; A. *Pers.* 337. Chantraine 1968: 331 has it as 'symétrique négatif' of *aekôn*, connected to *ekousios* ' "voluntaire"; in Lyr / Trag "de choise" au sens de "grace" ou "en vue de" '.
23. KRS frs. 89, 90. Barnes 1982: 5-13 prefers 'the comic overtones of "animator" to the theological overtones of "soul" ' in discussing Thales' argument.
24. KRS frs 175, 178, 185.
25. Lesher 1983: 8,15 comments on 'poetic epistemology' and its differences from Presocratic thought. KRS frs 186-9 on Xenophanes' limits to human knowledge; on Heraclitus and Alcmaeon, see KRS 205 and 439. Lloyd 1970: 14-15 sees a 'new critical spirit' in Thales and Solon. Solmsen 1949: 114 on 'natural causality' as a replacement for the spontaneous divine operation, also Guthrie 1962: 1: 29.
26. Irwin 2005a: 180, 175.
27. *Il.* 1.16: *kosmêtore laôn. Kosmos* and related forms in Homer: e.g. *kosmeô* as marshalling or ordering troops: *Il.* 2.554; 2.655; 2.704; 2.727; 2.806; 3.1; 11.48; 51; 12.85; 12.87; 17.205. *ou kata kosmon* as connected with violence: *Il.*5.759; 8.12; 17.205. *ou kosmôi* as not in order: *Il.* 12.225. *eu kata kosmon* as readying a sheep for a meal: *Il.* 24.622; cf. *apekosmeon* for a meal in *Od.* 7.232. *Kosmêtor* as a leader: *Il.* 1.16; 375; 3.236; *Od.* 18.152. Haubold 2000 on the need for a leader in Homeric society. Adkins 1985: 115; Linforth 1919: 198-200. Almeida 2003: 198 claims that *eukosma* is first in Solon; this may be so for the precise word, but the idea is Homeric. See the adverb *eukosmôs* at *Od.* 21.123, re Telemachus *hôs eukosmôs stêse*; also Hes. *Op.* 628.
28. *Il.* 2.214: *ou kata kosmon*. The single example of speech in the *Iliad* as *ou kata kosmon* may be compared to *Od.* 8.179, 489; 14.363; 20.181. For *kosmos* and speech in the archaic poets: e.g. Simon. 11.23-4; Sol. 1.2. In the Presocratics see Parm. B8.52. For good counsel as a Homeric virtue, Schofield 1999, ch. 1.
29. *Od.* 7.127; *Il.*14.187, as Hes. *Th.* 573; 587; *Op.* 72,76. Hesiod fr. 26.21 (MW), heavily restored, may describe an *anthea euôdea* 'sweet-smelling blossom' as *kosma*.
30. Kahn 1985: 220-1. Kahn 1985: 224-7 on *kosmos* in early philosophic texts.
31. E.g. *Il.* 2.655, 688. See Kahn 1985: 221.
32. Fränkel 1975: 102, who observes a 'similar tendency' in Linnaeus.

Notes to pages 19-26

33. Hes. *Op.* 306. A similar idea is later expressed in Xenophon's *Oeconomicus*, e.g. the arrangement of ship's tackle and household utensils at 8.17-20.

34. Beauty or utility: Critias 2.8 Dionysus of Chalcus 1.5. Political and social: elegist Melanthius 1.2; Thgn. 677, 947 (attr. by Bergk to Solon).

35. Hahn 2001: 175.

36. Kirk 1970: 337.

37. Hussey 1995: 543 n. 7.

38. Noted by Mülke 2002: 102, who shows earlier links between *hêmeteros* and *oikos, dôma, basileus* and *paterôn pateres*, in contrast to Solon's innovation.

39. Parker 1995, ch. 4, for the Solonian festival calendar. Lys. 30.18-19 calls on the ancestral laws of religious sacrifices. Ostwald 1986: 138 on state officials assigned post-Solon to administer cults and festivals, citing Arist. *Ath. Pol.* 21.6.

40. Bowra 1938: 101 argues that 'this attempt to see an ordered pattern of life' in poem 27 is 'the best argument for its authenticity'.

41. Irwin 2005a: 105-6.

42. Hahn 2001: 97f. for the plan views and elevation views of sixth-century temple architects, and the connections to cosmologies. Hippodamus of Miletus may have adopted such views of the physical, social and legal aspects of the town, and to apportion them according to a plan. Arist. *Pol.* 1267b22f. for the Peiraeus; for Thurii, D.S. 12.10.7.

2. 'To know all things': psychic qualities and the *polis*

1. Dihle 1982: 20f. for general discussion of the differences; 145-9 for the words as synonymous in Hellenistic and Roman times; 175 n. 5 for citations.

2. Chantraine 1968: 189, 315: *boulomai* is 'désirer, préférer'; *ethelô* is 'consentir à, accepter'. LSJ entry *ethelô* I.3 has *ouk ethelôn = aekôn* for *Il.* 4.300. Bowra 1938: 93 interprets wealth which comes *ouk ethelôn* in poem 13.13 as 'it comes uncertainly because against its real nature'.

3. Masaracchia 1958: 210.

4. *Timôsin* is problematic; various emendations have been suggested. The use here is certainly related to the actual attainment of wealth, not merely a person's view of it or attempts to attain status from it. See Chapter 5.

5. For the contrast see also *Il.* 3.232, 12.350, 13.741. *Od.* 17.185 expresses the idea: 'my king commands (*epetellen*) .. I'd rather (*bouloimên*) ...'.

6. Chantraine 1968: 224: *gignôskô*: 'apprendre, connaître à force d'efforts'. Linforth 1919: 133 translates: 'I am not unaware', although *gignôskô* may denote a more active process of 'recognition'. Vox 1984, citing Masaracchia 1958: 273, 280, notes the emphatic use of *gignôskô*, and places *kai ... keitai* in parentheses; with *gaian* as the object of *gignôskô* and *esorôn*. Solon thus gains a perspective similar to Zeus. McEwen 1993: 34-5 notes the connection between *gnômôn*, a thing by which one knows, or one who knows, and *gignôskô*; the latter refers in Homer primarily to the interpretation of signs, including birds: *Od.* 2.159. Nagy 1983 on *noêsis*.

7. LSJ, I.2 have 'Comp. And Sup , of things, *more* or *most important, taking precedence ... higher, more important*'. Hdt. 5.63.2: for the affairs of the gods as more venerable than those of man. S. *OT* 1365, no evil greater (*presbuteron*) than another.

8. Noussia 2001a: 258 connects *aigae* to *paschein* 'to suffer' in *Il.* 24.522f.

9. Wickersham 1991: 25f.

10. On the metaphor of the meal, Linforth 1919: 198-9; Halberstadt 1955: 199; Schmitt-Pantel 1992: 36-7; Anhalt 1993: 79-82, 93.
11. Fisher 1992.
12. Noussia 2001a: 196.
13. As Sullivan 1989: 138-9 observed, line 4.7, 'the *noos* of the leaders of the people is unjust', 'is associated with justice and its opposite, *hubris*'; *noos* here functions as the seat of the 'thoughts, plans and will of the leaders', and 6.4 is connected to 4.7-9 as a clarification in terms of *noos*.
14. Irwin 2005a: 217.
15. Noussia 2001a: 283 compares line 9.4 to *Od.* 10.231, in which Odysseus' men follow Circe *'aidreiêsin'*, 'per stoltezza del pensiero', 'by stupidity'. Solon would probably not agree with the Fagles or Fitzgerald translations, in which 'innocence' leads, or 'innocents' follow.
16. Doyle 1984: 36-46; Abel 1943. Vlastos 1995: 33-4 was right to say that 'there is no evidence that he thinks *of* a concept of social causality but he certainly thinks with one'.
17. Examples of *koros* in Homer are at *Il.* 13.636 and 19.221; *Od.* 4.103. Examples of related forms in Homer: *korenummi*, *Il.* 16.747 fulfilling hunger; *Il.* 22.427, *Od.* 4.541, 10.449, 20.59 for gluts of tears; *Il.* 22.509, *Od.* 10.411 for animals sated by food; *Od.* 14.28 for boar sent to town to satisfy the suitors; *Od.* 14.46 for drinking wine to satiety. *Akor-* forms also speak of being satisfied with respect to war, battle and menace, *Il.* 12.335, 13.621, 13.639, 14.479, 20.2; and hard work, *Il.* 7.117. Helm 1993: 5-8 details usage in Homer, and shows Hesiod's consistency with Homer.
18. Hes. *Op.* 33.
19. Hes. *Th.* 593.
20. E.g. *Il.* 19.167. Presocratic philosophers emphasize the contrast between *koros* and its opposites. Heraclitus, for example, often sets *koros* against *chrêmosunê*, *limos* and the like; Kahn 1979 fragments LXVII (= DK 33), CXX (= DK 65), CXXIII (= DK 67 = KRS 204). Kahn observes that references to *koros* in Heraclitus recall Solon.
21. As Balot 2001: 59 suggests. Helm 1993: 8 detects the first inklings of a change in meaning to 'excess' in two fragments of Alcman (164) and Sappho (144). Irwin 2005a: 210-20 for *koros,* its epic parallels and the contestations over its meaning, discussed in terms of social stratification. The question is not what is 'enough' or 'too much', but rather a 'positive or negative state' p. 218.
22. On *noos* see von Fritz 1943, 1993; Sullivan 1988a, 1989, 1995: 191-7; Krischer 1984. Mülke 2002: 112 comments on *adikos noos*, citing Sullivan 1989: 160, as one's 'inner nature'. To translate *'noos'* as 'mind' in any archaic thinker, at least before Parmenides, would be distinctly anachronistic.
23. Nagy 1983, 1990; Svenbro 1993.
24. Anhalt 1993: 69, n. 6.
25. Fränkel 1946 for 'subject to the changing day', and Dickie 1976 for the brevity of life. Gerber 1984 comments on the poem. Reinhardt 1916 compares Semonides 1 with Solon and Theognis, seeing the possibility of a metaphysical unification of the human and divine, through a proper sense of *to speudein* 'striving', as in Theognis 401-6 and Solon 13.65-70. Carson 1984 for discussion.
26. Hdt. 1.30-2. Harrison 2002: 34; Shapiro 1996; Sage 1985 on Solon and Croesus in Herodotus.
27. Pi. *N.* 7.1. Masaracchia 1958: 339 for the *hapax*. Gerber 1970: 139 for 'depth' in the lyric poets, as *poluphrôn* in Homer and *batheian* in *Il.* 19.125; also Snell

Notes to pages 34-39

1982: 17f. Heraclit. KRS fr. 232 for the *peirata* of the *psuchê*, which has a *bathus logos*. Linforth 1919: 217 for Pindar on *bathuphrôn*, and A. *Pers.* 142 *bathuboulon*. LSJ on *bouleêis* as 'of good counsel, sage'.

28. Griffith 1990: 196.
29. Irwin 2005a: 242-3.
30. Den Boer 1966, who claims this is an authentic fragment of Solon, citing Plu. *Sol.* 14.8: *kalon men einai tên turannida*. Den Boer is surely right to see *kalon* as sarcastic, given *ouk echein d' apobasin*, that there is no coming down.
31. Sullivan 1988a: 9-11. Similarly, Hdt. 5.97 has Aristagoras attempt to persuade the Spartan ephor and the Athenian assembly. Rather than 'political naïveté', as How and Wells 1975 comment, Herodotus may be offering an important insight into how groups affect an individual's decisions.
32. Fränkel 1975: 229.
33. McGlew 1993: 102.
34. Noussia 2001a: 351 reads 'non giustamente' or 'non opportunamente'.
35. *Il.* 1.207. Often after speech, e.g. *Od.* 23.141, or *Il.* 5.201. The middle form (*peithomenos*, or *peithomenoi*) plus a dative of something other than a man or a god exists in persuasions 'by words', 'by the portents and aid of the gods', *Il.* 1.33, 150; 23.157. In the *Odyssey*, 'the inescapable necessity of old age' is at 17.177; 23.644-5. To be persuaded is optional: *Od.* 9.44, men did not obey; Hes. *Sc.* 450, Ares did not persuade; *h. Ap.* 418 a ship did not obey; *Hymn to Hermes* 132, Hermes' *thumos* was not persuaded. *Iliad* 4.408 contrasts those 'persuaded by the signs and portents of the gods' with those 'destroyed by their own recklessness'. The few middle forms in the archaic poets are generally fragmented past definitive interpretation. Tyrt. 2.10; 19.11. Van Wees 1999a: 6-7 interprets Tyrt. 2 as exhorting obedience based on divine sanction. Sim. 7.3 has *peithônta*[. However, Bowra 1938: 72-8 sees Tyrt. 19.11 (which implied divine sanction) as *peisometh' êge*[*mosin* and an influence upon Solon 22a2. In Semonides 1.22-4 a speaker cites himself as the cure for those who abuse their *thumos* with troubles, 'if he is persuaded by me'.
36. Buxton 1982: 49. Scholars who favour 'being persuaded in' rather than 'obeying' in Solon's passages include Adkins 1985: 113; Jaeger 1966: 82 n. 1; Solmsen 1949: 112.
37. Democrit. B248. See Democrit. B181; Procopé 1989, 1990 commentary. Arist. *Mu.* 401a8-12 for Heraclit. B11, all animals pass through life 'persuaded by the statutes of the gods'. Heraclit. B33 connects *peithô* to *nomos*.
38. In Theognis: *peithomenos chrêmasi*, 194; *chalepêi diaboliê*, 324; *adikois ergmasi*, 380; *muthoisi*, 437, 746; *adikois andrasi*, 948; 1152 'by the speech of men', *rhêmasi anthrôpôn*, 1152, 1238a,b, 1262. Bergk 1882 attributes 945-8 to Solon.
39. Of eighteen instances of *peithomen-* in the *Palatine Anthology,* twelve are at the end of an elegiac line and refer to a dative: (Book)5.(epigram)89; 5.238; 6.50; 6.103; 7.51; 7.103; 7.249; 8.174; 9.778; 10.6; 10.40 (= Thgn. 1152,1238,1162); 11.433. 6.80 ends the line, without a dative.
40. Noussia 2001b.
41. Finkelberg 1998: 159-60. Mülke 2002: 114 on 4.9: *epistantai* is related to the German word *Wissen* 'knowledge, learning'. Compare the views of Allen 1949: 51-63 and Anhalt 1993: 20-2 n. 23 concerning wisdom and *sophia*. Solon 29 for *polla pseudontai aoidoi*.
42. As Pl. *Phdr.* 248d-e would put the *philosophos* and the *mousikos* on the same high level; Finkelberg 1998: 1-18.
43. Anhalt 1993: 69 and n. 6; Sullivan 1989: 140.

44. Most 1999: 338-9: Xenophanes cleared a space for his own views, as did Heraclitus. Loraux 1984 presents Solon as occupying a middle ground that is off-limits militarily to either side. See Anhalt 1993: 121 n. 9.

45. Greenhalgh 1972: 196 sees a 'cult of moderation' in Solon. Kahn 1998: 31 sees moderation as an alternative to the heroic ideal, beginning with warnings of excess in Hesiod and 'more fully developed' in Solon and the Seven Sages.

46. Greenhalgh 1972: 193.

47. Cairns 1993: 165-7. Cairns cites Hom *Il.* 22.104-7 as an instance of Hector's awareness that his future is based on something he has done that 'others will consider reprehensible'. Given *Il.* 6.441f., 'I would feel shame (*aideomai*) before the Trojans ... if I, like a coward, were to shrink from the fighting', Cairns 1993: 165 cannot be right in seeing Solon 32 as the first 'encounter' with *aideomai* in a conditional clause.

48. Cairns 1993: 166. Adkins 1960: 155, says that no one did this prior to Socrates.

49. Peikoff 1993: 251.

50. Kirk 1990 comment to *Il.* 444-6.

51. Discussions and dissensions on Solon's self-references include: Vox 1984; Sullivan 1988b: 2-7; Slings 1990; Goldhill 1991; Edmunds 1997; Finkelberg 1998, esp. 18-33; Atherton 1998; Irwin 2005a.

52. Democrit. B3,191 = KRS frs 593,594. Kahn 1998: 35 sees Democritus as internalizing the ideal of moderation, which Kahn 1998: 31 credited Solon with developing. Many scholars have focused on the presence – or not – of conscience in Solon. Guthrie 1965: 2: 494 positions Democritus, like Socrates, with conscience. Will 1958 sees no conscience in Solon; also Fränkel 1975: 224; Dodds 1951: 36-7; Anhalt 1993: 5. Bowra 1938: 75-7 sees conscience in Solon as a 'sense of *noblesse oblige*'. Treu 1968: 272 views Solon 33 as evidence for a deeper dimension of the soul prior to Heraclitus, and thus prior to Democritus.

53. KRS 1983: 432-3. Wheelwright 1999: 59, citing Heraclit. fr. 8, notes that *edizêsamên emeôuton*, 'I searched myself', requires both an inward and an outward look, when souls form communities.

54. Balot 2001 n. 3.

55. Rodgers 1971: 294 notes properly that the Greeks, in general, view action 'in the light of its consequences', not in terms of right and wrong on principle.

56. As Pl. *Chrm.* 164d-e connects *sôphrosunê* to *to gignôskein heauton ... to gar Gnôthi sauton kai to Sôphronei esti men tauton*. See Dihle 1982: 48-52.

57. As Arist. *EN* 1110a15 saw one as responsible for those actions for which the cause was within oneself. Adkins 1960: 27 n. 7 notes that 'Greek common sense' held to this view, which Aristotle later formulated.

3. 'In time, retribution surely comes': necessity, *dikê* and the good order of the *polis*

1. Irwin 2005a: 95.

2. Campbell 1982: 137.

3. Fragment 37 may belong with poem 36; Rhodes 1993: 178 comment to Arist. *Ath. Pol.* 12.5, citing Linforth 1919: 182. Stinton 1976; Anhalt 1993: 120-1 on fr. 37. Lavelle 2005 uses the fragment to support his conclusion that there were only two parties to the conflicts in Athens – an ill-organized *dêmos*, and the 'better sort' – and that 'Solon's poems show that the *dêmos* was sovereign' in empowering and removing leaders (14-15). This fails to account for the unclear referent to *dêmos*.

There is also no basis in Solon's verses for elevating 'the better sort' into a party unified by a single political agenda, interacting with the *dêmos* in an institutionalized manner.

4. Arist. *Ath. Pol.* 2 on the dichotomized factions.

5. Stanley 1999: 172f., agreeing with Rosivach 1992. Foxhall 1997; Lavelle 2005.

6. Morris 1987: 171. Almeida 2003: 210 thereby reads *astoi* in Solon 4.6 as 'the elite', whereas *astoi* actually means 'townsmen'. They are not self-evidently an aristocracy. Solon never says *agathoi* or *kakoi* in poem 4. Finley 1983: 2 insists that Solon 'acknowledged the centrality of class and class conflict'. Osborne 1996: 218 rather sees 'not primarily a matter of the rich struggling as a group against the poor as a group, but of individual citizen against citizen'. Sealey 1976: 114 sees a struggle between families, not classes. Miller 1969: 69 n. 11, sees everything as institutional prior to Solon; he left the people free to negotiate as they wished. Perhaps Solon freed individuals from ritualized strictures, allowing each man to pursue justice for himself.

7. For Plato (as much as it is possible to get with certainty to his views in the dialogues), justice is a type of harmony, and injustice an action that destroys the harmony, e.g. *Resp.* 4.443d-e. For Aristotle, it is rather a state of character that disposes people to act a certain way, e.g. *EN* 5.1 1129a1-12.

8. Noussia 2001a: 283 comments on the many possibilities for the lacuna before *noein*. Perhaps *peri*, the suggestion Noussia notes of Dindorf, would mean to consider everything 'deeply', rather than *kala*, 'nobly'.

9. Vlastos 1995: 33-4, who contrasts Solon with Sem. 7.37-40, in which the sea acts capriciously. But this should not be overstated. Semonides says a woman is 'like as' or 'even as' (*hôsper*) the sea, an analogy used to describe the woman, not the sea. This should not be elevated into a statement of capriciousness in nature. It is an analogy.

10. Hom. *Il.* 8.70 f.; 24.518-33, for the scales of fate that move independently of Zeus' will. Adkins 1960: 13: Poseidon reminds Zeus of limits to his sphere of powers: *Il.* 15.189. Limits to Zeus' power include *Il.* 22.178f., where Athena tells Zeus that he cannot save Hector – who is fated to die – and who does die only after Apollo deserts him.

11. *Pantôs* in the Presocratics and Sophists (omitting testimonia and Democrit. 1.5, which Taylor 1999 rejects): Antiphon B44, 54; Gorg. B11, 11a; Heraclit B137; Anaxag. B9; Parm. 4.9. LSJ credit Parm. B4 with the first use of *pantôs* without *ou*, ignoring Solon. Coxon 1986: 187-9 sees Parm. 4.3 *pantê pantôs* as an allusion to Heraclit. B41 *panta dia pantôn*. Diels traced the reduplications back to Heraclitus.

12. Campbell 1982: 236 comments: *pantôs* means 'at all events', 'assuredly'. A similar idea is in Heraclit. B137, *esti gar eimarmena pantôs*, one's lot is inevitable and comprehensive. LSJ stress the idea of 'absolutely', 'positively', 'assuredly' and 'at all hazards' in various uses of *pantôs*.

13. Contrary to Almeida 2003: 203.

14. Irwin 2005a: 176-7.

15. Scholars have argued energetically over the nature of *dikê* in Hesiod and Solon. Vlastos 1995: 32; Solmsen 1949, esp. 107-23, and Jaeger 1966: 75-99 see Solon as an advance on Hesiod. To Gagarin 1973 and 1974, Solon creates no 'new kind of justice'; similarly Havelock 1978, who sees no principle of justice, only arguments over 'procedural rights'. Also: Gernet 1981: 228: 'l'idée de la Justice comme celle d'une puissance divin'. Lloyd-Jones 1971: 44-5 on the personified

Hesiodic *Dikê*, 'who acts only through human judgements, and through external visitations of the gods', and the Solonian *Dikê*, 'immanent in the workings of the universe'. Readings also include von Fritz 1943 and 1993; Fränkel 1946 and 1993; Rodgers 1971; Dover 1974; McKirahan 1994.

16. Kalimtzis 2000: xiii, 5 and n. 13.

17. *Dikê* in Homer is relatively unimportant; see Gagarin 1974: 87. Leaf's comment to *Il.* 11.832 has the Centaur Cheiron as 'most civilized', 'the most conversant with *dikê*, the traditional order of society'.

18. Gagarin 1973: 89,93, who also, in his 1974 article, sees the 'proper behaviour' sense of *dikê* falling out of use in the archaic period. Vlastos 1995: 32-6 for Hesiod's two tiers of justice as 'belonging to the order of magic' and existing 'in natural terms'.

19. Ostwald 1973: 677.

20. West 1996 comment. Cf. *Il.* 2.374; 4.291 for taking a city by main force. Of course 'gift-receiving' judges were not necessarily taking bribes, but perhaps being paid for their services.

21. Gagarin 1974: 190-2, n. 33.

22. Mülke 2002: 157 comment refers to *Il.* 16.387, *skolias krinôsi themistas*. A similar phrase is at Hes. *Op.* 221.

23. Gentili and Cerri 1988: 18-19 n. 40, for a general, and common, description of *dikê* as equilibrium. Yet the equilibrium is not an end to movement. The seesaw need never stop rocking back and forth.

24. For poem 4 as reversing Hesiod's just and unjust cities, Jaeger 1966: 96f.; cf. Solmsen 1949: 117; Manuwald 1989: 7; Irwin 2005a.

25. Jaeger 1966: 94.

26. Dickie 1984 for the two aspects of *hêsuchia*. The archaic opposition of *hêsuchia* to *hubris* is followed by a classical opposition to *sôphrosunê*. Thgn. 48 for *hêsuchia* as a virtue of the *polis* that must be protected.

27. Jaeger 1966:95; Andrewes 1938: 89.

28. Ostwald 1969: 76-9.

29. Myres 1947: 81. For the personal vs social distinction: Ostwald 1969: 85-95. Andrewes 1938: 89. Stier's 1928: 234-5 idea that *eunomia* is opposed to *dusnomia* in Hesiod and Solon and opposed to *anomia* in Hdt. 1.65 is superseded by Ostwald's social–personal distinction. Jaeger 1966: 95. Thuc. 4.76.2 on Boeotia. Corcyra in Thuc. 3.81-5 comes closest to complete social *anomia*. N.b. the effects on the meanings of words; thought and discourse collapse amidst such violence.

30. Erasmus 1960: 58.

31. West 1997 comment to Hes. *Th.* 902, citing Andrewes 1938: 89f., and Arist. *Pol.* 4.8 1294a3.

32. Halberstadt 1955: 202 links specific items in praise of *Eunomiê* to topics presented earlier. See also Jaeger 1966: 92; Ostwald 1969: 67-8; Siegmann 1975: 278-80; Adkins 1985: 122-3; Manuwald 1989: 7.

33. Rodgers 1971: 289, 294; Havelock 1978: 250-2.

34. Anaximen.: KRS frs 140-3, 158.

35. Parm. B4 argues against this cycle using the terminology *pantôs* and (*ou*) *kata kosmon*: Coxon 1986: 187-9.

36. KRS fr. 250, perhaps the first expression of natural law, although Striker 1996 warns against assuming that natural justice implies natural law. KRS 1983: 211 identify the gnomic forms of Heraclitus' advice with the Delphic maxims *gnôthi sauton* and *mêden agan*, identified with Solon in the *Suda* (*s.v.* 776 *Solôn*). The scribe's uncertainty of the attribution is evident in *pheretai autou apo-*

phthegma tode. KRS fr. 227 n. 1 compare Solon 16 and Heraclitus with respect to *gnômê*, cf. fr. 247. Thgn. 335, 401 is aware of these maxims, cf. 219, 657. Reinhardt 1916: 130f. connects these to Sol. 13.34, reading *speudein*.

37. Ostwald 1973: 679 for a 'norm' in poem 36.

4. 'A *kosmos* of words': archaic logic and the organization of poem 4

1. Kennedy 1994: 3. For Solon and rhetoric, see Johnson 1982; Walker 2000; Stoddard 2002.

2. Edmonds 1931 translates fr. 1 as 'an ornament of words', so Gerber 1999: 'an adornment of words'. West 1993: 74 emphasizes the order: 'adopting ordered verse', as does Knox 1985: 147 'a pattern of verse'. So Perrin 1967 translates Plu. *Sol.* 8.2. Similarly: Orph. E1; Parm. B8.52; Democr. B2.

3. Discussions used include von Fritz 1943, 1993; Fränkel 1975; Sullivan 1988b, 1989; Lesher 1999; Most 1999.

4. Speech delivered in 1396; in Copeland and Lamm 1958: 333-6.

5. See Kilmer and Develin 2001: 134. Svenbro 1993 ch. 1 follows Nagy 1990 ch. 8 in a discussion of *sêma* and *noêsis*, and the movement from reading symbols to recognizable sounds. Svenbro pp. 14-15 notes that *kleos* was exclusively oral.

6. Halberstadt 1955: 200-1 for a three-stage analysis.

7. Noted in Mülke 200: 107.

8. For *to habra pathein*, 'experiencing luxurious life': Semonides 7.57; Thgn. 474. Treu 1968: 273 credits Sappho.

9. Mülke 2002: 113 notes the parallel between *algea polla pathein* here, and *Od.* 9.53, *hin' algae polla pathoimen*.

10. Keaney 1992: 72-3.

11. *Il*. 24.599-620. See Willcock's comment. Fränkel 1975: 519: 3.3-2 on Sol. 13.17-25.

12. As in Arist. *Ath. Pol.* 7.1-2; e.g. Keaney 1992: 76.

13. Anhalt 1993: 102 n. 60; also Adkins 1985: 118; Linforth 1919: 201; Jaeger 1966: 91. Thuc. 2.49.5 is the first appearance of *helkos* as 'sore'.

14. Thgn. 51-2 connects *emphuloi phonoi* to *stasies* and *mounarchoi*.

15. Jaeger 1966: 96. Gerber 1970 comments on the ring composition.

16. *Od*. 11.445: At *Od*. 1.229, a 'sensible' man is opposed to the suitors; 4.21: Nestor's 'clever' sons. Not in Hesiod.

17. Thgn. 501.

18. *Il*. 5.326; 14.92; *Od*. 8.240; 19.248. Not in Hesiod.

19. Linforth 1919: 179 comments to fr. 4c line 4: *artia* is like *hugiês* 'in its figurative senses'. Fränkel 1975: 222: *artia* 'designates what is proper and right'.

20. Literary parallels to *euthunei de dikas skolias*: Hes. *Op*. 221, 250, 264; Thgn. 40; Pi. *P*. 4.153.

21. See *Il*. 4.111; 15.260-1; *Od*. 8.260; 9.134; 10.103. LSJ note 'smooth, polish, of a worker in horn or stone, grind, crush, smooth away. Metaphorical smoothing, such as Hdt. 8.142 or Solon 4.32, depends upon the literal meaning.

22. Fränkel 1975: 519: 3 3-2.

23. Hussey 1990: 16-17 finds such scepticism. Zellner 1994: 308-10 criticizes this position: 'The reason for the skepticism is supposed to be that humans are not present to all things [and cannot observe all things] ... This would fall short of the "we do not know anything", but is still radically skeptical.' On archaic ideas of knowledge, Lesher 1983, 1991, 1994, 1999.

24. Fränkel 1993: 118-31.
25. Anhalt 1993 ch. 1. As we shall see, a different interpretation of Solon 13 is possible.
26. Peikoff 1993: 127. The term 'concrete-bound' was first used by Ayn Rand, to describe a mental process that does not function on an active, conceptual level, but is rather stuck on the level of immediate perception. Rand 1973: 199.
27. The classic article here is Perry 1937. Fowler 1987: 53 opines that philologists 'have prematurely declared it [lyric poetry] deficient'. Vegetti 1999 argues against any concept of 'cause' into the fifth century.
28. Henderson 1982: 27-9, who bases his work on Prier 1976, who uses Jung, Cassirer and Lévi-Strauss to support a 'synthetic' vision that is alleged to resist Aristotelian analysis. Less abstrusely, Lattimore 1947: 162 sees a progression of imagery to build a vivid picture.
29. See 'Prediction', Schuessler in *IESS* 12: 418-23. Causation does not require a separation in time: 'linguistic arguments to the contrary do not affect this use'.
30. Adkins 1972b on *alêtheia*, truth, values and possible etymology.
31. Fränkel 1975: 519: 3.3-2 for passages showing general / particular relationships.
32. This may also be a precursor to the later ideas of *phusis*: 'the argumentative form of the concept of *phusis* is the claim of natural necessity': Hussey 1995: 535, who cites Arist. *Met.* 1.10 993a13-24 on implicit 'causes'.
33. Pl. *Chrm.* 154d-55a.

5. '*Moira* brings good and evil': *bios* and the failure of *Dikê*

1. Scholarly debate on poem 13 has been intense, especially over its subject, structure and theme – or lacks thereof. In terms of its subject, Wilamowitz 1913 sees the desire for wealth; similarly Reinhardt 1916 emphasizes the striving. Bowra 1938: 99 sees 'human error', but later (1966: 73) thinks that Solon 'shows how'. Knox 1985: 148 sees prosperity. Gerber 1997: 115 sees wealth as his 'primary theme', as 1970: 124. Stoddard 2002 sees an ironic change for a didactic purpose. Structurally, Lattimore 1947: 161-79 sees a 'self-generating series of ideas' with 'no subject'; sections are 'fast at one end, free at the other'. Gerber 1970: 124 sees 'ideas in the process of formation'. Fränkel 1975: 236 sees no new world of thought and form, for he is not a true poet, and no comprehensive system, for he is no philosopher. Anhalt 1993: 34 sees an 'internal logic', discernible without an externally imposed structure. A division in the poem, at line 34, has been often noted: Noussia 2001a, also Noussia 1999. Mülke 2002 sees lines 33-6 as an 'antithese' to the previous; also Gerber 1997: 115; Vox 1984: 515. Thematically, Greene 1944: 36-9 sees a concern with *dikê*, 1-32, and *moira*, 33-76. Allen 1949 rather sees a unified whole, based on the need for wisdom. Sicking 1998: 7-14 finds sections, based on a single purpose. In his view, lines 7-70 are an analysis of *atê*, and a confirmation of the need for wisdom. Fowler 1987: 53 f. cautions against assuming that an organization was intended for poem 13; 80: Gentili: 1988: 49; Henderson 1982 agree.
2. Vlastos 1995: 32-56. Adkins, 1985: 124, answers Vlastos by placing Solon within a Homeric mode of thought: 'Solon has one vocabulary for both political and distributive justice'. Manuwald, 1989: 1 cites Vlastos' *Zweiteilung* (bifurcation) as the first rejection of Jaeger's *Vergeltung und Strafe* (Retaliation and Strife) thesis. Balot 2001: 58 sees the basis for a new view of 'distributive justice', although Balot does not say that Solon understood justice in political and distributive forms.

Notes to pages 75-83

3. Vlastos 1995: 46-7. Manuwald 1989: 12 sees a first in Greek literature here. But *Il.* 4.160-3 has a penalty fall on women and children; Hes. *Op.* 282-5 sees descendents as obscure forever; Thgn. 203-8 for inherited debts; Arist. *Ath. Pol.* 2.2 for 'the poor, their children and women were enslaved' prior to Solon. Bowra 1938: 95; Adkins 1972a: 43. Dover 1974: 260 notes the 'suppleness' of Solon's doctrine: its 'utility' could explain a range of results to follow unjust actions. Dover cites Lys. 6.20: the god does not punish everyone at once (that is human justice), but rather 'descendants of impious men, because of the wrong done by their ancestors'.

4. Hopper 1967: 143 rather sees crops as primary.

5. Solmsen 1949: 107-8 and van Wees 1999b stress the realism in Solon's observations, from different perspectives.

6. LSJ: *Bios* (and *biotos*) are 'mode of life'; 'lifetime'; 'livelihood, earning a living'.

7. Specific passages connecting such products to work (*erga* and related forms) include Hes. *Op.* 42-4; 229-32; 306-7; 314-16; 394-400; 576-81. In 314-16, for instance, Hesiod counsels Perses to turn to your work (*eis ergon*) and attend to your livelihood (*meletas biou*). 394-400 enjoins a person to work (*ergazeu*) the work (*erga*), else his family will be forced to seek sustenance (*bioton*) through neighbours.

8. For *moira* and *death* in other elegiac and iambic poets: Thgn. 340, 820, 1300; Tyrt. 7.2; Callin. 1.15, as 119.2b. Adespota Iamblica 35.16 for connection to profit (*kerdos*) (fragmentary); Semonides 7.104 has both the *moira* of the divine and the *charis* of man. Homer has *moira* as a norm: E.g. *Od.* 17.335 and 580 for outside *moira* and according to *moira* (*para moiran* and *kata moiran*). Adkins 1960: 17-18 stresses the scales of *Il.* 8.70f. as 'fates of death', not 'fate' in a deterministic sense.

9. Philo, *On the Creation of the World*, 104, says that Solon described these 'ages of life', *tas hēlikias*.

10. 27.3-4, 27.17-18. Marcovich 1967: 554 implies influence by Solon upon the Stoics through Heraclitus, connecting Sol. 27.3 to Heraclit. (testimonium) A18.

11. Sicking 1998: 9-10.

12. Various interpretations of the first lines of poem 13: Wilamowitz 1913; Linforth 1919; Christes 1986; Fowler 1987: 79. Finkelberg 1998: 162 for 13.1-2 as a calling for 'happiness and good fame'. Anhalt 1993: 13 n. 4 sees the address to the Muses as a typical archaic theme, see Nagy 1979: 271-2; Gentili 1988: 159; Noussia 2001a. Alt 1979: 390 notes that Solon follows Hesiod in praying for *sôphrosunê, die Einsicht in das Maß,* citing Hes. *Th.* 52f. and *Sc.* 206.

13. Wilamowitz 1913: 259 sees *chrêmata* in line 7 as identical to *olbos*. His Greek paraphrase of the poem uses *ploutos*. Anhalt 1993: 25: *olbos* is material wealth since true happiness cannot be responsible for *hubris*. Adkins 1972a: 53 holds that 'different types of gain' explains Solon's reintroduction of divine agency.

14. Björck 1942. Linforth 1919 deals with textual issues.

15. Lattimore 1947: 164. Anhalt 1993: 118f. differentiates simile and metaphor in Solon. Noussia 2001a: 198-200 cites multiple epic precedents for the storm, but also notes a possible connection between lines 19f. and natural philosophy, as described by Masaracchia 1958: 218f. See her note to 13.22, and Zeus' clearing of the high air in *Il.* 17.645.

16. As *Il.* 16.364-5. Janko 1992 comments: 'the cloud starts on Zeus' mountain-top and moves off the peak'. Linforth 1919: 231 warns against assuming that Solon would have seen the wind as rising up from the earth, dispersing the cloud, contra Wilamowitz 1913: 264 'Der Sturm kommt aus der Tiefe ...'.

17. Noussia 2001a: 198-200.

18. For *moira* or *terma* as death, see also Thgn. 340; Tyrt. 7.2; Callin. 1.15; as 119.2b; Thgn. 820, 1300; Adespota Iambica 35.16 is fragmentary. Fowler 1987: 44. Adkins 1960: 17-18 stresses the scales of *Il.* 8.70f. as 'fates of death', not 'fate'.

19. Thgn. 903-30 for death as thwarting the best-laid plans; 205-8 for debts and children.

20. Lattimore 1947: 164, 174 notes the inadequacy of the account preceding line 25. 13.8 needed expansion because 'it implied that punishment came immediately or simply; and Solon knows that this is not true'.

21. Contrasting in terms of values with Tyrt. 12.9. Campbell's 1982 comment notes the Homeric *oud' apo doxês* 'and not other (wise) than one expects'. For 'reputation' see also Solon fragments 1, 2, 3, 10, 21 and the hexameter fragment 31.

22. Donlan 1973: 5.

23. Allen 1949: 51.

24. Linforth 1919 comments to a 'plan' in 13.38.

25. Sicking 1998: 12 n. 8 is right to caution that a term such as *exopisô* in line 32, if translated as 'in the future', bears an image of something uncertain approaching from the rear.

26. 4.13; 13.43-62; 15; 24.1-6; 33; 34.1-2; 39; esp. 13.43. Peikoff 1991: 208 for a definition of value as subsuming a wide range of pursuits.

27. Given my hypothesis about the shift from *Dikê* to *Moira*, it is reasonable to personify *Dikê* in line 13.8. It is the sacred foundations of *Dikê* in poem 4 that men fail to guard, and that brings inevitable retribution to the *polis*.

28. Noussia 1999: 10 draws parallels between 13.63-6 and Hes. *Th.* 904-6, as well as to *Il.* 527-8, the twin jars of good and evil.

29. Theognis 637 expressly connects hope (*elpis*) to risk; both are harsh forces (*chalepoi daimones*). *Kindun-* or *kinduni* is in Sapph. fr. 161, Alc. 138 (Bergk).

30. Noussia 1999: 12-13 (footnotes omitted).

31. Archilochus frs 16 and 178.1. Matheson 1994: 19-20 notes the development of *Tuchê* into a protector and goddess of good fortune as relatively late; *Tuchê* in Hes. *Th.* 360, as in the Homeric Hymn to Demeter, is a water nymph.

32. Noussia 1999: 12.

33. Slater 2001: 112 interprets 13.69-70 in comparison to Pi. *O.* 2.51, *paraluei / aphrosun[* as 'success frees one from being thought a fool'. But it is not plausible that Solon 13 is concerned primarily with what one is thought of, rather than what actually occurs, given the previous statements about how we are deceived about how things will turn out.

34. As per Manuwald 1989: 15 n. 58; Christes 1986.

35. Lattimore 1947: 166, 169.

36. Clement *Stromateis* 5.81 uses Sol. 16 and Emp. KRS fr. 396. *Stromateis* 5.129-30 has Hes. *Melam.* fr. 169 (Rzach 1902), Sol. 17, Hes. *Op.* 176-8, *Il.* 8.69 = 22.209, and Menander fr. 714K.

37. Ker 2000.

38. Perhaps as Heraclit. KRS fr. 250 speaks of human law as nourished by the one divine law. Thgn. 947, *partida kosmêsô*, may be Solonic.

39. Contra Manuwald 1989: 19, and Christes 1986, who see Solon as affirming the operation of *dikê*.

40. Discussed by Broadie 1999: 213-14.

41. Lloyd-Jones 1971: 36, citing Dodds 1951: 30.

42. Kahn 1998: 38.

43. Treu 1968: 273: 'zugleich aber ist dies die Zeit im griechischen Geistesleben, die das Auseinanderklaffen von Schein und Sein entdeckt hat'.
44. In particular, Shapiro 1996; Harrison 2002. Harrison finds 'Solonian philosophy' to be central to Herodotus, while noting that neither historical accuracy nor consistency in the *Histories* is to be expected.
45. Chiasson 1986. Sources are in Harrison 2002: 38-9 ns 17-20; on p. 50 for the quotation. This is of course a story by Herodotus, not Solon.
46. Shapiro 1996, n. 15 for scholars who have seen 'divine jealousy', *phthonos theôn*, as an attempt to maintain the proper relationships between the gods and men. N.b. Chiasson 1986: 220.
47. Harrison 2000: 32-3.
48. Pl. *Tim.* 20d f.; *Crit.* 110a-b.
49. Pl. *Crit.* 108c-d.

6. 'We will not exchange our excellence': *Moira* and wealth

1. Adkins 1985: 132.
2. Thgn. 227-9.
3. Arist. *Pol.* 1.8 1256b31-7, quoting Solon 13.71. Thgn. 227-9.
4. Linforth 1919: 240. Helm 1993: 5 discusses lines 13.71-6 similarly. Campbell 1982: 240: 'of wealth no limit is set up visible for men'. Thgn. 693-4: 'for it is difficult to know a proper measure, whenever material goods (*esthla*) are present'.
5. On hierarchy in Greek values Adkins 1972a: 7. Linforth 1919: 211 sees 'inseparable' and 'separable' values. Donlan 1973: 4, 74 sees wealth in Homer as subordinated to bravery, but essential to *aretê*. Solon sets wealth and *aretê* in opposition.
6. Foxhall 1997: 121-2 sees Solon as maintaining elite rule, and his equation as 'positively paternalistic'. For a less cynical view, Osborne 1996: 221.
7. Accepted by Morris and other new classical archaeologists, from their interpretations of the grave evidence; Almeida 2003 follows.
8. Anhalt 1993: 79-81, citing *Od.* 18.16-18, states: 'For Solon, immoderate consumption poses the essential threat to Athens' stability'; see Thgn. 757-64.
9. Adkins 1972a: 55 applies the Homeric values to poem 33.
10. Fragment 4b, preserved as indirect discourse in Arist. *Ath. Pol.* 5.3. the term 'love of silver' (*philarguria*) is reconstructed from 'love of money' (*philochrêmatia*) in Plu. *Sol.* 14.
11. Campbell 1982: 333-6 for commentary, drawing on Bowra 1953: 1-14. See Sicking 1998: 18, for instance, for a new ethical connotation in archaic *aretê*.
12. A. *Eu.* 313 for the Chorus of Furies, who deny they will act against anyone holding out 'clean hands'. *Od.* 22.462 has Telemachus say that he would not end the lives of the suitors 'by a clean death', *katharôi thanatôi*, given their crimes. Demosthenes would ask for an oath, that 'I have lived a holy life, pure and unstained (*hagisteuô kai eimi kithara kai hagnê*) of pollution.
13. Books 1 and 3 describe 25 of 42 cases as fatal. Lloyd 1978: 16-17.
14. Rosivach 1992 for *isomoiria* directed at the *dêmos* as anachronistic in Solon's time.
15. The disputed *timôsin* is accepted by West 1993: 77, who translates this contentious passage as riches that mortals 'cultivate with violence'. Linforth 1919 cites ten alternate readings. Lattimore 1947 accepts *metiôsin*. Precedent for *timôsin* is in Hes. *Op.* 15-16, the Deep Strife which men 'honour from compulsion by the counsels of immortals'.

Notes to pages 104-110

16. Personified in epic poetry she is the goddess of mischief, *Il.* 19.91-3, quoted in Pl. *Smp.* 195d; Hes. *Th.* 230.

17. Hamilton 1977: 185-8 for the gods as the *autôn*. West 1974: 181 sees human action as the cause of *atê*. Linforth 1919: 241-2, Lattimore 1947: 179 and Sicking 1998: 13 prefer *kerdea* as the antecedent – which comes from the gods and from unsparing human effort, such as fishing.

18. McEwen 1993: 13-15.

19. Donlan 1973: xiii views the archaic 'aristocratic ideal' as a defence against challenges. Greenhalgh 1972: 200 for Solon 6.3-4 as the first reasoned ethical justification of an aristocratic principle against a challenge. Claiming a shift to cooperative values: Adkins 1962; McKirahan 1994: 358; Bryant 1996: 95.

20. Noted by Sicking 1998: 9.

21. Hes. *Op.* 42, in Chapter 1.

22. Henderson 1982 accepts this view.

23. Lattimore 1947: 162, who sees evidence for honesty: 179.

24. Allen 1949. Sicking 1998, who finds three categories of interpretation.

25. Stoddard 2002.

7. 'I set them free': tyranny, slavery and freedom

1. Arist. *Ath. Pol.* 9.

2. As Patrick Henry framed the issue in a speech on 23 March 1775: 'The question before the house is one of awful moment to this country. For my own part, I consider it as nothing less than a question of freedom or slavery; and in proportion to the magnitude of the subject ought to be the freedom of the debate'. In another unintended parallel to Solon, he also blasts reliance on false hope: 'Mr. President, it is natural to man to indulge in the illusions of hope. We are apt to shut our eyes against a painful truth, and listen to the song of that siren till she transforms us into beasts ... I am willing to know the whole truth; to know the worst, and to provide for it.'

3. Parker 1998 observes no semantic distinction between *turannos*, *basileus* and *anax* prior to Solon 32 and 33, and sees Archilochus 19 as the first use of *turannos*. Other discussions used here: McGlew 1993; Cawkwell 1995; Gouschin 1999. Rihll 1989: 280 notes that anti-tyrannical discourse developed later, and may have affected views of Solon through history. The horses in Hdt. 3.80-3 may be parodying the democratic assembly of Athens. Archilochus 19 and 23; Alcaeus 70; Thgn. 823, 1181 and 1204. The ambiguous position of Heiron of Syracuse in Pindar is a great window into a fifth-century poet's reaction to a tyrant.

4. Noussia 2001a: 283 comments on the many possibilities for the lacuna before *noein*. Perhaps *peri*, the suggestion Noussia notes of Dindorf, would mean to consider everything 'deeply', rather than 'nobly'.

5. Similar to Thgn. 946: *chrê gar m' artia panta noein*, 'for one must know all things well', which Bergk 1882 attributes to Solon.

6. *monarchou*: D.L. 1.50; Plu. *Sol.* 3.6; D.S. 9.20.2. *turannou*: Diodorus Siculus 19.1.4. McGlew 1993: 89 accepts *monarchia*, and calls tyranny 'the domination of the city by a single individual'. But, Solon says 'your raised *these men [toutous]*'. Rihl 1989 n. 45 thinks this means those who 'administered and executed the law'.

7. See Alcaeus decontextualized fragment 6a27 for *monarchian*, and S271a5 for *monarch[*. *Monarchia*: Hdt. 1.55.1; 3.80.3; 3.82.3; 3.82.4; 7.154.1. In favour of *monarchou*: Thgn. 51 for *mounarchoi*, attested in multiple manuscripts; see

Campbell 1982 note. For *monarchêi*, Arist. *Pol.* 5.6 1307a2, citing Tyrt. *Eunomia* (in Jacoby *FGrH* 580 fr. 1).

8. Editors accepting *rhumata:* in editions of Solon: Tyler 1894, Hudson-Williams 1926, Diehl 1949, Edmonds 1931, West 1998, Gentili and Prato 1979; in Plutarch: Perrin 1967, following Sintenis and Bekker; in Diodorus Siculus: Oldfather 1985, following Volger-Fischer. Accepting *rhusia* in Diodorus Siculus: Long 1964. Linforth 1919's comment, citing Wilamowitz 1893: 2: 312, rejects *rhumata* given *toutous* and *rhumata* as plural; Rihll 1989 follows. Noussia 2001a favours *rhumata* as 'baluardi' ('bulwarks') to maintain their power. Mülke 2002 accepts *rhumata*, drawing parallels to Solon's defences in other passages.

9. The only epic use of *ta rhusia*, *Il.* 11.674, is based on existing power; see Willcock 1978 comment. Hainsworth 1993 has 'pledges seized as surety for repayments, or simply booty seized in reprisal'. The scholiast to *Il.* 11.674 links *rhusi' elaunomenos* 'driving off his cattle' with *antenechurazomenos*, 'taking counterpledges'.

10. Fränkel 1950 comments on a similar problem regarding Helen in A. *Ag.* 535: 'how can Helen be designated as 'compensation' or as 'pignus', when she was certainly not seized by way of securing some other legal claim'? Fränkel notes the usual meaning in LSJ of 'stolen property taken back as compensation for the theft', and details its uses in *Il.* 11.674; A. *Supp.* 412, 728; S. *OC* 858; S. *Ph.* 959. Kamerbeek 1984 comments to S. *OC* 858-9: *rhusion* 'pledge, security' is followed by *thêseis* 'deposit, pay', relationships of reciprocity based on exchanges of value.

11. Rihll 1989: 286. Sources linking them with Pisistratus: Plu. *Sol.* 3.6; 30.3; D.S. 9.20.2; D.L. 1.50, 51. However, the only mid-sixth-century vote we know of was to grant bodyguards to Pisistratus; Arist. *Ath. Pol.* 14.1; Hdt. 1.59.5. See Ostwald 1986: 4. Rihll 1989: 279 n. 12 also notes that *rhuma* principally signifies spears and bodyguards, while tradition remembered *korunêphoroi* 'club-bearers'. But spears are also specified for the Pisistratids (Thuc. 6.56.2; 57.1,4; 58.2); and given that *rhuma* is otherwise attested only later than Solon, he may be speaking poetically, without distinguishing spears from clubs.

12. Rihll 1989: 278; 1991: 117, 123.

13. Harris 1997 on later commentators as introducing ideas such as 'securities'.

14. Gagarin and Woodruff 1995: 29. Gouschin 1999 for the *prostatês* as an established feature of the sixth century. Cawkwell 1995 argues against tyrants coming from the people.

15. Cawkwell 1995: 77 notes as 'improbable' the Pisistratids' dwelling permanently on the Acropolis. Boersma 1970: 14f. finds only small buildings between 570 and 550 BC, and no building activity between 546 and 528/7.

16. For archaic stones, Agora Inscriptions I5510, I5675, I7039. Shear in *Hesperia* 8 1939: 205-6 and *Hesperia* 9 1940: 266-7. By the fifth century a sacred boundary is shown for the Temple of Neleus, and for the Asklepeion Spring House: *IG* 1³ 84, *IG* 1² 874. Travlos 1971: 332-9 for the Temple of Kodros (Neleus); 138-9 for the Spring House. The *horoi* stones of the fourth to second centuries convey 'mortgages', an idea anachronistic to archaic Greece. The Loeb translation of Arist. *Ath. Pol.* 12.4 comments anachronistically: 'posts marking mortgaged estates'. Todd 1993: 252 n. 22 properly dismisses Solon's *horoi* in fourth-century studies.

17. Gerber 1997: 114 sees the *alôpêx*, the *aimulos anêr* and the *monarchos* of fragment 9 as referring to the tyrant.

18. Noussia 2001a: 292 reads the verb *auxanein* as 'rendre grande', an action of a divinity. See *Od.* 13.360; Hes. *Op.* 6; Pi. *O.* 8.88.

19. On freedom and of slavery as concepts: Finley 1968: 72; Patterson 1982: 340;

Pohlenz 1966: 3-9. Ober 1989: 62 n. 23 cautions that the peasants may not welcome emancipation that takes away their source of capital. An increase in foreign slavery in Attica at this time has become accepted by many historians today. However, the dearth of evidence leaves open the possibility that scholars have been influenced more by Marx and Engels than by primary evidence: Engels 1972: 178: in the 80 years after Solon, 'Instead of exploiting their fellow citizens in the old brutal way, they [the Athenians] exploited chiefly the slaves and the non-Athenian customers'. See Finley 1980: 87-8; Garlan 1988: 38-9; Cartledge 1997; Garnsey 1996: 4. I will always remember Professor A.J. Graham for a private discussion of this issue, including his energetic cry that the distinction between a 'slave' and a 'free man' is of 'enormous antiquity'. Raaflaub 2004: 25 notes that distinctions of status, esp. free men versus slaves, is at least as early as the seventh century BC.

20. Lesky 1996: 127. Fränkel 1975: 226-7 for a comparison with speeches in tragedy.

21. Linforth 1919: 185 for the 'corroborative testimony' of the Black Earth. A scholium to Pi. *O.* 1.127 attributes *summarturei* to Epimenides.

22. Podlecki 1975 discusses the causes of his *apodêmia*.

23. Solon's is the first extant use of *ekdikôs*. For *ekdikôs* and *dikaiôs* as a legal distinction see Woodhouse 1938: 132; Gagarin 1974: 192; Ehrenberg 1973: 57; Havelock 1978: 251-4; Blaise 1995: 32. Linforth 1919's comment is instructive: *ekdikôs* and *dikaiôs* are used 'with reminiscence of the primitive meaning of *dikê*, the custom of the community. They mean, therefore, "legally" and "illegally", not "deservedly" and "undeservedly" '. Solon, Linforth maintains, here expresses no opinion as to the 'absolute justice or injustice of selling men into slavery for debt'. Strictly true for the passage, but Solon's fundamental claim is that slavery of all kinds is wrong, legal or not.

24. Willcock 1984, comments to 21.40, as also 58, 102 and 454, for the confusion and the various verb forms used.

25. Arist. *Rh.* 1.5 1361a20. Cook, writing in *ESS* 11: 521, participates in the confusion surrounding ownership: 'The assertion that a person owns an object is a summary way of stating that he has an exceedingly complex aggregate of legal rights which relate to the object, and that indirectly all the facts necessary to give him these rights exist'. That 'sold' meant for a sum of value: *Il.* 17.225f.; 18.291-2; 21.71-9. An epic precedent for sale overseas is in *Il.* 21.34-113, where Lycaon reveals that he has been sold overseas many times.

26. Harris 2002: 415-35.

27. The enslaved overseas are *hientas*, 'uttering' speech: see comment in Gerber 1970. See *Il.* 3.152. With *glôssa*: S. *El.* 596; Hdt. 9.16; Thuc. 3.112.

28. Responding to Rhodes 1993, comment to *Ath. Pol.* 12.4 (= Solon 36.8-9).

29. *Tromeô* has no other appearance in archaic elegiac and iambic poetry. In epic, e.g. *Il.* 7.151 for *etromeon kai edeidisan*, 'they were all trembling and afraid'.

30. Tandy and Neale 1996: 39f., citing Gernet 1981: 147. Moore 1983's comment to Arist. *Ath. Pol.* 12.4 distinguishes χρείους 'debts' from χρειοῦς 'dire necessity'. Rhodes 1993 comment to Arist. *Ath. Pol.* sees the textual problems in the line, accepts χρειοῦς, and concludes that Solon was misunderstood in antiquity also.

31. Rihll 1991: 121 discusses the passage in terms of slavery at home or abroad.

32. Rickert 1989: 17-34. Among *anagkê* passages with force underlying the necessity Rickert cites *Od.* 22.330-1, 344-53; Hdt. 9.17.1; Thuc. 7.57.1-10.

33. The regional strongmen described by Harris 1997: 103-12 would have been the most powerful of the Mafia-chiefs, as described by van Wees 1999b; 2000.

34. Arist. *Ath. Pol.* 16.5.

35. Russo et al. 1992 comments on *Od.* 22.423: an early meaning of *doulosunê* was 'concubinage'. The women might have lessened their responsibility by not sleeping with the suitors. Was Solon's *polis* in bed with the tyrants?

36. Tyrt. frs 6 and 7, preserved in Pausanias 14.4, relate the physical and psychological domination imposed upon the Messenians. Fragment 7:
   wailing for their masters, they and their wives alike,
   whenever the dreadful allotted death came upon [their masters].

37. LSJ omit the use of *douleuousa* by Solon.

38. Finley 1985, for later economic terms such as *prasis epi lusei*. L'Homme-Wéry 1996: 37 sees Solon 36 as based on a war with Megara over Eleusis, with the *horoi* stones defining the boundary, and 'freedom' as liberation from foreigners. But this is a Homeric, not a Solonian, conception, and is based upon a historical reconstruction that is unsupported in ancient sources.

39. For the fifth century, Hansen 1999: 76 cites Democr. B251 for 'self-determination' in a man who is *eleutheros*. Pohlenz 1966: 1-2: 'his essential feeling is not a fear that puts him on the defensive, but a positive will to live, an urge to shape his life within the limits imposed by the order of the universe'.

40. Not mentioning *eleutherê / eleutherous* in commentaries on poem 36: Kenyon 1892; Sandys 1912; Linforth 1919; Masaracchia 1958; Campbell 1982; Gerber 1970; Rhodes 1993; Anhalt 1993. Even Noussia 2001a does not discuss these terms. Mülke 2002 comments on the passages. Pohlenz 1966: 7: Solon and the Athenians learned 'to appreciate the importance of freedom in the purely political sphere'.

41. Raaflaub 2004: 23, considering Homer's *Iliad*, sees the 'day of freedom' formula as primarily the 'moment of experience'. He notes, p. 28, that '*Eleutheros* in Homer never designates the status of individuals or a group among the free or dominant part of society in contrast to those who are free or dependent'. He cites as a reason, that the position of elites in Homeric society 'afforded no means by which freedom could attain a high value', p. 31.

42. Hom. *Il.* 6.455, 528; 16.831; 20.193. *Od.* 15.403-84 for the enslaved Greek Eumaeus. Hes. *Th.* 54 for *Eleuthêros* as a geographic location. Alcaeus 72.12; Thgn. 538, 916, 1380. Pi. *O.* 12.1 has 'Zeus deliverer'.

43. Endorsed by most editors, including West 1998, Campbell 1982: 252; Rhodes 1993: 176; Noussia 2001a: 359. The alternative is *nomou*, found in the Berlin papyrus, accepted by Blaise 1995; Myres 1947. Irwin 2005a discusses lines 36.15-17 in isolation from the rest of the poem, using comparisons from tyrannical discourse in Homer, Hesiod, Herodotus, et al.

44. Hes. *Th.* 385, 902. Noussia 2001a: 359 comment to 36.15 has related passages in the *Odyssey*.

45. 'Joints' between timbers: *Od.* 5.248, 361. Anhalt 1993: 76 on *Il.* 22.255, witnesses and guardians 'of agreements', *harmoniaôn* (cited in Chapter 1).

46. *Bia* in Solon: 32.2; 34.8; 36.16; 37.4. *Turannos* and related words: 32.2; 34.8; 33.6; 37.4. *Bia* is described but not named at 33.5 as *plouton aphthonon labôn*. The passage best illustrating the role of the *euthuntêr* 'straightener' is Theognis 39-52, discussed in Irwin 2005a: 226.

47. Campbell 1982: 245 for passages prior to Solon.

48. Ostwald 1969: 18-19.

49. Noted by Sealey 1994: 55. Laws as lists: see Jones 1956; Stroud 1979; Hölkeskamp 1992.

50. Noted by Linforth 1919 comment to line 36.19, that 'When Solon came to write this present line, he was confronted by a new political condition: disputes

Notes to pages 125-129

were now to be settled, not by the personal decision of a magistrate, but in accordance with the written law'. Solon thus wrote not *eutheias dikas* 'just decisions', but *eutheian dikên*, 'impartial justice'. But the change is not to democracy – for where has Solon granted power to the people? – but rather from an unwritten subjective sense of *dikê* to objective, written statutes.

51. S. fr. 683. Sandys 1912, Linforth 1919 with a variant reading. Anhalt 1993: 122-4 observes the Homeric *kentron* as a tool of impulse, never of constraint.

52. As a goad: A. *Pr.* 323; an incentive in line 691, and in Pi. fr. 124a.4. As torture: Hdt. 3.130. As a stinger: Ar. *V.* 225, 407, 420, 423; Arist. *PA* 683a12, *HA* 501a32; E. *Supp.* 242; on Socrates, e.g. Pl. *Phdr.* 91c. Hesychius 2232 connects *kentrênekês* with *peithomenos*: *tois kentrois eikontas kai peithomenos*. S. *OT* 809, 318. Eupolis 94 = Kassel and Austin 102. Szegedy-Maszak 1993: 209 compares 36.22 to Thuc. 2.65.8: [Pericles] *kateiche to plêthos eleutherôs*, interpreting the adverb as indicating Pericles' lack of concern for the assembly's approval. Cf. Rusten 1989 comment to 2.65.8: *eleutherôs* here denotes frankness and lack of flattery. Thgn. 847-50 connects the *ochus kentron* and the *dêmos keneophrôn*. For orators, see Pl. *R.* 564b. Also E. *Supp.* 240-3. D. XXVI *Against Aristogeiton* 2, 25.52.

53. See Rhodes 1993 comment to 36.20: *kakophradês to kai philoktêmôn*, fragment 36.21, compared to *Il.* 23.483, *Aian, neikos ariste, kakophradês*. Given Rhodes' general view that Solon did not use force, his comment stresses the persuasive aspects of the office, as well as the wilful evil that the alternative to Solon embraces. Linforth 1919 reads intentionally 'wrong-minded' as 'malignant' and 'unscrupulous', similar to Rhodes. But Linforth sees a greater use of power, as a driver over animals needs to 'use the curb as much as to ply the lash'.

54. E.g. from Judaic tribal law: Schiffman 1983: 'If a man has informed against his people and has delivered his people up to a foreign nation, and has done evil to his people, then you shall hang him on a tree and he shall die. On the evidence of two witnesses he shall be put to death and they shall hang him on the tree'. From the code of Hammurabi: 'If a builder has built a house for a man and his work is not strong, and if the house he has built falls and kills the householder, let the builder be killed.' Edwards 1921, #229.

55. Wolff 1946 for the thesis that the law was used to restrain the accuser, not the accused.

56. West 1998 notes several versions of this proverb.

57. Ostwald 1969 remains the most comprehensive account of *nomos* and *thesmos* in the classical period. Rhodes 1993: 177 comment to Arist. *Ath. Pol.* 12.4 on *thesmos* versus *nomos* in Solon 36.

58. For the fluid nature of tyrannical discourse, see McGlew 1993.

59. d'Entrèves 1967 for a discussion of force, power and authority; authority, in essence, is legal force (power) that is morally legitimated.

60. Arist. *Pol.* 1.2 1253a29f. Translation Sinclair 1982.

61. Szegedy-Maszak 1978 for the stages of the lawgivers' legends.

62. Hes. *Op.* 274-85.

63. On the idea of 'acceptance' consider Fogel 1989: 201: the lack of discussion of slavery through history indicates its deep acceptance.

Solon's Fragments

Translated by John David Lewis

Numbering is based on West 1998. A few short, or dubious, fragments have been omitted: West 4b, 22, 30a, 33a, 35, 41, 45, 46. [Square brackets] indicate an editorial insertion, or point of conjecture given the limitations of the surviving Greek text.

Fragment 1
>I have come as a herald from lovely Salamis,
>composing song, a *kosmos* of words, instead of speech.

Fragment 2
>Would that I were a Pholegandrian or a Sikinite,
>changing my fatherland of Athens.
>For suddenly this would be said by men,
>'This is a man of Attica, the forfeiters of Salamis.'

Fragment 3
>Let us go to Salamis, fighting for the lovely island,
>ridding ourselves of terrible shame

Fragment 4
>Our city will never be destroyed by a dispensation
> from Zeus or the plans of the blessed immortal gods
>for truly a great-hearted daughter of a mighty father
> Pallas Athena holds her hands over it.
>The townsmen themselves by their foolishness desire
> to destroy the great city, persuaded by material goods,
>and the mind of the people's leaders is unjust; they are about
> to suffer many pains from great hubris.
>For they do not understand how to restrain their excess
> nor to order the present festivities of the banquet in calmness.
>   . . . .
>They grow rich, persuaded by their unjust deeds.
>   . . . .
>Sparing the wealth of neither public nor sacred treasuries
>with rapaciousness they rob from one another,
> and fail to guard the sacred foundations of Justice
>who silently knows what is and what was,
> and, in time, surely comes to exact retribution later.
>And now this inescapable wound comes to the entire city,
> which falls swiftly into an evil slavery.

Solon the Thinker

It awakens civil strife and sleeping tribal war,
   which destroys the beautiful youth of many;
and from its troubles the much-loved city is swiftly
   worn out, friendships destroyed in unjust factions.
These evils turn on the people; and of the poor
   many are brought into foreign lands,
sold and bound in shameful fetters.
. . . .
Thus the public evil comes to the house of each man,
   it jumps high over the court-yard fence, breaks down
the locked door, and finds any man for certain,
   even if he flees into the farthest corner of his bedroom.
These things my heart prompts me to teach the Athenians:
   how Lawlessness brings the worst evils to the city, and
Lawfulness manifests good order and everything perfect,
   and often puts fetters on the evil-doers.
It smoothes what is rough; quells anger, dims hubris
   and shrivels the flowering bud of arrogant destruction.
It straightens crooked judgments, calms
   overbearing deeds, stops the deeds of civil strife,
and stops the anger of grievous conflict. It is by this
   that all things to men are perfect and reach their peak.

Fragment 4a

   I come to know, and many pains lie in my heart
      As I look on my most ancient land of Ionia
   declining

Fragment 4c

   You, calm yourselves in your hearts,
      who drag yourselves into an excess of material goods,
   moderate your over-bearing mind; for we will not
      be persuaded, nor will things turn out right for you

Fragment 5

   To the people I gave as many privileges as belonged to them
      neither taking away their honour nor overextending it
   And those who had power and were magnificent due to wealth,
      I saw to it that they had nothing shameful.
   I stood with a powerful shield around both sides,
      not permitting either to claim an unjust victory.

Fragment 6

   In this way the people would follow their leaders best,
      neither allowed to overreach nor oppressed too much.
   For excess breeds hubris, whenever great wealth follows
      men whose understanding is flawed

Fragment 7

   [For] in matters of great importance it is hard to please everyone

Solon's Fragments

Fragment 9
> The force of snow and hail comes from a cloud
>   and thunder from a flash of lightning.
> But the ruin of the city comes from unjust men
>   and the people fall into the slavery of a tyrant by ignorance.
> Having raised these men up it is [not] easy
>   to restrain them later. Now it is right to know all things [well].

Fragment 10
> A short time will show the townsmen whether I am crazy
>   with the truth coming out into the middle

Fragment 11
> If by your own actions you have suffered these most grievous calamities
>   do not place the blame for your lot on the gods.
> You yourselves increased the power of these men, providing them with
>   arms,
>   and this is why you have dreadful slavery.
> Each one of you walks in the steps of a fox,
>   but all together your mind is empty.
> You look to the tongue and words of a wily man,
>   and fail to see his deeds or the facts

Fragment 12
> The sea is stirred up from a wind; and if something does
>   not move it, it is the justest (most calm) of all things

Fragment 13
> Hear, O Muses, shining daughters of Olympian Zeus,
>   and Memory, my prayer.
> Grant me prosperity from the blessed gods, and always
>   to have a good reputation to all men.
> To be sweet to my friends, and bitter to my enemies,
>   Respected by one, and a terror to the others.
> I want to have money, but to get it unjustly
>   I am not willing; for justice surely comes later.
> Wealth which the gods give remains with man,
>   steadfast from the deepest foundation to the top,
> but that which men honour by hubris comes not with proper order,
>   but persuaded by unjust deeds
> does not follow willingly, but swiftly mixes with calamity.
>   It begins from small start, as a fire,
> at first it is minor, in the end devastating.
>   For the works of hubris do not abide for mortals
> but Zeus looks upon the end of all things, and suddenly
>   as a spring wind scatters the clouds
> which moves the depths of the swelling sea,
>   ravaging the lovely works of man
> along the wheat-bearing land, reaches the high seat
>   in the heavens and makes the sky clear,

Solon the Thinker

and the strength of the sun shines over the fair rich
   land, and there is not a cloud to be seen.
Such is the retribution of Zeus. Not upon each thing
   as a mortal man does he become angry,
it never escapes him when a man holds evil
   in his heart, in the end he surely becomes visible.
One man gets what he deserves right away, another later; some
   flee, and if they escape the onrushing fate of the immortals
it comes surely sometime. The innocents pay for the deeds
   or their children or their family thereafter.
We mortals, both noble and base, think we understand,
   and each of us expects that things are going well;
Until experience hits us. Then we wail forthwith, and even to this
   Gaping open-mouthed we are entertained by foolish hopes.
One man, oppressed by miserable disease
   deems he will be healthy, he plans this.
Another man, being lowly, thinks himself high;
   and the ugly man thinks he is handsome.
If a man is poor, violated by poverty,
   he thinks he will surely possess great wealth
Men pursue their livings in different ways. One fishes in the sea,
   using ships to bring home profit;
battered by the merciless winds,
   he places no regard upon life.
Another man ploughs the many-treed land for a year,
   working the curved plough for hire.
Another man, having learned the works of Athena
   and Hephaistos of many crafts, gathers a livelihood with his hands.
Another one, taught the gifts of the Olympian Muses,
   is an expert at the metre of lovely poetic wisdom;
King Apollo far-shooter makes another man a seer,
   he knows the evil coming upon man from afar,
if the gods are witnesses. Surely neither augury
   nor sacred rites can protect against one's allotted fate.
Other men, holding the many potions of Paion
   treat the sick; and there is no certain end to their efforts.
Often from a little pain comes a deep disease
   and he cannot be released from it by gentle remedies;
another one, in the grip of a deep debilitating disease,
   he cures by placing his hands on him.
Moira brings good and evil to mortals,
   the gifts of the immortal gods may not be escaped.
There is risk in all actions, and no one knows
   how something, having started, will end up.
But one man, attempting to do well but not seeing ahead
   falls into great and difficult calamity,
to another acting badly the god grants good luck in all things,
   releasing him from his folly.
Of wealth no limit lies revealed to men,
   for those of us who have the greatest standard of living

work twice as hard. Who can be satisfied in every way?
  The immortals bring profit to mortals,
but calamity arises from these things, which,
  when Zeus sends retribution, passes from one man to another.

Fragment 14
  No mortal is blessed, but all are wretched
    whom the sun looks down upon.

Fragment 15
  Many evil men grow rich, and good men grow poor.
    But we will not exchange our excellence
  for their wealth, since the one abides forever,
    but possessions jump from one man to another.

Fragment 16
  It is most difficult to know the measure of wisdom, which
    alone holds the end of all things.

Fragment 17
  The mind of the immortals is hidden in every way from men

Fragment 18
  I grow old always learning many things,

Fragment 19
  And now may you and your descendants inhabit this city
    ruling over Solioi for a long time.
  And may violet-crowned Cypris send me away
    from your renown island unscathed in a swift ship.
  May she bring favour and glory on this settlement
    and a good return to my homeland.

Fragment 20
  But if you will be persuaded by me, take this out —
    don't begrudge me, because I think better than you —
  and changing it, Ligiastades, sing this way:
    'May I meet my allotted death at eighty.'

Fragment 21
  May death not come to me tearlessly, but may I leave my
    friends with sorrow and pain when I die,

Fragment 22a
  Tell flaxen-haired Critias to listen to his father,
    for he will not be persuaded by an erring role-model.

Fragment 23
  The man is happy who has dear boys, single-hoofed horses,
    hunting dogs and a friend in a foreign land.

Fragment 24
>He is equally rich is he who has much silver
>>and gold, and wheat-bearing plains
>and horses and mules, and he who has this alone,
>>to live pleasantly in stomach and sides and feet,
>and when this comes, a season for woman and child
>>to live with proper youthful vigour.
>This is wealth to mortals; for no one
>>carries to Hades all their surpluses of money,
>nor can he pay a ransom and escape death,
>>deep disease, or encroaching evil old age.

Fragment 25
>[until] he falls in love with a boy in the flower of youth,
>>of desirable thighs and sweet lips.

Fragment 26
>Now the deeds of the Cyprus-born, of Dionysus and of
>>the Muses, are dear, which bring good cheer to men,

Fragment 27
>A child, while still immature and foolish, grows a fence of
>>teeth and loses them in the first seven years.
>When the god completes the next seven years,
>>signs appear of oncoming puberty.
>In the third period his body is growing, his chin gets a
>>down, and his skin changes colour.
>In the fourth hebdomad everyone is at best strength,
>>and men show signs of manly virtue.
>In the fifth season marriage comes to a man's attention,
>>and he looks for a line of sons to follow after him.
>In the sixth the mind of man is most practised in all things,
>>nor does he desire to do foolish things.
>In the seventh and eighth periods his mind and tongue
>>are at their best for fourteen years.
>In the ninth years he is yet capable, but his tongue and wisdom
>>are weaker with respect to great excellence.
>And if he comes upon a measured end in the tenth period,
>>he would not have his fated death unseasonably.

Fragment 28
>At the mouth of the Nile, near Canopus' shore.

Fragment 29
>Poets tell many lies.

Fragment 30
>Hearken to the officials, both right and wrong

Solon's Fragments

Fragment 31
    First let us pray to King Zeus son of Chronos
    to bring good luck and renown to the statutes.

Fragment 32
        If I spared my fatherland
    and did not grasp tyranny and implacable violence,
    staining and disgracing my reputation,
    I am not ashamed. For in this way I think that I shall
    be superior to all men.

Fragment 33
    'This man Solon is a shallow thinker and a fool;
    for the gods give him great goods, but he does not take them.
    He throws a great net around his prey, but then does not draw it in
    He has neither good sense nor the will to use it.
    Had I come upon power, taking lavish wealth
    and subjecting the Athenians to tyranny for one day only,
    I'd be willing to be flayed into a wineskin later, my family obliterated.'

Fragment 34
    They came as upon plunder, and held hope of riches,
    and each one of them expected to find much wealth,
    and that I, babbling smoothly, would show a rough disposition.
    But they spoke foolishly then, and now, angry at me,
    they all look askance as upon an enemy.
    But it is not necessary. For whatever I said, I have done with the gods,
    I did not take pointless measures, nor did it please me
    [to compel] with the force of tyranny nor to subject
    my rich fatherland to an equality of shares between good and evil men.

Fragment 36
    I brought the people together for these reasons,
    How did I stop before I accomplished them?
    In the court of Time these things will be witnessed
    by the testimony of the great mother of the Olympian
    gods, Black Earth, from whom I drew
    up the boundary stones stuck in everywhere;
    earlier she was enslaved, now she is free.
    Many men I brought up to their divinely-founded
    fatherland, men sold, one illegally,
    another legally, and others fleeing their debts,
    by forcible necessity, no longer speaking an Attic-tongue,
    as men wandering everywhere;
    and others holding a shameful slavery,
    now trembling before their masters,
    I set them free. By my own power,
    fitting together force with justice,
    these things I did, and I came through as I promised.
    And statutes alike to the base man and to the noble
    fitting straight justice onto each man's case

Solon the Thinker

these I wrote. But had another man than I taken the goad,
an evil-thinking and power-hungry man,
he would not have restrained the people.
For if I acquiesced to whatever things were pleasing to my enemies,
and then shifted to what the other side thought,
this city would be widowed of many men.
On account of these things, making a defence in all directions,
I stood, as a wolf among many hounds.

Fragment 37

If it were necessary to chide the people openly,
Whatever they now have they never could have known
In their dreams ...
And those who were greater and stronger
Would praise me and make me their friend.
[For if some other man, it is said, happened upon this honour]
He would not have restrained the people, nor stopped
until he stirred up the milk and took off the cream.
But I, on account of these things, as in a no-man's land,
stood, a boundary stone.

Fragment 38

They are drinking; and some are eating cakes,
others of them bread, and others gouroi mixed
with lentils. No pastry is missing there which
the dark earth brings forth to men, but
everything is present in abundance.

Fragment 39

Some work for mortar, others silphium,
others vinegar,

Fragment 40

One [works for] pomegranate seed, another sesame.

Bibliography

Abel, D.H. (1943), 'Genealogies of ethical concepts from Hesiod to Bacchylides', in *Transactions of the American Philological Association* 74: 92-101.
Adkins, A.W.H. (1960), *Merit and Responsibility: A Study in Greek Values* (Oxford).
Adkins, A.W.H. (1972a), *Moral Values and Political Behaviour in Ancient Greece from Homer to the End of the Fifth Century* (London).
Adkins, A.W.H. (1972b), 'Truth, ΚΟΣΜΟΣ, and ΑΡΕΤΗ in the Homeric poems', in *Classical Quarterly* 22: 5-18.
Adkins, A.W.H. (1985), *Poetic Craft in the Early Greek Elegists* (Chicago and London).
Allen, A.W. (1949), 'Solon's prayer to the muses', in *Transactions of the American Philological Association* 80: 50-65.
Almeida, J. (2003), *Justice as an Aspect of the Polis Idea in Solon's Political Poems: A Reading of the Fragments in Light of the Researches of New Classical Archaeology* (Leiden).
Alt, K. (1979), 'Solons Gebet zu den Musen', in *Hermes* 107: 389-406.
Andrewes, A. (1938), 'Eunomia', in *Classical Quarterly* 32: 89-102.
Anhalt, E.K. (1993), *Solon the Singer: Politics and Poetics* (Lanham).
Anton, J.P. and Preus, A. (eds) (1983), *Essays in Ancient Philosophy*, vol. 2 (Albany).
Atherton, C. (1998), *Form and Content in Didactic Poetry* (Bari).
Badian, E. (ed.) (1967), *Ancient Society and Institutions: Studies Presented to Victor Ehrenberg on his 75th Birthday* (New York).
Balot, R.K. (2001), *Greed and Injustice in Classical Athens* (Princeton).
Barnes, J. (1982), *The Presocratic Philosophers*, rev. edn (London, Boston, Melbourne and Henley).
Bergk, T. (1882), *Poetae Lyrici Graeci*, 4th edn (Leipzig).
Björck, G. (1942), 'A propos de Solon 1,11', in *Eranos* 40: 177-81.
Blaise, F. (1995), 'Solon Fragment 36W. Pratique et fondation des norms politiques', in *Revue des Etudes Grecques* 108: 25-37.
den Boer, W. (1966), 'A new fragment of Solon?', in *Mnemosyne* 19 ns 4: 46-7.
Boersma, J.S. (1970), *The Athenian Building Policy from 561/0 to 405/4* (Groningen).
Bowie, E.L. (1993), 'Lies, fiction and slander in early Greek poetry', in Gill and Wiseman (eds): 1-37.
Bowra, C.M. (1938), *Early Greek Elegists* (London).
Bowra, C.M. (1953), *Problems in Greek Poetry* (Oxford).
Brannan, P.T. (ed.) (1975), *Classica et Iberica: A Festschrift in Honor of The Reverend Joseph H.-F. Marique, S.J.* (Worcester, MA).
Broadie, S. (1999), 'Rational theology', in Long (ed.): 205-24.
Brock, R. and Hodkinson, S. (eds) (2000), *Alternatives to Athens: Varieties of Political Organization and Community in Ancient Greece* (Oxford).

Brunschwig, J. and Lloyd, G.E.R. (eds) (2000), *Greek Thought: A Guide to Classical Knowledge*, tr. under the direction of C. Porter (Cambridge, MA and London).
Bryant, J.M. (1996), *Moral Codes and Social Structure in Ancient Greece: A Sociology of Greek Ethics from Homer to the Epicureans to the Stoics* (Albany).
Burn, A.R. (1960), *The Lyric Age of Greece* (London).
Buxton, R.G.A. (1982), *Persuasion in Greek Tragedy: A Study of Peitho* (Cambridge).
Cairns, D. (1993), *Aidos: The Psychology and Ethics of Honour and Shame in Ancient Greek Literature* (Oxford).
Calhoun, G.M. (1927), *The Growth of Criminal Law in Ancient Greece* (Berkeley).
Campbell, D.A. (1982), *Greek Lyric Poetry: A Selection of Early Greek Lyric, Elegiac and Iambic Poetry*, new edn (London).
Carawan, E. (1998), *Rhetoric and the Law of Draco* (Oxford).
Carson, A. (1984), 'How bad a poem is Semonides Fragment 1?', in Gerber (ed.): 59-71.
Cartledge, P.A. (1997), *The Greeks: A Portrait of Self and Others*, rev. edn (Oxford).
Cartledge, P.A. (1998), 'Introduction: Defining a Kosmos', in Cartledge, Millett and von Reden (eds): 1-12.
Cartledge, P.A., Millett, P. and von Reden, S. (eds) (1998), *Kosmos: Essays in Order, Conflict and Community in Classical Athens* (Cambridge).
Case, T, 'Chronology of the Solonian Legislation', in *Classical Review* 2: 241-2.
Cavarnos, C. (1996), *The Seven Sages of Ancient Greece: The Lives and Teachings of the Earliest Greek Philosophers, Thales, Pittacus, Bias, Solon, Cleobulos, Myson, Chilon* (Belmont, Ma.).
Cawkwell, G. (1995), 'Early Greek tyranny and the people', in *Classical Quarterly* 45: 73-86.
Centre G. Glotz (1984), *Aux Origines de l'Héllenisme de la Crète et la Grèce: Hommage à Henri van Effenterre* (Paris).
Chantraine, P. (1968), *Dictionnaire Etymologique de la Langue Grecque: Histoire des Mots* (Paris).
Chiasson, C.C. (1986), 'The Herodotean Solon', in *Greek, Roman and Byzantine Studies* 27: 249-62.
Christes, J. (1986), 'Solon's Musenelegie', in *Hermes* 87: 163-90.
Coldstream, J.N. (1977), *Geometric Greece* (London).
Coldstream, J.N. (1984), *The Formation of the Greek Polis: Aristotle and Archaeology* (Opladen).
Cooper, J.M. (ed.) (1997), *Plato: Complete Works* (Indianapolis).
Copeland, L. and Lamm, L. (eds) (1958), *The World's Great Speeches* (New York).
Coxon, A.H. (1986), *The Fragments of Parmenides* (Amsterdam).
Croiset, M. (1903), 'La morale et la cité dans les poésies de Solon', in *Comptes Rendus de l'Academie des Inscriptions et Belles-Lettres*: 581-96.
Dickie, M.W. (1976), 'On the meaning of ἐφήμερος', in *Illinois Classical Studies* 1: 7-14.
Dickie, M.W. (1984), '*Hesychia* and *hybris* in Pindar', in Gerber (ed.): 83-109.
Diehl, E. (1949), *Anthologia Lyrica*, vol. 1 (Lipsiae).
Diels, H. and Kranz, W. (1951/52), *Die Fragmente der Vorsokratiker*, 3 vols (Berlin).
Dihle, A. (1982), *The Theory of Will in Classical Antiquity* (Berkeley, Los Angeles and London).
Dodds, E.R. (1951), *The Greeks and the Irrational* (Berkeley).

Bibliography

Donlan, W. (1973), *The Aristocratic Ideal in Ancient Greece: Attitudes of Superiority from Homer to the End of the Fifth Century* BC (Lawrence).
Dougherty, C. and Kurke, L. (eds) (1993), *Cultural Poetics in Archaic Greece: Cult, Performance, Politics* (Cambridge).
Dover, K.J. (1974), *Greek Popular Morality in the Time of Plato and Aristotle* (Berkeley and Los Angeles).
Doyle, R.E. (1984), *ATH: Its Use and Meaning* (New York).
Easterling, P.E. and Knox, B.M.W. (1985), *Cambridge History of Classical Literature: I: Greek Literature* (repr.) (Cambridge).
Edmonds, J.M. (1931), *Elegy and Iambus* (Cambridge, MA).
Edmunds, L. (1997), 'The Seal of Theognis', in Edmunds and Wallace (eds): 29-48.
Edmunds, L. and Wallace, R.W. (eds) (1997), *Poet, Public and Performance in Ancient Greece* (Baltimore and London).
Edwards, C. (tr.) (1921), *The Hammurabi Code* (London).
Ehrenberg, V. (1973), *From Solon to Socrates: Greek History and Civilization during the Fifth and Sixth Centuries* BC, 2nd edn (London).
Ehrhardt, A. (1959), *Politische Metaphysik von Solon bis Augustin I: Die Gottesstadt der Griechen und Römer* (Mohr).
Emlyn-Jones, C. (1980), *The Ionians and Hellenism: A Study of the Cultural Achievements of the Early Greek Inhabitants of Asia Minor* (London, Boston and Henley).
Engels, F. (1972 [1884]), *Origins of the Family, Private Property and the State in the Light of the Researches of Lewis H. Morgan* (London).
d'Entrèves, A.P. (1967), *The Notion of the State* (Oxford).
Erasmus, H.J. (1960), 'Eunomia', in *Acta Classica* 3: 53-64.
Everson, S. (ed.) (1990), *Epistemology* (Cambridge).
Everson, S. (ed.) (1998), *Ethics* (Cambridge).
Fagles, R. (1996), *The Odyssey* (New York).
Fine, J.V.A. (1951), 'Horoi', in *Hesperia* Supplement 9.
Finkelberg, M. (1998), *The Birth of Literary Fiction in Ancient Greece* (Oxford).
Finley, M.I. (1968), *Slavery in Classical Antiquity: Views and Controversies*, repr. edn (Cambridge).
Finley, M.I. (1980), *Ancient Slavery and Modern Ideology* (London).
Finley, M.I. (1983), *Politics in the Ancient World* (Cambridge).
Finley, M.I. (1985), *Studies in Land and Credit in Ancient Athens, 500-200* BC, 2nd edn (New Brunswick).
Fisher, N.R.E. (1992), *Hybris: A Study in the Values of Honour and Shame in Ancient Greece* (Warminster).
Fitzgerald, R. (1963), *The Odyssey* (New York).
Fogel, R.W. (1989), *Without Consent or Contract: The Rise and Fall of American Slavery* (New York).
Fowler, R.L. (1987), *The Nature of Early Greek Lyric: Three Preliminary Studies* (Toronto, Buffalo and London).
Foxhall, L. (1997), 'A view from the top: evaluating Solonian propertied classes', in Mitchell and Rhodes (eds): 113-39.
Foxhall, L. and Lewis, A.D.E. (eds) (1996), *Greek Law in its Political Setting* (Oxford).
Fränkel, E. (1950), *Aeschylus: Agamemnon* (Oxford).
Fränkel, H. (1946), 'Man's "ephemeros" nature according to Pindar and others', in *Transactions of the American Philological Association* 70: 131-45.

Fränkel, H. (1975), *Dichtung und Philosophie des frühen Griechentums*, tr. M. Hadas (Oxford).
Fränkel, H. (1993), 'Xenophanes' empiricism and his critique of knowledge', in Mourelatos (ed.): 118-31.
Freeman, K. (1926), *The Work and Life of Solon* (London).
French, A. (1956), 'The economic background to Solon's reforms', in *Classical Quarterly* 6: 11-25.
French, A. (1963), 'Land tenure and the Solon problem', in *Historia* 12: 242-7.
von Fritz, K. (1943), 'ΝΟΟΣ and NOEIN in the Homeric poems', in *CP* 38: 79-94.
von Fritz, K. (1993), 'ΝΟΥΣ, NOEIN and their derivatives in pre-Socratic philosophy (excluding Anaxagoras)', in Mourelatos (ed.): 23-85.
von Fritz, K. and Kapp, E. (1974), *Aristotle's Constitution of Athens and Related Texts* (New York).
Furley, D.J. and Allen, R.E. (eds) (1970), *Studies in Presocratic Philosophy*, vol. 1 (London).
Gagarin, M. (1973), '*Dikê* in the *Works and Days*', in *Classical Philology* 68: 81-94.
Gagarin, M. (1974), '*Dikê* in Archaic Greek thought', in *Classical Philology* 69: 186-97.
Gagarin, M. (1986), *Early Greek Law* (Berkeley).
Gagarin, M. and Woodruff, P. (1995), *Early Greek Political Thought from Homer to the Sophists* (Cambridge).
Garlan, Y. (1988), *Slavery in Ancient Greece*, tr. J. Lloyd, rev. and exp. edn (London).
Garnsey, P. (1996), *Ideas of Slavery from Aristotle to Augustine* (Cambridge).
Gentili, B. (1988), *Poetry and Its Public in Ancient Greece: From Homer to the Fifth Century*, tr. A.T. Cole (Baltimore and London).
Gentili, B. and Cerri, G. (eds) (1988), *History and Biography in Ancient Thought* (Amsterdam).
Gentili, B. and Prato, C. (1979), *Poetarum Elegiacorum Testimonia et Fragmenta* (Leipzig).
Gerber, D.E. (1970), *Euterpe: An Anthology of Early Greek Lyric, Elegiac and Iambic Poetry* (Amsterdam).
Gerber, D.E. (1984), 'Semonides, Fr. 1 West: a commentary', in Gerber (ed.): 125-35.
Gerber, D.E. (ed.) (1984), *Early Greek Poetry and Philosophy: Studies in Honour of Leonard Woodbury* (Chico, CA).
Gerber, D.E. (1991), 'Early Greek elegy and iambus', in *Lustrum* 33: 7-225.
Gerber, D.E. (1997), *A Companion to the Greek Lyric Poets* (Leiden, New York and Köln).
Gerber, D.E. (1999), *Greek Elegiac Poetry* (Cambridge, MA).
Gernet, L. (1981), 'Les bases de la cité classique', in *Quaderni di Storia* 13: 228-35.
Goldhill, S. (1991), *The Poet's Voice: Essays on Poetics and Greek Literature* (Cambridge).
Gouschin, V. (1999), 'Pisistratus' leadership in A.P. 13.4 and the Establishment of the Tyranny in 561/60 BC', in *Classical Quarterly* 49: 14-23.
Greene, W.C. (1944), *Moira: Fate, Good and Evil in Greek Thought* (Cambridge, MA).
Greenhalgh, P.A.L. (1972), 'Aristocracy and its advocates in Ancient Greece', in *Greece and Rome* 19: 190-207.
Griffith, M. (1990), 'Contest and contradiction in early Greek poetry', in Griffith and Mastronarde (eds): 185-207.

Bibliography

Griffith, M. and Mastronarde, D.J. (eds) (1990), *The Cabinet of the Muses: Essays on Classical and Comparative Literature in Honor of Thomas G. Rosenmeyer* (Atlanta).
Guthrie, W.K.C. (1962, 1965, 1969), *A History of Greek Philosophy*, vols 1, 2 and 3 (Cambridge).
Hahn, R. (2001), *Anaximander and the Architects* (Albany).
Hainsworth, B. (1993), *The Iliad: A Commentary, Books 9-12* (Cambridge).
Halberstadt, M. (1955), 'On Solon s "Eunomia" ', in *Classical Weekly* 48: 15: 197-203.
Hamilton, R. (1977), 'Solon 13.74 ff. (West)', in *Greek, Roman and Byzantine Studies* 18: 185-8.
Hamilton, A., Madison, J. and Jay, J. (2005), *The Federalist*, ed. J.R. Pole (Indianapolis and Cambridge).
Hammer, D. (2004), 'Ideology, the symposium, and archaic politics', in *American Journal of Philology* 125.4: 479-512.
Hansen, M.H. (1999), *The Athenian Democracy in the Age of Demosthenes*, repr. edn (London).
Harris, E. (1997), 'A new solution to the riddle of the seisachtheia', in Mitchell and Rhodes: 103-12.
Harris, E. (2002), 'Did Solon abolish debt-bondage?', in *Classical Quarterly* 52.2: 415-35.
Harrison, T. (2002), *Divinity and History: The Religion of Herodotus*, repr. edn (Oxford).
Haubold, J. (2000), *Homer's People: Epic Poetry and Social Formation* (Cambridge).
Havelock, E.A. (1957), *The Liberal Temper in Greek Politics* (London).
Havelock, E.A. (1978), *The Greek Concept of Justice: From its Shadow in Homer to its Substance in Plato* (Cambridge, MA and London).
Helm, J.J. (1993), 'Koros: from satisfaction to greed', in *Classical World* 87.1: 5-11.
Henderson, W.J. (1982), 'The nature and function of Solon's poetry: Fr. 3 Diehl, 4 West', in *Acta Classica* 25: 21-33.
Hodkinson, S. and Powell, A. (eds) (1999), *Sparta: New Perspectives* (London).
Hölkeskamp, K-J. (1992), 'Written law in archaic Greece', in *Proceedings of the Cambridge Philological Society* 38: 87-117.
Hopper, R.J. (1967), 'The Solonian "crisis" ', in Badian (ed.): 139-46.
Hopwood, K. (ed.) (1999), *Organised Crime in Antiquity* (London).
How, W.W. and Wells, J. (eds) (1975), *A Commentary on Herodotus*, vol. 2 (Oxford).
Hudson-Williams, T. (1926), *Early Greek Elegy* (Cardiff and London).
Hussey, E. (1972), *The Presocratics* (London).
Hussey, E. (1990), 'The beginnings of epistemology: from Homer to Philolaus', in Everson (ed.): 11-38.
Hussey, E. (1995), 'Ionian inquiries: on understanding the Presocratic beginnings of science', in Powell (ed.): 530-49.
Irwin, E. (2005a), *Solon and Early Greek Poetry: The Politics of Exhortation* (Cambridge).
Irwin, E. (2005b) Review of Mülke (2002), in *Bryn Mawr Classical Review* 2005: 05: 26.
Jaeger, W. (1947), *The Theology of the Early Greek Philosophers* (Oxford).
Jaeger, W. (1966), *Five Essays*, tr. A.M. Fiske (Montreal).
Janko, R. (1992), *The Iliad: A Commentary*, vol. 4, books 13-16 (Cambridge).

Johnson, W.R. (1982), *The Idea of Lyric: Lyric Modes in Ancient and Modern Poetry* (Berkeley).
Jones, J.W. (1956), *The Law and Legal Theory of the Greeks: An Introduction* (Oxford).
Kahn, C.H. (1979), *The Art and Thought of Heraklitus: An Edition of the Fragments with Translation and Commentary* (Cambridge).
Kahn, C.H. (1985 [1960]), *Anaximander and the Origins of Greek Cosmology*, 1st paperback edn (New York).
Kahn, C.H. (1998), 'Pre-Platonic Ethics', in Everson (ed.): 27-48.
Kalimtzis, K. (2000), *Aristotle on Political Enmity and Disease* (Albany).
Kamerbeek, J.C. (1984), *The Plays of Sophocles: Commentaries, Part VII: The Oedipus Coloneus* (Leiden).
Kassel, R., and Austin, C. (1986), *Poetae Comici Graeci*, vol. 5 (Berlin).
Keaney, J.J. (1992), *The Composition of Aristotle's Athenaion Politeia: Observation and Explanation* (New York and Oxford).
Kennedy, G.A. (1994), *A New History of Classical Rhetoric* (Princeton).
Kenyon, F.G. (1892), *Aristotle on the Constitution of Athens*, 3rd edn (London).
Ker, J. (2000), 'Solon's theoria and the end of the city', in *Classical Antiquity* 19.2 (2000): 304-29.
Kilmer, M.F. and Develin, R. (2001), 'Sophilos' vase inscriptions and cultural literacy in archaic Athens', in *Phoenix* LV.1-2: 9-43.
Kirk, G.S. (1970), 'Some problems in Anaximander', in Furley and Allen (eds): 323-49.
Kirk, G.S. (1990), *The Iliad: A Commentary*, vol. 2 (Cambridge).
Kirk, G.S., Raven, J.E. and Schofield, M. (1983), *The Presocratic Philosophers: A Critical History with a Selection of Texts* (Cambridge).
Knox, B.M.W. (1985), 'Solon', in Easterling and Knox (eds): 146-53.
Krischer, T. (1984), 'νόος, νοεῖν, νόημα', in *Glotta* 62: 141-9.
Kurke, L. (1992), 'The politics of ἁβροσύνη in archaic Greece', in *Classical Antiquity* 11.1: 91-120.
Laistner, M.L.W. (1923), *Greek Economics: Introduction and Translation* (London and Toronto).
Lattimore, R. (1947), 'The first elegy of Solon', in *American Journal of Philology* 68.1: 161-79.
Lavelle, B.M. (2005), *Fame, Money and Power: The Rise of Peisistratos and 'Democratic' Tyranny at Athens* (Ann Arbor).
Leaf, W. (1960), *The Iliad*, vols 1 and 2, 2nd edn (Amsterdam).
Lehmann-Haupt, C.F. (1912), *Solon of Athens* (Liverpool).
Lesher, J.H. (1983), 'Xenophanes' skepticism', in Anton and Preus (eds): 2: 20-40.
Lesher, J.H. (1991), 'Xenophanes on inquiry and discovery: an alternative to the 'Hymn to Progress' reading of Fr. 18', in *Ancient Philosophy* 11.2: 229-48.
Lesher, J.H. (1994), 'The emergence of philosophical interest in cognition', in *Oxford Studies in Ancient Philosophy* 12: 1-34.
Lesher, J.H. (1999), 'Early interest in knowledge', in Long (ed.): 225-49.
Lesky, A. (1996), *History of Greek Literature*, tr. J. Willis and C. de Heer (London).
Lévêque, P. and Vidal-Naquet, P. (1996), *Cleisthenes the Athenian: An Essay on the Representation of Space and Time in Greek Political Thought from the End of the Sixth Century to the Death of Plato*, tr. D.A. Curtis (Atlantic Highlands, NJ).
Lewis, J. (2005), 'Slavery and lawlessness in Solonian Athens', in *Dike* 7: 19-40.

Bibliography

L'Homme-Wéry, L.M. (1996), *La Perspective Eleusinienne dans la Politique de Solon*, Geneva.
Liddell, H.G., Scott, R. and Jones, S. (1994), *A Greek-English Lexicon* (Oxford).
Linforth, I.M. (1919), *Solon the Athenian* (Berkeley).
Lloyd, G.E.R. (1970), *Early Greek Science: Thales to Aristotle* (London).
Lloyd, G.E.R. (1978), *Hippocratic Writings* (Harmondsworth).
Lloyd, G.E.R. (1987), *The Revolutions of Wisdom: Studies in the Claims and Practice of Ancient Greek Science* (Berkeley, Los Angeles and London).
Lloyd, G.E.R. (2000), 'Images of the World', in Brunschwig and Lloyd (eds): 20-38.
Lloyd-Jones, H. (1971), *The Justice of Zeus* (Berkeley, Los Angeles and London).
Long, A.A. (ed.) (1999), *The Cambridge Companion to Early Greek Philosophy* (Cambridge).
Long, H.S. (1964), *Diogenis Laertii: Vitae Philosophorum* (Oxford).
Longo, C.P. (1988), 'Sulla legge "Soloniana" contro la neutralitè', in *Historia* 37: 374-9.
Loraux, N. (1984), 'Solon au milieu de la lice', in Centre G. Glotz (ed.): 199-214.
Manuwald, B. (1989), 'Zu Solons Gedankenwelt', in *Rheinisches Museum* 132: 1-25.
Manville, P.B. (1990), *The Origins of Citizenship in Ancient Athens* (Princeton).
Marcovich, M. (1967), *Heraclitus: Greek Text with a Short Commentary* (Merida, Venezuela).
Martin, R.P. (1993), 'The Seven Sages as Performers of Wisdom', in Dougherty and Kurke (eds): 108-28.
Martina, A. (1968), *Solone: Testimonianze sulla Vita e l'Opera* (Rome).
Masaracchia, A. (1958), *Solone* (Firenze).
Matheson, S.B. (1994), 'The Goddess Tyche', in Matheson (ed.) (New Haven): 18-33.
Matheson, S.B. (ed.) (1994), *An Obsession with Fortune: Tyche in Greek and Roman Art* (New Haven).
Matthiessen, K. (1994), 'Solon's Musenelegie und die Entwicklung des griechischen Rechtsdenkens', in *Gymnasium* 101: 385-407.
McEwen, I.K. (1993), *Socrates' Ancestor* (Cambridge, MA).
McGlew, J. (1993), *Tyranny and Political Culture in Ancient Greece* (Ithaca and London).
McKirahan, R.D. (1994), *Philosophy Before Socrates* (Indianapolis).
Meier, C. (1990), *The Greek Discovery of Politics*, tr. D. McLintock (Cambridge, MA and London).
Merkelbach, R. and West, M.L. (1999), *Fragmenta Hesiodea*, Sandpiper edn (Oxford).
Miller, M. (1969), 'The accepted date for Solon: precise, but wrong?', in *Arethusa* 2: 62-86.
Milne, J.G. (1930), 'The monetary reforms of Solon', in *Journal of Hellenic Studies* 50: 179-85.
Milne, J.G. (1945), 'The economic policy of Solon', in *Hesperia* 14: 230-45.
Mitchell, L. and Rhodes, P.J. (eds) (1997), *The Development of the Polis in Archaic Greece* (New York).
Moore, J.M. (1983), *Aristotle and Xenophon on Democracy and Oligarchy* (London).
Morris, I. (1987), *Burial and Ancient Society* (Cambridge).
Morris, I. (1994), 'Archaeologies of Greece', in *Classical Greece: Ancient Histories and Modern Archaeologies* (Cambridge).

Morris, I. (2000), *Archaeology as Cultural History: Words and Things in Iron Age Greece* (Malden, MA).
Most, G. (1999), 'The poetics of early Greek philosophy', in Long (ed.): 332-62.
Mourelatos, A.P.D. (ed.) (1993), *The Presocratics* (New York).
Mülke, C. (2002), *Solons politische Elegien und Iamben (Fr. 1-13, 32-37 West): Enleitung, Text, Übersetzung, Kommentar* (Leipzig).
Murray, O. (1990), 'Cities of reason', in Murray and Price (eds): 1-28.
Murray, O. (ed.) (1990), *Sympotica: A Symposium on the Symposium* (Oxford).
Murray, O. (1991), 'History and reason in the ancient city', in *British School at Rome* 59 ns 46: 1-13.
Murray, O. (1993), *Early Greece*, 2nd edn (London).
Murray, O., and Price, S. (eds) (1990), *The Greek City from Homer to Alexander* (Oxford).
Myres, J.L. (1927), *The Political Ideas of the Greeks* (London).
Myres, J.L. (1947), 'Eunomia', in *Classical Review* 61: 80-2.
Nagy, G. (1979), *The Best of the Achaeans: Concepts of the Hero in Ancient Greek Poetry* (Baltimore and London).
Nagy, G. (1983), 'Σῆμα and νόησις: some illustrations', in *Arethusa* 16: 35-55.
Nagy, G. (1990), *Greek Mythology and Poetics* (Ithaca).
Noussia, M. (1999), 'The profession of physician (Solon fr. 1,57-66 Gent.-Pr.^{2} = 13,57-66 W.^{2})', in *Eikasmos* 10.9-20.
Noussia, M. (2001a), *Solone: Frammenti dell'Opera Poetica* (Milano).
Noussia, M. (2001b), 'Solon's symposium (Frs 32-4 and 36 Gentili-Prato = 38-40 and 41 West)', in *Classical Quarterly* 51.2: 353-9.
Ober, J. (1989), *Mass and Elite in Democratic Athens* (Princeton).
Oldfather, C.H. (1985), *Diodorus Sicilus: Library of History, I-2.34* (Cambridge, MA).
Osborne, R. (1996), *Greece in the Making: 1200-479 BC* (London).
Ostwald, M. (1969), *Nomos and the Beginnings of Athenian Democracy* (Oxford).
Ostwald, M. (1973), 'Ancient Greek ideas of law', in *Dictionary of the History of Ideas*: 673-85.
Ostwald, M. (1986), *From Popular Sovereignty to the Sovereignty of Law: Law, Society and Politics in Fifth-Century Athens* (Berkeley).
Page, D.L. (1975), *Poetae Melici Graeci* (Oxford).
Parker, R. (1983), *Miasma* (Oxford).
Parker R. (1995), *Athenian Religion: A History* (Oxford).
Parker, V. (1998), 'Τύραννος. The semantics of a political concept from Archilochus to Aristotle', in *Hermes* 126: 145-72.
Patterson, O. (1982), *Slavery and Social Death: A Comparative Study* (Cambridge, MA, and London).
Peikoff, L. (1993), *Objectivism: The Philosophy of Ayn Rand* (New York).
Perrin, B. (1967), *Plutarch Parallel Lives: Theseus et al* (Cambridge, MA).
Perry, B. (1937), 'The early Greek capacity for viewing things separately', in *Transactions of the American Philological Association* 68: 403-27.
Podlecki, A. (1975), 'Solon's sojourns', in Brannan (ed.): 31-40.
Pohlenz, M. (1966), *Freedom in Greek Life and Thought: The History of an Ideal* (Dordrecht).
de Polignac, F. (1995), *Cults, Territory and the Origins of the Greek City-State*, tr. J. Lloyd (Chicago and London).
Powell, A. (ed.) (1995), *The Greek World* (London and New York).

Bibliography

Pozzi, D.C. and Wickersham, J.M. (eds) (1991), *Myth and the Polis* (Ithaca and London).
Prier, R.A. (1976), *Archaic Logic: Symbol and Structure in Heraclitus, Parmenides and Empedocles* (The Hague).
Procopé, J.F. (1989), 'Democritus on politics and the care of the soul', in *Classical Quarterly* 39: 307-31.
Procopé, J.F. (1990), 'Democritus on politics and the care of the soul: appendix', in *Classical Quarterly* 40: 21-45.
Raaflaub, K. (2004), *The Discovery of Freedom in Ancient Greece* (Chicago and London).
Rand, A. (1973), 'The Missing Link', in The Ayn Rand Letter II.16-17: 195-204.
Reinhardt, K. (1916), 'Solons Elegie εἰς ἑαυτόν', in *Rheinisches Museum* 27: 128-35.
Rhodes, P.J. (1993), *A Commentary on the Aristotelian Athenaion Politeia,* repr. with corr. and adds (Oxford).
Rich, J. and Wallace-Hadrill, A. (eds) (1991), *City and Country in the Ancient World* (London).
Rickert, G. (1989), *EKΩN and AKΩN in Early Greek Thought* (Atlanta).
Rihll, T.E. (1989), 'Lawgivers and tyrants (Solon Frr. 9-11 West)', in *Classical Quarterly* 39: 277-86.
Rihll, T.E. (1991), "ΗΕΚΤΗΜΟΡΟΙ: partners in crime?', in *JHS* 111: 101-27.
Rodgers, V.A. (1971), 'Some thoughts on Δίκη', in *Classical Quarterly* 21: 289-301.
Roebuck, D. (2001), *Ancient Greek Arbitration* (Oxford).
Rosivach, V.J. (1992), 'Redistribution of land in Solon, Fragment 34 West', in *Journal of Hellenic Studies* 112: 153-7.
Rudberg, G. (1952), 'Solon, Attika Attisch', in *Symbolae Osloenses* 29: 1-7.
Ruschenbusch, E. (1966), 'ΣΟΛΩΝΟΣ ΝΟΜΟΙ: die Fragmente des solonischen Gesetzwerkes, mit einer Text und Überlieferungsgeschichte', *Historia* Suppl. 9 (Wiesbaden).
Russo, J., Fernandez-Galiano, M., and Heubeck, A. (1992) *A Commentary on Homer's Odyssey: Volume III, Books XVII-XXIV* (Oxford).
Rusten, J.S. (ed.) (1989), *Thucydides: The Peloponnesian War*, book 2 (Cambridge).
Rzach, A. (1902) *Hesiodi: Carmina* (Lipsiae).
Sage, P.W. (1985), 'Solon, Croesus and the theme of the ideal life' (PhD Diss., Johns Hopkins University: Baltimore).
Sandys, J.E. (ed.) (1912), *Aristotle's Constitution of Athens* (London).
Schiffman, L.H. (1983), *Sectarian Law in the Dead Sea Scrolls* (Providence).
Schmitt-Pantel, P. (1990), 'Sacrificial meal and symposion: two models of civic institutions and the archaic city?', in Murray (ed.): 14-33.
Schmitt-Pantel, P. (1992), *La Cité au Banquet* (Rome).
Schofield, M. (1999), *Saving the City: Philosopher-Kings and Other Classical Paradigms* (Cambridge).
Sealey, R. (1976), *A History of the Greek City States 700-338 BC* (Berkeley).
Sealey, R. (1994), *The Justice of the Greeks* (Ann Arbor).
Shapiro, S. (1996), 'Herodotus and Solon', in *Classical Antiquity* 15.2: 348-66.
Sicking, C.M.J. (1998), *Distant Companions: Selected Papers* (Leiden).
Siegmann, E., (1975), 'Solons Staatselegie', in *Perspektiven der Philosophie 1* (Amsterdam): 267-81.
Sills, D.L. (ed.) (1968), *The International Encyclopedia of the Social Sciences* (New York).
Sinclair, T.A. (tr.) (1982), *Aristotle: The Politics*, revised and re-presented by T.J. Saunders (London and New York).

Slater, W. (2001), 'Gnomology and criticism', in *Greek, Roman and Byzantine Studies* 41: 99-121.
Slings, S.R. (1990), 'The I in Personal Archaic Lyric: An Introduction', in Slings (ed.) (1990): 1-30.
Slings, S.R. (ed.) (1990), *The Poet's I in Archaic Greek Lyric: Proceedings of a Symposium held at the Vrije Universiteit Amsterdam* (Amsterdam).
Smyth, H.W. (1972), *Greek Grammar*, rev. G.M. Messing (Cambridge, MA).
Snell, B. (1982), *The Discovery of the Mind: The Origins of European Thought* (Oxford).
Snodgrass, A.M. (1977), *Archaeology and the Rise of the Greek City-State* (Cambridge).
Snodgrass, A.M. (1981), *Archaic Greece: The Age of Experiment* (London).
Snodgrass, A.M. (1991), 'Archaeology and the study of the Greek city', in Rich and Wallace-Hadrill (eds).
Solmsen, F. (1949), *Hesiod and Aeschylus* (Ithaca).
Stanley, P.V. (1999), *The Economic Reforms of Solon* (Scripta Mercaturae).
Stier, H.E. (1928), 'Nomos Basileus', in *Philologus* 83: 225-58.
Stinton, T.C.W. (1976), 'Solon, Fragment 25', in *Journal of Hellenic Studies* 96: 159-62.
Stoddard, K. (2002), 'Turning the tables on the audience: didactic technique in Solon 13 W', in *American Journal of Philology* 123.2: 149-68.
Striker, G. (1996), *Essays on Hellenistic Epistemology and Ethics* (Cambridge).
Stroud, R. (1979), *The Axones and Kyrbeis of Drakon and Solon* (Berkeley).
Sullivan, S.D. (1988a), *Psychological Activity in Homer* (Ottawa).
Sullivan, S.D. (1988b), 'Noos and vision: five passages in the Greek Lyric poets', in *Symbolae Osloenses* 63: 7-17.
Sullivan, S.D. (1989), 'A study of the psychic term νόος in the Greek lyric poets (excluding Pindar and Bacchylides)', in *Emerita* 57: 129-68.
Sullivan, S.D. (1995), *Psychological and Ethical Ideas: What the Early Greeks Say* (Leiden, New York and Köln).
Svenbro, J. (1993), *Phrasikleia: An Anthropology of Reading in Ancient Greece*, tr. J. Lloyd (Ithaca and London).
Szegedy-Maszak, A. (1978), 'Legends of the Greek lawgivers', in *Greek, Roman and Byzantine Studies* 19: 199-209.
Szegedy-Maszak, A. (1993), 'Thucydides' Solonian Reflections', in Dougherty and Kurke (eds): 201-14.
Tandy, D.W. and Neale, W.C. (1996), *Hesiod's Works and Days: A Translation and Commentary for the Social Sciences* (Berkeley and Los Angeles).
Taylor, C.C.W. (1999), *The Atomists: Leucippus and Democritus: Fragments: A Text and Translation* (Toronto, Buffalo and London).
Thomas, R. (1996), 'Written in stone? Liberty, equality, orality, and the codification of law', in Foxhall and Lewis (eds): 9-31.
Todd, S.C. (1993), *The Shape of Athenian Law* (Oxford).
Travlos, J. (1971), *Pictorial Dictionary of Ancient Athens* (New York).
Treu, M. (1968), *Von Homer zur Lyrik* (München).
Tyler, H.M. (1894), *Selections from the Greek Lyric Poets* (Boston).
Vegetti, M. (1999), 'Culpability, responsibility, cause: philosophy, historiography and medicine in the fifth century', in Long (ed): 271-89.
Vlastos, G. (1995), *Studies in Greek Philosophy*, ed. D.W. Graham (Princeton).
Vox, O. (1984), 'Le muse mute di Solone (e lo specchio del suono)', in *Belfagor* 38: 515-22.

Bibliography

Walker, J. (2000), *Rhetoric and Poetics in Antiquity* (Oxford).
Wallace, R. (1983), 'The date of Solon's reforms', in *American Journal of Ancient History* 8: 81-95.
van Wees, H. (1999a), 'Tyrtaeus' *Eunomia*', in Hodkinson and Powell (eds): 1-41.
van Wees, H. (1999b), 'The mafia of early Greece: violent exploitation in the seventh and sixth centuries BC', in Hopwood (ed.): 1-51.
van Wees, H. (2000), 'Megara's mafiosi: timocracy and violence in Theognis', in Brock and Hodkinson (eds): 52-67.
West, M.L. (1974), *Studies in Greek Elegy and Iambus* (Berlin and New York).
West, M.L. (1993), *Greek Lyric Poetry: The Poems and Fragments of the Greek Iambic, Elegiac and Melic Poets (excluding Pindar and Bacchylides) down to 450 BC* (New York).
West, M.L. (1996), *Hesiod's Works and Days*, Sandpiper edn (Oxford).
West, M.L. (1997), *Hesiod's Theogony*, Sandpiper edn (Oxford).
West, M.L. (1998), *Iambi et Elegi Graeci ante Alexandrum Cantati* II, Sandpiper edn (Oxford).
Wheelwright, P. (1999), *Heraclitus* Sandpiper edn (Oxford).
Wickersham, J.M. (1991). 'Myth and Identity in the Archaic Polis', in Pozzi and Wickersham (eds): 16-31.
von Wilamowitz-Möllendorf, U. (1893), *Aristoteles und Athenes* (Berlin).
von Wilamowitz-Möllendorf, U. (1913), *Sappho und Simonides* (Berlin).
Will, F. (1958), 'Solon's consciousness of himself', in *Transactions of the American Philological Association* 89: 301-11.
Willcock, M.M. (1978 and 1984), *The Iliad of Homer*, vols 1 and 2 (Basingstoke and London).
Williams, B. (1993), *Shame and Necessity* (Berkeley, Los Angeles and London).
Wilson, W. (1994), *The Papers of Woodrow Wilson*, vol. 5, ed. A.S. Link et al. (Princeton).
Wolff, H.J. (1946), 'The origin of judicial litigation among the Greeks', in *Traditio* 4: 31-87.
Woodhouse, W.J. (1938), *Solon the Liberator: A Study of the Agrarian Problem in Attica in the Seventh Century* (Oxford).
Zeller, E. (1931), *Outline of the History of Greek Philosophy*, tr. L.R. Palmer, ed. W. Nestle, 13th edn (London).
Zellner, H.M. (1994), 'Skepticism in Homer?', in *Classical Quarterly* 44: 308-15.

Index

Greek text passages are listed by line only if they appear in the main body of the text.

Abel, D.H., 136n.21; 140n.16
Adespota Iambica, 148n.18; 147n.8
Adkins, A.W.H., 8, 25; 136nn.21, 27;
  137nn.8, 9, 11, 15; 138n.27; 141n.36;
  142nn.48, 57; 143n.10; 144n.32;
  145n.13; 146nn.2, 30; 147nn.3, 8, 13;
  148n.18; 149nn.1, 5, 9; 150n.19
Aeschylus: Athena's new tribunal and laws
  119, 130; Cassandra's prophecy, 32;
  Dikê, 138n.17; divine thought, 137n.5;
  goad, 125; 154n.52; good counsel,
  140n.27; hekêti, by will of gods, or on
  account of things, 138n.22; Helen's
  seizure, 151n.10; pollution, 149n.12;
  tuchê, 138n.19
agathos/ agathoi, 'good man/ men', 44-6,
  53, 84, 96-7, 99, 100, 102, 122; 143n.6
agôn, 'contest', 2, 5-7, 12, 34, 36, 40, 45,
  105, 109, 127, 131; 135nn.5, 8
aisa, 'fate, lot', 14-15, 131; 137n.15
Alcaeus, risks, 148n.29; tyranny, 109;
  150n.3; aristocratic *ethos*, 122;
  monarchy, 150n.7; slavery, 153n.42
Alcmaeon, 138n.25
Alcman, 140n.21
alêtheia, 'truth', 1-2, 35, 40, 69-71, 91-2;
  146n.30
Allen, A.W., 107; 141n.41; 146n.1; 148n.23;
  150n.24
Almeida, J., 135nn.3, 7; 136n.12; 138n.27;
  143nn.6, 13; 145n.37; 149n.7
Alt, K., 147n.12
Amasis of Egypt, 112
Anaxagoras, 143n.11
Anaximander, 8, 23; 136n.23
Anaximenes, 8, 59; 144n.34; cyclical
  world-view, 59, 105
ancestral laws and constitution, 128;
  139n.39
Andrewes, A., 57; 135nn.11, 21; 144nn.27,
  29, 31

Anhalt, E.K., 15, 39, 69; 135n.3; 136n.15;
  137nn.11, 12; 140nn.10, 24; 141nn.41,
  43; 142nn.3, 44, 52; 145n.13; 146nn.1,
  25; 147nn.12-13, 15; 149n.8;
  153nn.40, 45; 154n.51
anomia, 'lawlessness', 56-7, 131; 144n.29
Antiphon, 143n.11
Apollo, 15-16, 25, 38, 48, 87, 102; 143n.10
Archilochus, 109; 148n.31; 150n.3
Aristagoras, 141n.31
aristocratic *ethos* or ideal, 7, 26, 122;
  136n.114; 150n.19
aristocratic and traditional prerogatives,
  11, 23, 27, 58, 98, 103, 108, 114,
  118-20, 123, 127-9; 136n.14
Aristophanes, 42; 154n.52; stinger as goad,
  125
Aristotle 1, 3, 16, 30, 76, 97, 108; 146n.28;
  stasis, 51; stinger, 125
  Constitution of the Athenians: social
    classes and factions, 45; 143n.4;
    Draco, 136n.1; Epimenides and Cylon,
    137n.7; state cults, 139n.39; Solon, 36;
    142n.3; ring composition, 63-4;
    145n.12; slavery, 147n.3; 152n.28;
    love of sliver, 100; 149n.10; Solon's
    democratic reforms, 150n.1;
    Pisistratus' bodyguards, 151n.11;
    'mortgage stones', 151n.16; forcible
    necessity and debts, 152n.30;
    Pisistratus' courts, 152n.34; laws,
    nomos and *thesmos*, 154n.57
  History of Animals, and *Parts of
    Animals*, 154n.52
  Metaphysics: causes, 146n.32
  Meteorology, 146n.32
  Nicomachean Ethics, 46, 59;
    responsibility, 142n.57; character,
    143n.7
  On the Universe, 141n.37
  Politics, 10, 127; city planning, 139n.42;

174

Index

laws, 144n.31; wealth, 149n.3; monarchy, 151n.7; justice, 154n.60
Rhetoric: ownership, 152n.25
artios / artia, 'proper', 30, 56, 58, 67-8; 145n.19; 150n.5
Ascra, 31
associative thinking, 65, 70, 106
astos / astoi, 'townsman, townsmen', 24, 77-9, 113, 131; 143n.6; citizens, 14, 25, 28, 31, 38, 40, 55, 57, 61-5, 68, 96, 120, 130; 143n.6; 152n.19
atê, 29, 31, 56, 68, 71, 74, 77, 89, 92, 102, 104-6, 131; 146n.1; 150n.17
Athena, 14-17, 29, 32, 37, 49, 61, 63-5, 67, 87, 108, 119, 130, 133; 137n.12; 138n.18; 143n.10
Athenaeus, 135n.2
Athens, 1, 7-8, 21, 43, 52, 80; as agonistic, 2; buildings, 138n.18; 151n.15; civil strife in, 11, 14, 27, 47, 61-2, 66, 69, 79, 100, 116; 149n.8; divinely-founded, 115; factions in, 39, 42, 45, 84; 135n.8; 142n.3; freedom in, 129; and Herodotus, 109; institutions, 3; law in, 119, 123-4, 130; and Megara, 120; political order, 26, 57-8, 60, 96, 103, 108, 110, 128; 150n.3; religious rituals in, 138n.18; self-supporting and independent of gods, 9, 15-17, 20, 23, 124; Solon brings wisdom to, 94, 105, 114; Solon's exile from, 116; venerable, 25-6
Atherton, C., 142n.51
Attic language and discourse, 2, 6, 38, 100, 114-16, 118, 121-2; 135n.6
Attica, 4, 11, 25, 38, 96, 100, 118-20, 128; 152n.19
authority, 13, 16, 88, 97, 107, 119; 154n.59; Solon's authority, 23, 113, 116, 127

'Boundless', 105
Bacchylides, 138n.22
Balot, R.K., 40; 135n.5; 140n.21; 142n.54; 146n.2
Barnes, J., 138n.23
bathuphrôn, 'deep-thinker', 33-4; 140n.27
Bergk, T., 139n.34; 141n.38; 148n.29; 150n.5
bia / biê, 'hands-on physical force', 24, 27, 34, 53, 118, 122-4, 126, 128, 132; 153n.46

Bias of Priene, 136n 23
bios / bioton, 'lifestyle, earning a living', 13, 16, 74, 77-80, 82, 84, 89, 90, 92-4, 98, 101, 107, 131; 147nn.6-7; different ways of earning a living, 86-8; *bios*-perspective, 97
Björck, G., 147n.14
Blaise, F., 152n.23; 153n.43
Blok, J. and Lardinois, A., 135n.3
Boer, W. den, 141n.30
Boersma, J.S., 151n.15
Boiotia, 4, 57n.29
boulêeis, 'good of counsel', 33-4
boulomai and *ethelô*, 24-5; 139nn.2, 5
boundary stone, see *horos*
Bowie, E.L., 136n.19
Bowra, C.M., 136n.15; 139nn.2, 40; 141n.35; 142n.52; 146n.1; 147n.3; 149n.11
Broadie, S., 148n.40
Bryan, W.J., 145n.4
Bryant, J.M., 150n.19
Burn, A.R., 135n.2
Buxton, R.G.A., 37; 141n.36

Cairns, D., 39; 142nn.47-8
Calhoun, G.M., 3; 135n.10
Callinus, 4, 66; 148n.18; *moira*, 147n.8
Campbell, D.A., 137nn.9, 11, 15; 142n.2; 143n.12; 148n.21; 149nn.4, 11; 150n.7; 153nn.41, 43, 47
Carawan, E., 135n.10
Carson, A., 140n.25
Cartledge, P.A., 138n.21; 152n.19
Case, T., 135n.1
cause, causality, causal connections, 18, 29, 31, 35, 46-7, 54-5, 67, 69-72, 82-4, 87, 89-90, 92, 94-5, 99, 104-5, 107, 111, 114, 117, 124; 138n.25; 146nn.27, 29, 32; social causality, 140n.16
Cavarnos, C., 136n.2
Cawkwell, G., 150n.3; 151nn.14, 15
Cerri, G., 144n.23
Chaerephon, 72
chance, see *tuchê*
Chantraine, P., 138n.22; 139nn.2, 6
Chiasson, C.C., 149nn.45-6
chrêmata, 'property, or 'wealth'', 97; 147n.13 ; 149n.10; *agatha*, 'goods', 36
Christes, J., 147n.12; 148nn.34, 39
Cicero, 1; 135n.2

175

Index

classes, social, 27, 45-6; 143n.6
classical archaeology, 3, 11; 135nn.3, 7; 136n.12; 149n.7
Clement of Alexandria, 91; 148n.36
Cleobis and Biton, 94
Coldstream, J.N., 136n.12
concrete-bound, 70-2
conflict, 21, 38, 45, 56, 61, 71, 100, 113-14, 120, 122, 127, 133; 142n.3; 143n.6; conflict and harmony as a principle, 16; see disease
conscience, 29, 126; 142n.52
constitution/ constitutional, 1, 7, 54, 60, 79, 108-10; 154n.50
contest, see *agôn*
cosmology, 7-8, 11, 23; 137n.2
Coxon, A.H., 143n.11; 144n.35
Critias, 72, 94; 139n.33
Croesus, 3, 33, 35, 93, 96, 102; 140n.26
Croiset, M., 136n.21
Cyclops, 57
Cylon, 11; 137n.7

dais, 'ceremonial meal', 42, 58, 61, 66; 140n.10
debts, 3, 53, 76, 97, 115, 118; 147n.3; 148n.19; 152n.30; debtor's prerogatives, 57, 76; debt slavery, 3, 108; vs. debt bondage, 117
deceptions, 5-7, 37, 86-7, 112, 123, 126, 129; 137nn.5, 6; 148n.33; divine deception, 13
Declaration of Independence, 5, 108
deilos, 'base' or 'cowardly', 44, 85, 102
Delphi, 14
Delphic maxims, 41; 142n.56; 144n.36
democracy, 3, 110
Democritus, 39-41; 136n.22; persuasion and law, 37; 141n.37; introspection/ moderation, 59; 142n.52; ancestral laws, 127-8; ordered speech, 145n.1; free man's self-determination: 153n.39
Democritus fr. 259, 128
dêmos, 'the people', 27-8, 34, 37, 44-5, 61-4, 77, 80, 82, 100, 112-13, 120; 142n.3; 149n.14
Demosthenes, 1, 126; 149n.12; 154n.52
Dickie, M.W., 140n.25; 144n.26
Diehl, E., 151n.8
Diels, H. and Kranz, W., 140n.20
Diels, H., 143n.11

Dihle, A., 137n.3; 139n.1; 142n.56
dikê, 'justice', 2, 5, 7, 9, 16-18, 20, 29, 34, 42-4, 46-65, 72, 74-96, 103-4, 106-8, 112-16, 119-24, 126-31; 135n.15; 143n.15; 144nn.18, 23; 146n.1; 148nn.27, 39; 152n.23; 154n.50; natural and volitional senses, 53-4, 103, 123
Diodorus Siculus: monarchy, 150n.6; Pisistratus and Solon, 151n.11; *rhumata* and *rhusia*: 151n.8
Diogenes Laertius: monarchy, 150n.6; Pisistratus and Solon, 151n.11
Dionysus of Chalcus, 139n.33
disease, 44, 65, 86-7, 98, 101-2, 133; vs. conflict theory, 51
disputes and dispute mediation, 21, 23, 30, 45, 49-52, 54, 59, 103, 124; 153n.50
divine interventions, 5, 9, 11, 13-17, 31, 42, 51-5, 87-8, 91-4, 122, 126
divine jealousy, 93-4; 149n.46; divine hostility, 92
divine will, 9, 11, 13, 17; and *moira*, 92-3
Dodds, E.R., 92; 142n.52; 148n.41
Donlan, W., 148n.22; 149n.5; 150n.19
Dover, K.J., 144n.15; 147n.3
doxa, 'expectation' or 'reputation', 44, 69, 77, 80-1, 85, 100, 131
Doyle, R.E., 140n.16
Draco, 11, 111-12; 136n.1
Dusnomia, 'lawlessness' or 'disorder', 9, 27, 56-7, 59, 61-3, 66-8, 105, 108, 119, 125, 127, 132; 144n.29

earth/ Black Earth, 11-12, 14, 19, 52, 63, 76, 87, 92, 103, 114-16, 120-1, 131; 137n.8; 152n.21
economic interpretations, 3; 135n.11
Edmonds, J.M., 145n.2; 151n.8
Edmunds, L., 142n.51
Edwards, C., 154n.54
Egypt, 14, 94, 112; 137n.7
Ehrenberg, V., 152n.23
Ehrhardt, A., 136n.21
Eleusis, 153n.38
Eleutheros (locale), 153n.42
eleutheros, eleutheria, 'free man'/ 'freedom', 6-7, 9, 52, 77, 100, 108-9, 118, 120-2, 126-30, 132; 151n.19; 153nn.39, 42; 154n.52; political freedom, 6, 121-2; 153nn.39-41; in modern rhetoric, 150n.2

Index

Emlyn-Jones, C., 136n.21
Empedocles, 91; 148n.36
Engels, F., 151n.19
Entrèves, A.P. d', 154n.59
ephêmeros, 'a person living upon the moment', 33; 140n.25
Epictetus, 95
Epimenides, 11, 14; 137n.7; 152n.21
episkopos, 'overseer', 15-16; 138n.18
Erasmus, H.J., 57; 144n.30
ethos, 'custom' or 'habit', 16, 26, 122
Eumaios, 153n.42
Eunomiê, 'lawfulness', 1, 9, 20, 27, 46 51-2, 54-8, 61, 63, 67-8, 72, 75, 77-8, 90, 100, 105, 108, 121, 124-5, 129 132; 144nn.29, 32
euphrosunê, 'festivities', 20, 21, 26-7, 42, 62, 64, 101
Eupolis, 125; 154n.52
Euripides, 125; 138n.22; 154n.52
Eurycleia, 120
exiles, 61, 83-4, 112, 117-19 Solon's exile, 116; 152n.22; a lawgiver's exile, 127

factions and groups, 11, 23, 28, 31, 38-9, 43, 45-6, 51, 60, 62, 64, 66, 111; 135n.8; 143nn.4, 6; 153n.41
Fagles, R., 140n.15
fatalism, 9, 80, 90, 94-5, 130; 147n.8; 148n.18
fate, see *aisa*, *moira*
Federalist Papers, 108; 135n.2
festive calendar, 20, 49, 91-2; 139n.39
Finkelberg, M., 141nn.41-2; 142n.51; 147n.12
Finley, M.I., 143n.6; 151n.19; 153n.38
Fisher, N.R.E., 140n.11
flood myth, 94
Fogel, R.W., 154n.63
Fowler, R.L., 137n.11; 146nn.1, 27; 147n.12; 148n.18
Foxhall, L., 143n.5; 149n.6
Fränkel, E., 151n.10
Fränkel, H., 7, 35, 68; 136nn.20, 21; 137n.9; 138n.32; 140n.25; 141n.32; 142n.52; 144n.15; 145nn.3, 11, 19, 22; 146nn.1, 24, 31; 152n.20
free/ freedom, see *eleutheros*
Freeman, K., 135n.3
French, A., 135n.11

Fritz, K. von, 8, 13; 136nn.20, 25; 137nn.4, 5; 140n.22; 144n.15; 145n.3

Gagarin, M., 51-2, 112; 135n.10; 143nn.15, 17; 144nn.18, 21; 151n.14; 152n.23
Garlan, Y., 152n.19
Garnsey, P., 152n.19
genre, 2, 4-5, 20; 136n.15
Gentili, B., 136n.15; 144n.23; 146n.1; 147n.12; 151n.8
geras, 'gifts' or 'offices', 100
Gerber, D.E., 135n.3; 137n.9; 140nn.25, 27; 145nn.2, 15; 146n.1; 151n.17; 152n.27; 153n.40
German idealism, 50
Gernet, L., 118; 143n.15; 152n.30
gnômosunê, 'judgment based on maxims', 91
goad, see *kentron*
Goldhill, S., 142n.51
Gorgias, 143n.11
Gouschin, V., 150n.3; 151n.14
Graham, A.J., vii; 152n.19
Greene, W.C., 146n.1
Greenhalgh, P.A.L., 39; 142nn.45-6; 150n.19
Griffith, M., 6; 136n.19; 141n.28
Guthrie, W.K.C., 136n.23; 138n.25; 142n.52

Hahn, R., 139nn.35, 42
Hainsworth, B., 151n.9
Halberstadt, M., 140n.10; 144n.32; 145n.6
Hamilton, R., 150n.17
Hammer, D., 136n.14
Hammurabi, 128; 154n.54
Hansen, M.H., 153n.39
harmonia, 54, 122-3; 137n.12; 153n.45
Harris, E., 151n.13; 152nn.26, 33
Harrison, T., 94; 136n.21; 140n.26; 149nn.44, 45, 47
Haubold, J., 138n.27
Havelock, E., 4, 50; 136nn.13, 21, 22; 143n.15; 144n.33; 152n.23
Hebraic and Near Eastern laws, 126; 154n.54
hekastos, 'each one of us', 32, 35, 40-4, 65, 84, 110, 122
helkos, 'wound', 43-4, 65; 145n.13
Helm, J.J., 140nn.17, 21; 149n.4
Henderson, W.J., 135n.6; 137n.9; 146nn.1, 28; 150n.22

177

Index

Henry, Patrick, 150n.2
Heraclitus, 147n.10; ethical views, 142n.44; introspection, 142n.52; knowledge, 138n.25; 140n.27; 144n.36; *koros*, 140n.20; law, 59; 141n.37; 144n.36; 147n.38; 148n.38
Herodotus, 141n.31; 145n.21; 150n.3; 152n.27; gods as venerable, 139n.7; Croesus, 3, 33, 102; 140n.26; 'Solonian philosophy', 93-4; 149n.44; tyranny, 109; 153n.42; *anomia*, 144n.29; Solon's exile, 116; monarchy, 150n.7; goad, 125; 152n.52; fatalism, 130; Pisistratid bodyguards, 151n.11; necessity, 152n.32
Hesiod, on aggrandizing men, 151n.18; *Atê* as goddess, 150n.16; *bios*, lifestyle, 77, 92, 96, 106; 147n.7; 150n.21; Clement of Alexandria, 91; 148n.36; obligations, 118; political order, 44, 58; 144n.31; Eleutheros, 153n.42; deceptive language, 137n.16; *dikê* and justice, 49, 51-2, 55; 138n.17; 143n.15; 145n.20; divine intervention, 12-14, 16-18, 47, 55; 137n.5; divine genealogy, 122; 153n.44; good and evil, 148n.28; *koros*, 29-30; 140nn.18-9; *kosmos*, 138nn.27, 29; 139n.33; literary tradition and comparison, 1, 4, 5; 136n.21; 140n.17; moderation, 145n.45; *noos* and *phrên* 8, 13, 31-2, 91; 137n.5; 147n.2; penalty on descendents, 147n.3; persuasion, 37; 141n.35; laws, 128; 144n.22; 154n.62; self-reference, 11; strife, 149n.15; *tuchê*, 89; 148n.31; tyrannical discourse, 153n.43; will, 137nn.3, 5
Works and Days 3-4, 47-9, 54-6: 12
hêsuchiê, 'calmness', 9, 27, 31, 55-6, 58, 62-3, 77, 100, 108, 129, 132; 144n.26
Hesychius, *kentron* and persuasion, 154n.52
Hieron of Syracuse, 150n.3
Hippocratic medicine, 101; 149n.13
Hippodamus of Miletus, 139n.42
Hobbes, T., 5
Hölkeskamp, K-J., 153n.49
Homer: Achilles' rage, 44; aggrandizing men, 151n.18; *Atê* as goddess, 150n.16; bird signs, 139n.6; cleverness, 145n.16; and Hesiod, 140n.17; crimes, 149n.12; *dikê*/ justice, 143n.15; 144nn.17, 20; divine genealogy, 122; 153n.44; divine intervention, 15-17, 47-8, 55; 136n.21; 137n.11; *doxa*, 'expectation', 131; *episkopos* as spy or cargo, 138n.18; gods' power, 94; 143n.10; 148n.18, forcible necessity, or the goad, 125-6; 152n.32; 154nn.51-2; prudence, 67-8; 145n.18; good and evil, 148n.28; *harmonia* and agreements: 137n.12; 153n.45; human shortcomings, 62; 140n.15; 154n.53; *koros*, 29-30; 140n.17; *kosmos*, 18-19; 138nn.27-9, 31; literary/ intellectual tradition, 1, 2, 4, 8, 59; luxurious life, 145n.9; values, 20; mode of thought, knowing and *noêsis*, 32, 62, 69, 91; 139n.6; 146n.2; 148n.36; moderation, 49; 149n.8; *moira*, 89; 147n.8; *pathein*, 139n.8; penalty on descendents, 147n.3; language and persuasion, 37; 137n.16; 141n.35; psychic qualities, 13; 137n.4; 140n.27; *rhusia*, 151nn.9, 10; reputation and 'seeming': 85; 148n.21; ring composition, 64; 145n.11; slavery and freedom, 120; 152nn.24-5, 27; 153nn.35, 38, 42; smoothing rough things, 145n.21; standards, 39-40, 96, 100-1; 142nn.47, 50; 145n.50; 148n.21; statutes, 144n.22; storm, 147nn.15-16; Thersites, 19, 103; trembling, 152n.29; two cities, 56; tyrannical discourse, 153n.43; wealth, 97; 'will' of gods and men: 25; 138n.22; 139nn.2, 5
Iliad 13.570-2: 24
Homeric Hymns: persuasion, 37; 141n.35; *pantos*, *Hymn to Apollo*, 48; *tuchê*, *Hymn to Demeter*, 148n.31
Hopper, R.J., 147n.4
horos/ *horoi*, 'boundary stone(s)', 7, 63, 83, 103, 113, 115-16, 120; 151n.16; 153n.38; boundary between gods and men, 48, 113, 128
How, W.W. and Wells, J., 141n.31
hubris, 'arrogance', 2, 6, 15, 17, 20, 24-31, 35-9, 42, 46, 48, 54-6, 58, 61-5, 68, 71-2, 74, 78, 80-2, 84, 90, 100-5, 108-9, 111, 114, 117, 119-23, 128, 132-3; 140n.13; 144n.26; 147n.13

178

Index

Hudson-Williams, T., 151n.8
Hussey, E., 20; 136nn.24, 26; 139n.37; 145n.23; 146n.32

independence, 40
intellectual context and history, 2-4, 7-9, 23, 60, 73, 93
Irwin, E., 4, 5, 17, 20, 28, 34, 42, 49; 135n.3; 136nn.14, 16-17, 19; 137n.11; 138n.26; 139n.41; 140nn.14, 21; 141n.29; 142nn.1, 51; 143n.14; 144n.24; 153nn.43, 46
isomoiria, 'equal shares', 27, 36, 103; 149n.14

Jaeger, W., 50, 56, 67; 136n.21; 137nn.11-15; 141n.36; 143n.15; 144nn.24, 25, 29, 32; 145nn.13, 15; 146n.2
Janko, R., 147n.16
Jefferson, T., 5
Johnson, W.R., 145n.1
Jones, J.W., 153n.49
jury courts, 2-3, 108, 124
justice, also see *dikê*, 1, 4, 12, 20-1, 26 28, 31, 35, 38-9, 42-3, 46, 48, 50-6, 58-9, 63, 67-8, 71-6, 89, 92-3, 103-4, 107-9, 113-14, 118-19, 122-30, 131; 140n 13; 143nn.6, 7, 15; 144nn.18, 36; 146n.2-3; 152n.23; 154n.50

Kahn, C.H., 17, 19, 93; 136n.23; 137n.14; 138nn.22, 30, 31; 140n.20; 142nn.45, 52; 148n.42
Kalimtzis, K., 51; 144n.16
Kamerbeek, J.C., 151n.10
Kassel, R. and Austin, C., 154n.52
Keaney, J., 63-4; 145nn.10, 12
Kennedy, G.A., 145n.1
kentron, 'goad', 99, 125-6; 153n.50
Kenyon, F.G., 153n.40
Ker, J., 148n.37
kerdos/ kerdea, 'profit', 104, 134; 147n.8; 150n.17
Kilmer, M.F. and Develin, R., 145n.5
kindunos, 'risk', 88-9; 148n.29
Kirk, G.S., 20; 139n.36; 142n.50
Kirk, Raven and Schofield, 40-1, 59, 91; 137n.5; 138nn.23-25; 140nn.20, 27; 142nn.52-3; 144nn.34, 36; 148nn 36, 38

Kleisthenes, 15
Knox, B.M.W., 145n.2; 146n.1
koros, 'satiety' or 'excess', 9, 27-31, 36-7, 48, 60, 65, 68, 71, 92, 104-5. 132; 140nn.17, 20; changes meaning, 30; 140n.21
kosmos/ kosmein, 9, 11, 16-21, 23, 27, 39, 42, 46, 55, 59-61, 67, 77, 80-2, 91, 105, 107, 109, 124, 127, 130, 132; 138nn.21, 27-30; 144n.35; 145n.2
kratos/ kratein, 'power'/ 'to wield power', 3, 5, 28, 33, 53, 97, 123, 127; *krateron*, 'powerful', 45
Krischer, T., 140n.22
kudos, 'praise' or 'renown', 16, 19, 132
Kurke, L., 136n.14

L'Homme-Wéry, L.M., 153n.38
Laistner, M.L.W., 135n.11
Lattimore, R., 2, 82, 90, 106; 135n.4; 146nn.1, 28; 147n.15; 148nn.20, 35; 149n.15; 150nn.17, 23
Lavelle, B.M., 142n.3; 143n.5
law, see *nomos*
laws of Solon, 1, 3, 5, 8, 16, 21, 35, 44, 49, 50, 53, 55, 58, 68, 105, 108, 109, 116, 118-30; 135n.10; 138n.19; status after his exile, 127
Leaf, W., 137n.10; 144n.17
Lehmann-Haupt, C.F., 135n.11
Lesher, J.H., 136n.23; 138n.25; 145nn.3, 23
Lesky, A., 116; 136n.15; 152n.20
lifestyle, see *bios*
Linforth, I.M., 54, 97, 111; 135nn.3, 6, 7; 137n.12; 138n.27; 139n.6; 140nn.10, 27; 142n.3; 145nn.13, 19; 147nn.12, 14, 16; 148n.24; 149nn.4, 5, 15; 150n.17; 151n.8; 152nn.21, 23; 153nn.40, 50
Linnaeus, 138n.32
Lloyd, G.E.R., 136n.23; 137nn.2, 3; 138n.26; 149n.13
Lloyd-Jones, H. 92; 136n.21; 137n.11; 143n.15; 148n.41
Locke, J., 7, 108-9.
Long, A.A., 136n.26
Long, H.S., 151n.8
Longo, C.P., 135n.10
long-range perspective, 33-5, 39, 48, 53
Loraux, N., 142n.44
Lysias, 139n.33; 147n.3

179

Index

Madison, J., 1
Manuwald, B., 144nn.24, 32; 146n.2; 147n.3; 148nn.34, 39
Manville, P.B., 136n.12
Marcovich, M., 147n.10
martial *ethos*, values and poetry, 4, 7, 20, 26, 31, 66; 135n.3; 136n.14
Martin, R.P., 135n.2
Martina, A., 135n.10
Marx, K., 151n.19
Masaracchia, A., 24; 135n.3; 139nn.3, 6; 140n.27; 147n.15; 153n.40
Matheson, S.B., 148n.31
Matthiessen, K., 136n.21
McEwen, I.K., 139n.6; 150n.18
McGlew, J., 141n.33; 150nn.3, 6; 154n.58
McKirahan, R.D., 144n.15; 150n.19
meal, ceremonial, see *dais*
Megara, 2, 26, 109, 120; 153n.38
Meier, C., 136n.21
Melanthius, 139n.33
Memory, 32, 44, 49, 69, 78, 80, 82, 94, 96, 100, 107, 128
Menander, 2, 26, 91, 109, 120; 148n.36
Messenia, 153n.36
metaphor, 38, 42, 45, 49, 51-2, 61, 65-6, 69, 80, 82, 113-14, 116, 120, 126; 147n.15
metron, 'measure', 38, 68, 91
middle, 1, 2, 11, 63, 91; 142n.44
Miller, M., 135n.1; 143n.6
Milne, J.G., 135n.11
Mimnermus, 84
moderation, 28, 31, 36, 38-9, 46, 49, 54, 56, 62, 100-1, 103, 105, 124, 128-9; 142nn.45, 52; 149n.8
moira, 'lot' or 'fate', 7, 9, 14, 16, 74-96, 102-8, 110-11, 130, 132; 137n.15; 146n.1; 147n.8; 148nn.18, 27
monarchy, 6, 110; 145n.14; 153nn.6, 7
Moore, J.M., 152n.30
moral thought and standards, 7, 28, 31, 33, 39-41, 46, 55, 59, 90, 97, 99, 109, 116, 119, 129; 154n.59
Morris, I., 136nn.12, 14; 143n.6; 149n.7
Most, G., 142n.44; 145n.3
Mülke, C., 135n.3; 139n.38; 140n.22; 141n.41; 144n.22; 145nn.7, 9; 146n.1; 151n.8; 153n.40
Murray, O., 15; 136n.12; 137n.13
Muses, 80, 87; 147n.12
Myres, J. L., 136n.23; 144n.29; 153n.43

Nagy, G., 139n.6; 140n.23; 145n.5; 147n.12
natural events, 5, 13, 47, 82; not caused by human action in Solon, 17
natural law, 58; 144n.36; 148n.38
natural philosophy, 7, 59, 83, 91; 147n.15
naturalism, 15, 28, 47
necessity, 9, 17-18, 29, 35, 42, 46-8, 52-3, 55, 58-9, 71, 97, 99, 115, 117-21; 146n.30; psychic factors and, 27-8, 31, 38; forcible necessity, 6, 53, 55, 97, 115, 117-21; 146n.32; 152nn.30, 32; 'embedded', not authoritarian, 17
Niobe, 64
noêsis, 'recognition of signs', 25, 31, 35; 139n.6; 145n.5
nomos 'law', 93, 105; 136n.22; the ancestral law, 128; and *thesmos* 'statute', 127; 154n.57; *nomos* and persuasion, 141n.37; disputed reading of Solon 36.16: 153n.43
noos/ noein, 5, 7, 8, 13, 25-32, 35-42, 44, 48, 56, 60-3, 67-8, 71-4, 84, 89-93, 96-7, 99-100, 104-5, 110-14, 117, 123, 132; 150n.4; defined, 31; 140n.22; and virtue, 39, as cause of injustice, 35-7, 67, 72, 104-5, 114-15, 117, 132; 140n.13; 143n.8
Noussia, M., 27, 38, 83, 88-9; 135n.3; 138n.19; 139n.8; 140nn.12, 15; 141nn.34, 40; 143n.8; 146nn.1, 12; 147n.15, 17; 148nn.28, 30, 32; 150n.4; 151nn.8, 18; 153nn.40, 43, 44

Ober, J., 152n.19
oikos, 'home', 44, 58, 61, 66-7, 78, 105, 120, 133; 139n.38
olbos, 'riches', 77, 80, 85, 97, 133; 147n.13
Oldfather, C.H., 151n.8
order in all things, 91-2, 104; *pantos*, 143nn.11-12; *harmonia* as 'fitting together', 137n.12
Orphic texts, 138n.17; 145n.1
Osborne, R., 136n.12; 143n.6; 149n.6
Ostwald, M., 136n.22; 139n.39; 144nn.19, 28, 29, 32; 145n.37; 151n.11; 153n.48; 154n.57
ownership, 117; 152n.25

Palatine Anthology, 38; 141n.39
pantôs, 'in every way', 43, 47-8, 58-9, 72, 83, 96; 143nn.11-12; 144n.35

Index

Parker, R., 135nn.4, 10; 138n.18; 139n.39
Parker, V., 2, 6; 135n.4; 136n.18; 150n.3
Parmenides, 6, 69, 92-3; 140n.22; *kosmos* and *pantôs*, 143n.11; 144n.35; *kosmos*, verse and speech, 138n.28; 145n.1
pathein, 'to suffer' or 'experience', 33, 62-3, 69, 84-5, 90, 93, 102; 145nn.8-9
Patterson, O., 151n.19
Peikoff, L., 40, 70; 142n.49; 146n.26; 148n.26
Peiraeus, 139n.42
perceptual level of awareness, 6, 32, 69, 97
Pericles, 26, 116, 125
Perrin, B., 145n.2; 151n.8
Perry, B., 146n.27
Perses, 19, 29, 31-2
perspectives: on *dikê* vs. *bies*, 87, 97; on *dikê* as principle or procedure, 55; human vs. divine, 13, 88; on knowing vs. seeing, 69; on necessity, 59, 71; on poem 4, 64-6; on Athens, 9, 18, 21, 23, 56; on wealth, 99
persuasion, 36-40, 63-5, 107, 112, 122-6; 141nn.35-9
Philo Judaeus, 147n.9
Philoctetes, 77
Philocyprus of Soli, 79
phrên/ phrênas, 13, 26, 34, 61, 68, 133; 137nn.5, 6, 9; described, 13
phulê/ phulai 'tribe(s)', 15, 61, 66, 77, 133; 145n.14
phusis, 'nature', 136n.23; 146n.32
Pindar: *hekêti*, 'on account of', 138n.22; aggrandizing men, 151n.18; deep thinking, 34; 140n.27; 148n.33; Epimenides and the earth (scholium), 152n.21; goad, 154n.52; justice, 145n.20; tyranny, 109; 'Zeus Deliverer', 153n.42
pinuta, 'prudence', 56, 67-8
Pisistratus, 111-12, 116, 119; 135n.8; 151nn.11, 15
Plato, 1, 16, 32-3, 72-3, 76, 94, 99, 125-6; *Protagoras*: Seven Sages, 135n.2; *Laws*: dating, 137n.7; *Critias*: Egyptian priests, 137n.7; Memory, 149nn.48-9; *Symposium*: honour to Solon, 138n.19; *atê*, 150n.16; *Phaedrus*: philosophers and poets, 141n.42; goad, 154n.52; *Charmides*: 72; 142n.56; 146n.33; *Republic*:

justice, 143n.7; orators, 154n.52; *Timaeus*: 149n.48
ploutos, 'wealth', 28-9, 31, 33, 97, 105-7, 133; 147n.13; 149nn.4, 15; 153n.46
Plutarch, 1, 3, 16, 35, 45-6; *Life of Solon*: Seven Sages, 135n.2; Epimenides and Cylon, 137n.7; tyranny, 141n.30; ordered verse, 145n.2; love of silver, 149n.10; monarchy, 150n.6; *rhumata*, 151n.8; Pisistratus, 151n.11
Podlecki, A., 135n.1; 152n.22
poetic form, 1, 4-5, 14, 17-18, 68, 109
Pohlenz, M., 152n.19; 153nn.39, 40
Pol Pot, 128
polemos, 'war', 27, 29, 66, 77, 133
Polignac, F. de, 138n.18
polis, passim; *hemeterê polis*, 'our *polis*', 14; 139n.38
politeia, 'constitution', 3, 79, 110
pollution, 11, 50; 149n.12
Prato, C., 151n.8
Praxiteles, 10
Presocratic philosophers, 8, 16-17, 20, 46, 48, 132
Prier, R.A., 146n.28
Procopé, J.F., 141n.37
proof, 71-2
prostatês, 'man of political prominence', 99; 151n.14
Protagoras, 58
psychic factors, 6, 9, 13, 17, 20-3, 28-31, 38, 40-1, 46, 71, 99-100, 104-5, 108, 124, 131-2; and physical factors, 9, 99, 104-5, 117; in Homer, 137n.4
psychology, mass, 35; 141n.31

Raaflaub, K., 135n.9; 152n.19; 153n.41
Reinhardt, K., 136n.21; 140n.25; 145n.36; 146n.1
reputation, 148n.21
responsibility, 137n.11; 142n.57
rhetorikê, 'rhetoric', 5, 60, 123; 145n.1
Rhodes, P.J., 142n.3; 152nn.28, 30; 153nn.40, 43; 154nn.53, 57
rhumata/ rhusia, 'arms', 111-13; 151n.8-11
Rickert, G.A., 118; 137n.3; 152n.32
Rihll, T.E., 111-12; 135n.11; 150n.3; 151nn.8, 11, 12; 152n.31; 153n.6
ring composition, 61-5, 68, 105; 145n.15
Rodgers, V.A., 142n.55; 144nn.15, 33
Roebuck, D., 135n.8

Index

Roman law, 1, 76
Rosivach, V.J., 143n.5; 149n.14
Rudberg, G., 135n.6
Ruschenbusch, E., 135n.10
Russo, J. et al., 153n35
Rusten, J.S., 154n.52
Rzach, A., 148n.36

Sage, P.W., 140n.26
Salamis, see Solon
Sandys, J.E., 153n.40; 154n.50
Sappho, 140n.21; 145n.8; 148n.29
scepticism, 17, 69, 85, 92; 138n.25; 145n.23
Schiffman, L.H., 154n.54
Schmitt-Pantel, P., 140n.10
Schofield, M., 138n.28; see Kirk, Raven and Schofield
sea, as analogy, 31, 47, 49, 54, 78, 82, 131; 143n.9
Sealey, R., 136n.1; 143n.6; 153n.49
seasons, 12, 19-20, 31-2, 49, 79
seisactheia, 'shaking-off of burdens', 108
Semonides, human understanding as limited, 32-3, 83; 140n.25; analogy to the sea, 143n.9; life as luxurious, 145n.8; persuasion, 141n.35; *moira*, 147n.8; fr. 1.1-5: 32
Seven Sages, 1; 135n.2; 142n.45
Shakespeare, W., 7
Shapiro, S., 93; 140n.26; 149nn.44, 46
Sicking, C.M.J., 146n.1; 147n.11; 148n.25; 149n.11; 150nn.17, 20, 24
Siegmann, E., 144n.32
Simonides, 138nn.22, 8; 141n.35
Sinclair, T.A., 154n.60
Slater, W., 148n.33
slavery, incl. *doulosunê* and *douliê*, 3, 6-7, 9, 24, 27-30, 43-4, 47, 49, 52-4, 56, 64, 66, 77, 101, 108-11, 114-23, 126-8, 132; 146n.3; 151n.19; 152nn.19, 31; 153nn.35-7; set slaves free, 118; 152n.28
Slings, S.R., 142n.51
Snell, B., 136n.23; 140n.27
Snodgrass, A., 136n.12; 138n.18
society, 40, 50-1, 102, 104, 117, 127; defined, 57
Socrates, 29, 40, 59, 72, 95, 125; 142nn.48, 52
Solmsen, F., 50; 136nn.19, 22; 137n.3;
138n.25; 141n.36; 143n.15; 144n.24; 147n.5
Solon: dating, 1, 109, 111; 135n.1
 exile, and possible trial, 116; 152n.22
 and history of philosophy, 8, 46, 59, 91, 93, 95
 on lying poets, (rel. to fr. 29), 141n.41
 self-references, 1, 11, 25, 33-4, 36, 40, 45, 53-4, 60, 81, 85, 108, 113, 115-6, 121-2, 125; 142n.51
 Mimnermus criticized for the span he accords to human life (fr. 20), 79, 84,
 on the stages of life (fr. 27), 20, 31, 77, 79, 96; 139n.40; 147n.9
 testimonia to, 135n.10
 Ruler of Soli (on Cyprus) praised (fr. 19), 79, 132-3
 'tyranny is a lovely stronghold', (possible fr., 33a), 35; 141n.30
 uniqueness as a source, 2
 urges war with Salamis (frs 1, 2, 3), 2, 20, 26, 60, 133
 wisdom of, 33-5, 42, 48, 69, 74, 87, 94; 136n.23
Solon: text passages
 fr. 3.11-13: 24
 fr. 4.11: 37
 fr. 4.11-29: 43
 fr. 4.1-4: 14
 fr. 4.23-5: 115
 fr. 4.30-9: 55-6
 fr. 4.5-6: 24
 fr. 4.7-10: 26
 fr. 4a: 25
 fr. 4c: 36
 fr. 5.5-6: 45
 fr. 6: 27
 fr. 9.1-6: 47
 fr. 9: 109-10
 fr. 11.1-2: 14
 fr. 11: 110
 fr. 12: 47
 fr. 13.1-6: 80
 fr. 13.7-16: 81
 fr. 13.17-25: 82
 fr. 13.25-32, 83
 fr. 13.29-32, 63-6: 75
 fr. 13.33-5: 84
 fr. 13.35-42: 85
 fr. 13.43-62: 86
 fr. 13.63-6: 88

Index

fr. 13.67-70: 89
fr. 13.71-3: 96
fr. 13.71-6: 104
fr. 15: 97
frs 16, and 17: 90
frs 24 and 25: 98
fr. 30: 126
fr. 32: 34
fr. 33.5-7: 33
fr. 34: 35-6
fr. 36.1-15: 115
fr. 36.15-20: 122
fr. 36.20-7: 125
fr. 36.3-5, 52
fr. 36.8-11, 15-20: 53
fr. 37.9-10: 113
'Solonian Philosophy', 93-4; 136n.21; 149n.44
Sophists, 58; 143n.11
Sophocles: *hekêti*, 'by reason of', 138n 22; goad, 125; 154nn.51-2; search for knowledge, 33; security or pledges, 151n.10; speech and identity, 152n.27; venerable deeds, 139n.7
soul, 40-1
speudein, 'to hustle for a living', 86-7; 96-7; 104; 140n.25; 144n.36
standard of evaluation, dependent vs. independent, 39-40
Stanley, P.V., 143n.5
stasis, 'civil strife', 24, 27-9, 31, 39, 48, 51, 55, 57, 65-6, 72, 77, 95. 133, 77, 95, 104-5, 108, 123, 132-3; 145n.14
Stier, H.E., 136n.21; 144n.29
Stinton, T.C.W., 142n.3
Stoddard, K., 145n.1; 146n.1; 150n.25
Stoics, 33; 147n.10
Striker, G., 144n.36
Stroud, R., 135n.10; 153n.49
strung-on style, 70
Sullivan, S.D., 35, 39; 137n 4; 140nn.13, 22; 141nn.31, 43; 142n.51; 145n.3
Sunium Kouros, 10, 59, 127; 135n.3
sunoikism, 'political unification', 20, 115, 128
Svenbro, J., 140n.23; 145n.5
symposium, 4-5, 20-1, 23, 37-8, 60, 68, 100-1; 136n.14
Szegedy-Maszak, A., 154nn.52, 61

Tandy, D.W. and Neale, W.C., 118; 152n.30

Taylor, C.C.W., 143n.11
telos, 'goal' or 'end', 31, 79-80, 87, 91, 99, 106
Thales, 8, 17; 136n.23; 138nn.23, 25
Theognis, 28, 38, 68. 90, 109, 122; 139n.34; 140n.25; 144nn.26; 145nn.8, 14, 17, 20, 36; 147nn.3, 8; 148nn.18, 19, 29, 38; 149nn.2-4, 8; 150nn.3, 5, 7; 153nn.42, 46; 154n.52; persuasion, 141nn.38-9
thesmos/ thesmoi 'statute(s)', 116, 122-4, 127, 132; 144n.22
Thucydides, 152n.27; love of Athens, 26; Melian dialogue, 33; civil war, 144n.29; *helkos* as 'sore', 145n.13; Pisistratids, 151n.11; forcible necessity, 152n.32; Perikles and democracy, 154n.52
thumos, 'faculty of spirit', 13, 34, 40, 58, 83, 127, 132, 134
Thurii, 139n.42
time, 1, 33-5, 42-3, 48, 65, 71, 79-80, 84, 87, 91, 97, 116; 'Court of Time' 9, 52, 87, 115-16
Todd, S.C., 151n.16
tragedy, 2; 152n.20
Treu, M., 93; 138n.22; 142n.52; 145n.8; 149n.43
Troy, 16, 42
tuchê, 'chance' or 'luck', 16, 88-9, 95, 133; 138n.19; personified, 148n.31
Tyler, H.M., 151n.8
tyranny, 5-7, 9, 11, 14, 28, 33-6, 39, 44, 48-9, 102-3, 108-14, 117, 120, 122-3, 126, 128, 133; 150n.3; 151nn.3, 14, 17; 153nn.43, 46
Tyrtaeus, 4; 148nn.18, 21; 150n.7; *moira*, 147n.8; Messenia, 153n.36; obedience, 141n.35; values 146n.30; 148nn.21, 26; 149nn.5, 9; 150n.19

Vegetti, M., 146n.27
vengeance, 11, 13, 42, 51, 55, 58, 72, 84, 105, 118, 126-8
Vlastos, G., 8, 47, 50, 74-6; 136n.21; 140n.16; 143nn.9, 15; 144n.18; 146n.2; 147n.3
Vox, O., 139n.6; 142n.51; 146n.1

Walker, J., 145n.1
Wallace, R., 135n.1
wealth, see *ploutos*, *chrêmata*, *kerdea*, *olbos*

183

Index

Wees, H. van, 136n.12; 141n.35; 147n.5; 152n.33
West, M.L., 46, 51; 136n.15; 137nn.3, 6; 144nn.20, 31; 145n.2; 149n.15; 150n.17; 151n.8; 153n.43; 154n.56
Wheelwright, P., 138n.22; 142n.53
Wickersham, J.M., 139n.9
Wilamowitz-Möllendorf, U. von, 146n.1; 147nn.12, 13, 16; 151n.8
wilful/ volitional choices, 13-14, 16-18, 24-6, 49, 53-4; 154n.53
Will, F., 136n.21; 142n.52
Willcock, M.M., 145n.11; 151n.9; 152n.24
Williams, B., 136n.21
Wilson, W., 1; 135n.2
wisdom poet/ poetry, 6-7, 26, 34, 38-9
wisdom, '*sophia*', 14, 35, 86, 90-1, 107; 141n.41
Wolff, H.J., 154n.55

Woodhouse, W.J., 135n.3; 152n.23
Woodruff, P., 112; 151n.14
world-view, 1, 7, 11-12, 14-16, 18, 84; 137n.2

Xenophanes, 6-7; divine insight, 13; theology, 17; 158n.24; knowing and seeing, 69, 92; 138n.25; *noos*, 8; divine will, 136n.14; 137n.5; ethical views, 100; 142n.44
Xenophon, 139n.33

Zeller, E., 135n.2
Zellner, H.M., 145n.23
Zeus, 12-14, 16-18, 26, 29, 32, 44, 47, 49, 51-2, 55, 58, 72, 79-80, 82-4, 88-90, 92-3, 95, 103-4, 122, 125, 130; 137nn.3, 5, 6, 15; 138n.17; 139n.6; 143n.10; 147nn.15-6; 153n.42

www.ingramcontent.com/pod-product-compliance
Lightning Source LLC
Chambersburg PA
CBHW061835300426
44115CB00013B/2384